Introduction to Civil Aviation

Second Edition

Nawal K. Taneja
The Ohio State University

Lexington Books
D.C. Heath and Company/Lexington, Massachusetts/Toronto

New airbuses seen in the air together during a recent flight test. Top to bottom: A300-600R American Airlines; A310-300 Royal Jordanian Airlines; A320-200 Ansett Airlines of Australia. Front cover photo courtesy of Airbus Industrie of North America.

Library of Congress Cataloging-in-Publication Data

Taneja, Nawal K.
  Introduction to civil aviation.

  Bibliography: p.
  Includes index.
  1. Aeronautics, Commercial—United States. I. Title.
HE9803.A4T362 1989   387.7'0973   88–36396
ISBN 0–669–21020–X (alk. paper)

Published simultaneously in Canada
Printed in the United States of America
Casebound International Standard Book Number: 0–669–20418–8
Paperbound International Standard Book Number: 0–669–20419–6
Library of Congress Catalog Card Number 88–36396

The paper used in this publication meets the minimum requirements of American National Standard for Information Sciences—Permanence of Paper for Printed Library Materials, ANSI Z39.48–1984. ∞™

Year and number of this printing:

89 90 91 92 93 8 7 6 5 4 3 2 1

To my wife, Carolyn

Contents

Figures and Tables

Figures

Preface and Acknowledgments

The first edition of this book was directed at students interested in the U.S. civil aviation industry. The immediate stimulus behind its preparation was my need to teach a course in the Department of Aviation at The Ohio State University and the lack of an adequate textbook providing an overview of the major components of the aviation industry. Although several books examined particular aspects or components of the aviation system, none covered the overall system in sufficient detail to make students aware of major developments, constraints, issues, opportunities, and challenges. The first edition of *Introduction to Civil Aviation* was thus an attempt to meet those needs.

Since publication of the first edition, I have received numerous comments worldwide from students, faculty, government officials, and practitioners in the industry. Most of the comments fell into three categories: (a) The book focused almost entirely on U.S. domestic aviation, (b) parts of four chapters ("The National Airspace System," "The Airport System," "The Aeronautical Vehicle," and "Air Carriers") contained material too detailed for an "overview" book, and (c) a number of important points either were not raised at all or were mentioned cursorily. Examples of the first and third criticisms included lack of description of the International Civil Aviation Organization and its role in establishing standards governing air traffic control, personnel licensing, and instrument and airport design. Examples of the second criticism included definitions of airport financial performance measures, data sources for monitoring delay trends, information on aircraft performance, and descriptions of airport radar service area configurations and the decision-making process at selected *national* carriers. Despite the existence of a number of "rough spots," however, most of the readers who contacted me expressed a need for such an overview book.

Based on the expressed need for a book providing an overview of civil aviation and on the constructive criticisms received, I decided to produce this second edition of *Introduction to Civil Aviation*. In this edition, I have attempted to address as many of the criticisms as possible and at the same time to update the information contained in first edition. The result is a book that contains perhaps too much material for a one-quarter or one-semester course. For instructors concerned about the quantity of material covered, I recommend picking and choosing chapters to be covered on the basis of course objectives and instructors' personal interests.

There are many people to thank for their help, encouragement, and criticism: the faculty and staff of the Department of Aviation at The Ohio State University; Mr. Tom Bass, Head of Policy and Licensing Division, Civil Aviation Authority (United Kingdom); Mr. Donald W. Bauer, Regional Manager, Cessna/Citation; Mr. Donald J. Bennett, Director of 747/767 Marketing Management and Product Development, Boeing Commercial Airplanes; Mr. Geo R. Besse, Director of Government Affairs, International Air Transport Association; Mr. John N. Bradbury, Chief of the RAC/SAR Section, International Civil Aviation Organization; Mr. Thomas Craig, Director of Market Research, Boeing Commercial Airplanes; Ms. Ann W. Devers, Manager of Educational Programs, National Business Aircraft Association; Professor Rigas Doganis, Director of the Transport Studies Group, Polytechnic of Central London; Captain Lawrence E. Earhart, Trans World Airlines; Mr. Gunnar Finnsson, Chief of the Airport and Route Facility Management Section, International Civil Aviation Organization; Dr. William Fromme, Director of the Air Navigation Bureau, International Civil Aviation Organization; Ms. Anne Graham, British Airports Teaching Fellow, Polytechnic of Central London; Mr. Andy Hofton, Head of the Air Transport Group, Cranfield College of Aeronautics; Mr. James D. McCormick, Vice-President of Economic Affairs, Airport Operators Council International; Professor Michael Nolan, Department of Aviation Technology, Purdue University; Mr. Richard S. Shreve, Assistant Director of Cargo Services, Air Transport Association of America; Dr. Edward C. Spry, Senior Director of Industry Automation and Finance Services, International Air Transport Association; Mr. David A. Swierenga, Assistant Vice-President of Airline Industry Data, Air Transport Association of America; and Mr. Vladimir D. Zubkov, Director of Air Transport Bureau, International Civil Aviation Organization. I extend special thanks to John B. Fisher, a doctoral student at OSU, Mr. George R. Stearns, Staff Vice President Strategic Planning, Braniff, Inc., for reading, commenting on, and editing the entire manuscript, and Yvonne Holsinger, Learning Resources Associate at The Ohio State University Center for Teaching Excellence, for graphics. Finally, I express my appreciation to the staff at Lexington Books.

Abbreviations

AAIA	Airport and Airways Improvement Act of 1982
ADA	Airline Deregulation Act of 1978
ADAP	Airport Development Aid Program
ADF	automatic directional finder
ARTCC	Air Route Traffic Control Center
ARTS	automated radar terminal system
ASNA	Aviation Safety and Noise Abatement Act
ATA	Air Transport Association of America
ATC	air traffic control
ATCRBS	air traffic control radar beacon system
ATIS	automatic terminal information service
BAe	British Aerospace
CAA	Civil Aviation Authority (United Kingdom)
CAB	Civil Aeronautics Board
CAR	Civil Air Regulation
CDI	course deviation indicator
CLC	course line computer
CRS	computer reservation system
CRT	cathode ray tube
DME	distance-measuring equipment
DOT	Department of Transportation
EAS	Essential Air Service
EC	European Community
ECAC	European Civil Aviation Conference
FAA	Federal Aviation Administration

FAR	Federal Aviation Regulation
FBO	fixed-base operator
FMS	flight management system
FSS	flight service station
GA	general aviation
GATT	General Agreement on Tariffs and Trade
GNP	gross national product
GPS	global positioning system
HHI	Herfindahl-Hirschman Index
HOTOL	horizontal takeoff and landing
HSCT	high-speed commercial transport
HST	hypersonic transport
HUD	head-up displays
IATA	International Air Transport Association
ICAO	International Civil Aviation Organization
IFR	instrument flight rule
ILS	instrument landing system
INS	inertial navigation system
JAL	Japan Air Lines
LD	lower deck
loran	long-range navigation
MAP	Mutual Aid Pact (air carrier)
MLS	microwave landing system
NAS	national airspace system
NASA	National Aeronautics and Space Administration
NASP	National Airspace System Plan
NCS	Naval Communication Station
NDB	non-directional beacon
NOTAM	Notices to Airmen
NPIAS	National Plan of Integrated Airport Systems
NTSB	National Transportation Safety Board
NWS	National Weather Service
OAG	*Official Airline Guide*
O&D	origin and destination

OEW	operating empty weight
PANS	procedures for air navigation services
PATCO	Professional Air Traffic Controllers Organization
PICAO	Provisional International Civil Aviation Organization
R&D	research and development
RNAV	area navigation
SAR	search and rescue
SARP	standard and recommended practice
SAS	Scandinavian Airlines System
SMSA	Standard Metropolitan Statistical Area
SSR	secondary surveillance radar
SST	supersonic transport
STOL	short takeoff and landing
TACAN	tactical air navigation
TCA	terminal control area
TCAS	traffic alert and collision avoidance system
TDC	total distribution costs
TDWR	Terminal Doppler Weather Radar
TRACAB	terminal radar approach control in tower cab
TRACON	terminal radar approach control
TWA	Trans World Airlines
UDF	unducted fan
UHB	ultra high bypass
UHF	ultra high frequency
VFR	visual flight rule
VHF	very high frequency
VLF	very low frequency
VOR	very high frequency omnidirectional range
VORTAC	integrated VOR/TACAN facility

1
Historical Developments in Civil Aviation

This first chapter synthesizes, in roughly chronological order, significant historical developments in international civil aviation—airplanes, airports, regulations, and air traffic control. The chapter is divided into four sections, discussing (a) developments prior to 1938, from the early history of civil aviation to passage of the U.S. Civil Aeronautics Act of 1938; (b) developments from World War II to the introduction of jet service and passage of the U.S. Federal Aviation Act of 1958; (c) developments from 1958 to 1978, the year of airline deregulation in the United States; and (d) events around the world since U.S. deregulation. Although developments in the United States are discussed in greater detail than those in other parts of the world, it will be obvious by the end of this chapter that even though the U.S. air transportation system is now the largest in the world, many of the most significant breakthroughs in aviation have occurred in other parts of the world.

Developments Prior to 1938

From the dawn of history, the human mind has explored alternative ways to fly. According to Greek mythology, for example, Daedalus and his son Icarus created wings of feather—held together with wax—to fly out of a prison on the Isle of Crete. In the thirteenth century, Friar Roger Bacon, an English monk, argued that it was possible for the air to support a machine, his convictions based on the principles of buoyancy discovered by the Greek inventor Archimedes. During the sixteenth century, Leonardo da Vinci explored the concept of flapping wings. In eighteenth-century France, the Montgolfier brothers used the principle of rising smoke to design and construct the first hot air balloon,[1] and later, the Germans constructed balloons that transported mail and even passengers.[2] Toward the end of the 1800s, Otto Lilienthal of Germany began to construct gliders.[3] While such balloons and gliders generated a great deal of enthusiasm, they had serious payload and control limitations, which motivated the ongoing search for a true "flying machine."

During the nineteenth century, progress toward controlled, heavier-than-air, powered flight was held back for two reasons. First, prior to the work of Sir George Cayley in England, inventors had focused on the development of wing-flapping devices. Cayley's research, during the first half of the nineteenth century, put an end to this unproductive line of thought and advanced the idea of a fixed-wing craft. Second, although Cayley developed the necessary aerodynamic theory to design a human-carrying flight vehicle, the choice of the power plant during the second half of the nineteenth century was restricted to then-contemporary steam engines. Ultimately, it was the collective work of many individuals—among them, Sir George Cayley in England, Otto Lilienthal in Germany, and Octave Chanute, Samuel Langley, and Charles Manly in the United States—that led to the first successful controlled, heavier-than-air flight by the Wright brothers in 1903 at Kitty Hawk, North Carolina.

Publicity from the Wright brothers' flight in the United States and Louis Bleriot's flight across the English Channel in 1909 sparked a flurry of excitement throughout the two continents. Numerous scientific organizations, scientists, philanthropists, and expositions awarded substantial prize money for airplane "firsts." Pilots and designers from both continents competed fiercely for the money and legitimization of their designs. The most meaningful interest in the powered airplane emerged during World War I, when governments in both Europe and the United States began to appreciate the value of airplanes for military purposes. As a consequence, airplane development and production on both continents increased tremendously. Besides the increase in the sheer volume of aircraft production, airplane performance also improved substantially under the pressures of war.

By the end of World War I, the governments of leading countries in Western Europe had come to strongly support the development of air services for the public, partly because of the war-ravaged condition of ground transportation systems and partly because of the competitive nature of European nations. Moreover, many of the prerequisites for establishing an airline industry were present: war-surplus airplanes, ex-military pilots seeking civilian aviation-related employment, government financial support, and dedicated individuals who had faith in the future of commercial passenger transportation.[4] The situation in the United States, however, was quite different. The ground transportation system in the United States, unlike that in Europe, had not been affected by the war. There were fewer war-surplus airplanes, and intercountry rivalry was not an issue. Moreover, the airplane of the early 1920s offered no significant speed advantage over express trains, nor did it even begin to offer the luxury of American Pullman trains.[5] Consequently, most early attempts to offer regularly scheduled passenger air service in the United States failed.

Without full-fledged government support, the domestic aircraft industry in the United States was reduced to a small fraction of its wartime size. Nevertheless, despite minimal government support and a lack of public confidence, a number of aviation enthusiasts in the United States continued to design and build airplanes. These dedicated entrepreneurs were motivated not so much by the lure of profits as by a passion for aviation and a profound faith in its future. Drawing upon their irrepressible devotion to aviation and often using funds from their other business interests, these individuals pursued new aviation ventures fraught with enormous risks, most of which offered only minimal rewards. Their goal was simply to further the development of air travel.

Despite the lack of support by the U.S. government in the development of passenger services, the Post Office Department did consider the airplane a possible solution to the problem of long-distance mail transportation. Using army equipment and personnel, the Post Office Department in May 1918 inaugurated airmail service on the New York–Philadelphia–Washington route and, within a few months, took over the service. Within two years, the department and selected railroads had put into operation a combined transcontinental air/rail mail service between New York and San Francisco. Mail was flown during the day and transported by rail at night. Although the airmail business was not very successful over short distances, opportunities for long-haul transportation of the mail were great, particularly after the Post Office Department took the initiative to develop lighted airways so that airplanes could fly at night.

Through the early 1920s, the United States continued to have no coherent national aviation policy. Unlike European governments, the U.S. government had not yet come to support the development of passenger services. The Post Office Department, responsible for operating mail flights, likewise had not yet come to encourage the development of new airplanes. Although aircraft manufacturers tried to design new airplanes dedicated to the transportation of mail, the Post Office Department opted to use converted wartime airplanes, such as the de Havilland Four (DH-4), a 1916 British design mass-produced in the United States in 1918.[6] Even worse was the government's policy of owning the design rights to the relatively few airplanes it purchased. This policy made it unattractive, for competitive reasons, for a manufacturer to risk designing a totally new airplane for fear that the government might take the design and open the construction phase to competitive bids.[7]

With respect to the infrastructure, there were neither adequate airports nor navigational aids, other than the few fields operated by the military and those established by the Post Office Department. Nor were there air laws to ensure safety. This lack of a definitive national policy held back the growth of aviation. That President Coolidge ultimately became concerned about the United States' weakness in this area led to the appointment of the Aircraft Board, a body that was charged with assessing the condition of the aircraft industry and the aviation-related needs of the nation and with developing a long-range policy to fulfill those needs. The Aircraft Board's work facilitated six major events that strongly encouraged the development of the domestic aviation industry during this critical period.

1. The Air Mail Act of 1925—also known as the Kelly Act, for Congressman Clyde Kelly, chairman of the House Post Office Committee—transferred airmail operations to private carriers on the basis of competitive bids. This act encouraged commercial aviation by allowing the U.S. Post Office to contract with private companies (thereby allowing new airlines to be established) and by allowing airlines to develop passenger services using part of the airmail payments as subsidies.

2. Combining his interest in aeronautics with his interest in business ventures, automobile tycoon Henry Ford concluded in the mid-1920s that one way to provide a boost to the U.S. aircraft industry was to increase public demand for its products, which in turn required action to overcome the public's fear of flying. His company produced the famous Ford Trimotor (the "Tin Goose"), a reliable three-engine airplane. To demonstrate the safety of modern commercial airplanes, Trimotors were sent on "Ford Reliability Tours."[8] Not only did Ford's strategy help instill public confidence in commercial aviation, but the automobile maker went on to win mail routes in the Midwest. Ford's presence and financial commitment lent a great deal of credibility to the fledgling aviation industry.

3. The Air Commerce Act of 1926—a recommendation of the Aircraft Board—initiated government-backed development of civil airways and navigational aids and provided for safety regulations requiring that airplanes, pilots, and navigational facilities be registered, examined, and certified; in addition, it established air traffic rules, such as those governing safe altitudes for flights. These original Civil Air Regulations (CARs) were the predecessors of the current Federal Aviation Regulations (FARs) of the Federal Aviation Administration. The 1926 act thus relieved private carriers in the United States from having to make heavy investments in ground facilities for air navigation.

4. At the urging of the Aircraft Board, the government established a five-year plan (1926–31) to reequip the army and the navy air services with modern airplanes. This legislation provided a significant boost to the otherwise stagnant aircraft industry.[9]

5. The Guggenheim Fund for the Advancement of Aeronautics, established in 1926, sanctioned the development of schools of aeronautical engineering at New York University, Michigan, MIT, and Georgia Tech. In addition to conducting research, these schools produced such famous aircraft designers as Kelly Johnson of Lockheed and Wellwood Beall of Boeing. Other noteworthy achievements of the Guggenheim Fund were the financing of Lindbergh's forty-eight-state tour in the *Spirit of St. Louis,* which made the historic transatlantic flight, and a grant to Western Air Express, an airline formed in 1926, to initiate passenger service between Los Angeles and San Francisco.[10]

6. Charles Lindbergh's 1927 transatlantic flight greatly accelerated the

public's acceptance of air travel. His flight proved the reliability of airplane technology and, more than any other single event, aroused public interest in aviation.

Whereas the U.S. government's attention to aviation during the 1920s focused on airmail services, in Europe, where the war had destroyed a significant part of the ground transportation systems, the air transportation industry concentrated on the development of passenger services, a much different focus. Because transcontinental transportation in Europe involves crossing national frontiers, the need arose as early as 1919 to (a) establish principles of international law to regulate aerial navigation and each nation's sovereignty over its airspace, (b) make international air transportation convenient and more acceptable to passengers by standardizing the international system (for example, in traffic-handling procedures and forms), and (c) establish rules for air carrier accident liability in international air transportation. The Paris Convention of 1919 established the basic international law regarding commercial aviation—that is, that every nation has complete and exclusive sovereignty over the airspace above its territory—and instituted the International Commission for Air Navigation, which, as the predecessor of the current International Civil Aviation Organization, provided a mechanism for governments to hold discussions and standardize aviation facilities and services.

In the area of commercial air transportation, six European nations in 1919 jointly created an organization called the International Air Traffic Association (IATA), whose mission was to make international air transportation convenient and more acceptable to passengers by standardizing the international system—for example, through establishment of the standard airline ticket and the air waybill. The issue of accident liability in international air transportation was not resolved, however, until 1929, when more than sixty countries, including the United States, ratified the Warsaw Convention, which went into effect in 1933. This convention prescribed that an air carrier be held liable for damages for death or injury to passengers and loss or damage to baggage and goods. At that time, the liability was limited to $8,300 per person, although in the interim, the Warsaw Convention has been modified a number of times to raise the monetary limit.

Clearly, the development of the aeronautical vehicle was not the only matter to be addressed in the furtherance of the air transportation system. For sound development of the whole system, other components—such as airports and navigation devices—also needed to be improved and integrated into the system. Here, the importance in the United States of the Air Commerce Act of 1926 cannot be overstated. This act made the secretary of commerce responsible for promoting and fostering the development of commercial aviation and for regulating the business aspects of air transportation; further, it designated that the control and operation of airports, which for the most part had been privately owned and operated until the early 1920s, were the responsibility of municipal authorities.

The Air Commerce Act also affected the general aviation industry. Since the end of World War I, a number of ex-military pilots had been flying in air shows and giving short rides to the public for whatever price the market would bear. The Air Commerce Act required that these pilots become licensed and that their airplanes meet certain maintenance standards. As a result, many of these barnstormers decided to settle down and become fixed-base operators (as discussed in chapter 8).

Once it became clear that some form of government subsidy was required to invigorate the aviation industry—a conclusion of the Aircraft Board—the Kelly Act was amended to increase the indirect subsidy provided to airmail carriers. This was done by manipulating the method of their compensation. Using this strategy, the Post Office Department, under the leadership of Walter F. Brown, subsidized selected airlines so as to transform the industry from a random assortment of short, unconnected mail routes to a more stable, integrated, self-sufficient, nationwide airline system. It appears that Brown's plan was to set up three major transcontinental routes on the theory that the smaller carriers were undercapitalized and that nearly all of them were completely dependent on government contracts. This strategy was implemented by passage of the McNary-Watres Act of 1930 (the amended Kelly Act), which eliminated competitive bidding. In effect, the government awarded mail contracts as a form of subsidy to support carriers that were strong enough to contribute to the development of commercial aviation. In addition, mail payments were made on the basis of capacity flown, rather than amount of mail transported, thereby encouraging the industry to acquire faster, larger, and longer-range airplanes. Moreover, transport companies, some of which were owned by airplane manufacturers, began to consolidate and strengthen their operations.

Similarly in Europe—particularly in England, France, Holland, Belgium, and Germany—numerous airlines that by the mid-1920s had begun to offer passenger services now began to consolidate their operations to form stronger airlines. For example, the amalgamation in 1926 of a number of smaller German airlines produced Deutsche Luft Hansa, the largest airline in Europe. Two other characteristics of Luft Hansa not only indicated the differences in the development of airlines in Europe and the United States but also set the stage for future financial and operating practices for airlines in other parts of the world. First, the German government held about a third of the ownership of Luft Hansa, a development that signified the beginning of government-owned national airlines. Second, in 1927 Luft Hansa signed an agreement with Farman, a French airline, to offer joint services between the two countries, an arrangement that heralded the beginning of "pooling" agreements (discussed in chapter 6).[11]

Although significant research in aeronautical science had been performed in the United States and Europe during the 1920s, it was not until the beginning of the 1930s that the technological advances resulting from that research began to be implemented in the designs of new airplanes. For example, in 1933 the Boeing Airplane Company introduced its 247 transport airplane, which synthesized the latest trends in airplane design. Widely considered the first "modern" transport airplane, the Boeing 247 was a twin-engine, all-metal, low-wing (allowing the landing gear to retract into it) monoplane capable of comfortably transporting ten passengers and 400 pounds of cargo at a cruising speed of about 150 miles per hour (which reduced U.S. domestic coast-to-coast trip time to about twenty hours).

Recognizing the competitive advantage promised by this high-technology airplane, United Airlines placed an order for the first sixty Boeing 247s to be produced by Boeing. Since United's competitors could not get a Boeing 247 until United's order had been filled (about two years), they panicked and approached the Douglas Aircraft Corporation for a competitive design. TWA, for example, gave Douglas the contract to build the DC-1, a twelve-passenger, 150 mile-per-hour airplane with a nonstop range of about 1,000 miles. The prototype DC-1 also flew in 1933, just a few months after the Boeing 247. TWA made a few changes to the prototype (adding two more seats, for example) and placed an order for twenty (DC-2s). American Airlines' requirements (for example, fourteen berths) led Douglas to lengthen and widen the fuselage to accommodate either fourteen berths or twenty-one passengers. Thus, in 1936 the DC-3 (figure 1–1) was born and became available to the airlines that same year.

The DC-3, with a capacity of twenty-one passengers and a cruise speed of almost 200 miles per hour, became the first airplane to be operated profitably (due to its higher productivity—higher speed and higher capacity) by transporting only passengers. In other words, an airline that operated the DC-3 did not necessarily have to depend on mail contracts and subsidies. Among the advanced features of the all-metal DC-3 were a lighter, stress-carrying skin; air-cooled radial engines; controllable-pitch propellers; wing flaps; and retractable landing gear. It was an economical airplane for the airlines, and it was appealing to passengers because of its comfort and speed. This airplane was so popular among commercial and government users that more than ten thousand DC-3s were produced, including the version used by the U.S. Air Force, the C-47, and that used by the Royal Air Force, the Dakota.

In addition to the advances made in the development of landplanes during the 1930s, there was considerable interest—particularly by Pan American Airways in the United States and Imperial Airways in Great Britain (the predecessor of BOAC, now British Airways)—in large "flying boats" capable of operating at higher speeds and altitudes for commercial transoceanic service. In 1934, Sikorsky Aircraft introduced the S-42 "Clipper," a four-engine flying boat with a capacity of thirty-two, a speed of 160 miles per hour, and a range of about 2,500 miles. This vehicle was built to the specifications of Pan American, which put it into service in the Caribbean. Other manufacturers had also shown some interest in the development of flying boats. In 1935, the Glen Martin Company developed the M-130 "China

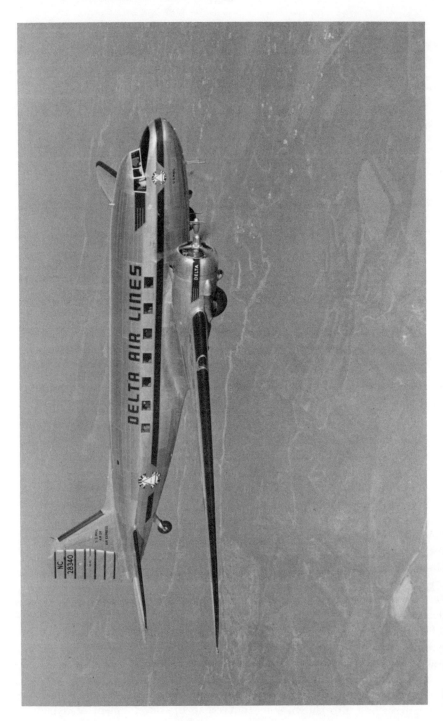

Figure 1–1. Douglas DC-3

Photo Courtesy of Douglas Aircraft Company

Clipper," a four-engine flying boat capable of carrying forty-eight passengers a distance of 3,000 miles at 160 miles per hour; Pan American inaugurated its transpacific service with this flying boat. Boeing developed the 314, capable of carrying seventy-four passengers, and Pan American used it to offer regular passenger service across both the Atlantic and the Pacific. Although these flying boats were technological marvels, their development costs were so high that manufacturers eventually turned their attention to the design of four-engine landplanes.

While revisions to the Kelly Act provided needed stability in the airmail business, which in turn fostered the development of advanced airplanes, it soon became obvious that the application of the Kelly Act was subject to abuse. The postmaster general was suspected of holding a series of meetings with major airlines for the purpose of allocating routes. Moreover, contracts were typically awarded not to the lowest bidder but to selected airlines. These activities brought charges of collusion and unfair mail awards by small independent airlines. A special investigative committee formed in 1933 found, among other things, that most of the mail contracts had in fact been awarded to selected carriers; as a result, President Franklin Roosevelt canceled all mail contracts between the Post Office Department and private carriers, directing the Army Air Corps to fly the mail instead. Yet shortage of equipment and experienced pilots, severe weather conditions, and unfamiliar routes led to an increase in operating costs and, worse, several tragic accidents. These developments forced the government to subsequently return airmail contracts to the airlines on a temporary basis and to seek remedial legislation to correct the flawed and biased process of awarding mail contracts.

Once again, the government faced the perplexing problem of how to simultaneously promote and regulate the industry. This problem was solved in part by the Air Mail Act of 1934 (the Black-McKeller Act), which set up a threefold control of the air transport industry: (a) Airmail contracts were to be awarded by the Post Office Department, (b) the Interstate Commerce Commission was put in charge of setting "fair and reasonable" airmail rates, and (c) the Department of Commerce was made responsible for the regulation of safety and the maintenance, operation, and development of the airway system.

The act contained three major provisions. First, although mail contracts were again awarded on the basis of competitive bidding, those carriers which had been accused of collusion during the 1933 investigation were not allowed to bid. This provision caused many of the affected carriers to change their corporate names. Second, because of the potential conflict of interest, the Air Mail Act of 1934 made holding companies illegal, thereby separating the historical affiliation between major airlines and airplane manufacturers. As a result, a division of the Boeing Airplane Company became United Airlines; North American split up two of its divisions, which became TWA and Eastern; and a division of AVCO became American Airlines. Third, the act established the five-member Federal Aviation Commission to study federal aviation policy and recommend future policy. The most important contribution of this commission was the creation of a separate agency to regulate the economic practices of the civil air transport industry.

Through the mid-1930s, substantial progress was also made by the general aviation industry. The British firm de Havilland pioneered the private airplane with the development of the de Havilland Moth in 1925, and the light-airplane industry thrived until the beginning of World War II.[12] In the United States, the Travel Air Manufacturing Company—started by Walter Beech and Clyde Cessna—was producing approximately 25 percent of all commercial airplanes toward the end of the 1920s.[13]

Pilot training was and continues to be one of the most important contributions of the general aviation industry. The U.S. Congress felt this activity to be so important that it appropriated $4 million to establish the Civilian Pilot Training Program at the nation's colleges, with the goal of training ten thousand pilots in the United States.[14] At about the same time, William Piper introduced the J-3 Piper Cub, a single-engine, fabric-covered, high-wing monoplane that ultimately became the most widely accepted airplane for training pilots. Availability of the J-3 Piper Cub, coupled with congressional funding for pilot training, brought immediate prosperity to the Piper Company.

The success of long-distance flights in general aviation also contributed to the promotion of civil aviation. Whereas in the late 1920s the interest of most aviators was in ocean crossings, during the 1930s the focus changed to around-the-world flights. Wiley Post, for example, made an around-the-world solo flight in 1933 in a Lockheed Vega monoplane, the *Winnie Mae*, in eight days.

Considerable advancement took place as well in the aviation infrastructure. For example, when one of the first airports opened at Croydon, England, in 1920, the first air traffic controller was a man using flags at the ends of runways. This rudimentary system was replaced in due course by light guns, and in 1930 the first radio-equipped control tower was established at the Cleveland airport in the United States.

The need to maintain safe separation standards between airplanes in flight came about as more airlines started operating without visual reference to the ground or to other aircraft. In 1935, public outcry following a TWA crash near Kansas City in which Republican Senator Bronson Cutting of New Mexico was killed prompted the Bureau of Air Commerce to establish a uniform and centralized air traffic control system. Since the bureau did not have the financial or human resources to accomplish this task, it asked airlines—in particular, American, Eastern, and TWA—to get the air traffic control system started at Newark, Cleveland, and Chicago, hoping the bureau itself could assume control of the system as soon as possible. In July 1936, the federal government took over the operation of these three air traffic control stations.[15] The government, however, continued to be blamed for accidents such as the one cited above. In addition, investment in the airline industry was shrinking, partly because of the losses experienced by the airlines (the result of fierce competition), coupled with the instability of mail routes. The stage was therefore set for new legislation that would stabilize commercial aviation. The result was passage of the Civil Aeronautics Act of 1938.

Developments between 1938 and 1958

Just prior to World War II, the civil aviation industry was beginning to take shape. In the United States, the Civil Aeronautics Act of 1938 placed all commercial air transportation regulation, both economic and safety, within one federal agency consisting of three separate bodies: (a) the Civil Aeronautics Authority, responsible for economic and safety regulations; (b) the Air Safety Board, responsible for investigating aircraft accidents; and (c) the Administrator of Aviation, responsible for carrying out the safety policies of the Civil Aeronautics Authority. This system replaced the older one under which the Air Mail Act of 1934 had allowed three separate agencies (with overlapping authority) to promote and regulate the development of commercial air transportation. The new system provided a clearer set of guidelines for the air transportation industry.

In Europe, where major airlines had developed in Britain, France, Holland, Belgium, and Germany, attention had turned to linking empires, most notably with colonial destinations in Asia and Africa. It is interesting to note that most of the major European airlines followed the same routes to Asia because of the existence of limited navigational aids at certain points along the route. Eventually these routes (for example, through Athens, Baghdad, Karachi, Calcutta, Rangoon, and Bangkok) became the main trade routes between the West and the East. Economically and politically important routes to Africa were developed by airlines from Britain (Imperial Airways), France (Air France), Belgium (SABENA), and Holland (KLM).

Germany, with the largest airline in Europe, had significant influence in Latin America. Indeed, the first airlines in Latin America—SCADTA in Colombia and LAB in Bolivia—had been established by German nationals and with German capital.[16] These airlines became successful very early in their development by demonstrating the value of air transportation in underdeveloped areas having severe geographical conditions—mountains, tropical swamps, and the like. SCADTA, for example, was able to carry passengers and mail between Barranquilla and Bogotá—a distance of about 650 miles— in about seven hours, as compared with transportation by land, which even in favorable conditions took about one week.[17] When German-controlled airlines (for example, SCADTA) attempted to establish service from points in South America to points in the United States, the U.S. government became concerned about allowing a foreign airline operate so close to the Panama Canal and therefore encouraged a U.S. airline to provide service to points in

South America.[18] This situation ultimately led to the expansion of Pan American.

World War II not only transformed the scope of airline operations but also influenced the aviation industry in other ways. First, with respect to airline operations, service was suspended or curtailed on many international and domestic routes, and a number of airlines, notably Pan American in the United States and Imperial Airways in Britain, became virtual extensions of the armed forces. Pan American, for example, was asked by the military to provide global operations and to build strategic airfields in Africa and South America. In Germany, Deutsche Luft Hansa, which had already become the largest airline in Europe prior to the onset of the war, was well positioned to expand its services; however, the war prevented the negotiation of a bilateral agreement that would have allowed Luft Hansa to begin service on the North Atlantic.

Second, the airplane manufacturing industry underwent dramatic structural changes as a result of both opportunities and pressures arising from the tremendous increase in the demand for military-use airplanes. Manufacturers of civil airplanes turned to the production of military airplanes. In the United States, all manufacturers expanded their facilities and looked to the automobile industry for added production capacity, through either subcontracting or licensing agreements. The relationship between aircraft manufacturers and the automobile industry was initially problematic; production techniques in the two industries were different, for example, and unions had serious concerns about safeguarding their rights. Recognizing that domestic airplane manufacturing capacity was inadequate, the federal government, through the Reconstruction Finance Corporation, built new facilities that were subsequently leased to individual companies. There were also many other wartime changes in how aircraft manufacturers conducted their business. Companies that before the war had been strong competitors now pooled their resources for the common good, and fixed-price contracts gave way to cost-plus-fee contracts. Although the manufacturing industry was doing well during the war, many manufacturers still remembered the costly lessons learned at the end of World War I and had legitimate concerns about the ramifications of a sudden termination of war-related government contracts. To relieve these concerns, the government established the Reconstruction Act, the Joint Contract Termination Board, and the Contract Settlement Act to ease the transition from war-related to peacetime airplane production. Defense considerations also led to the decision to upgrade existing airports and to build new airports, many of which reverted to civilian use at the end of the war.

Third, the war was responsible for the rapid advancement in airplane technology and in the aviation infrastructure. The most radical technological breakthrough was the introduction of the jet engine. The concept of jet propulsion had been independently developed by Frank Whittle in England in 1930 and by Hans von Ohain in Germany in 1935. In 1939 the Heinkel

178 flew in Germany, and in 1941 the Gloster E-28/39, powered by the Whittle jet engine, flew in England. The Whittle engine was the basis for the General Electric engine that powered the Bell XP-59A; this aircraft flew in October 1942 as the first jet operation in the United States. The war effort also led to technical refinements in other areas of aviation, including radio communications, navigational aids, instrument flying, and airport facilities. For example, although concepts relating to the development of radar can be traced back to the work of Guglielmo Marconi in 1922 and perhaps even earlier to the work of Heinrich Hertz in 1886, it was not until World War II that in both the United Kingdom and the United States radar was developed to a point that its installation along the east coast of Britain proved extremely valuable as an early warning system. Airport development also kept pace with the new demands of the war and advancing aircraft technology.

After the war, five major changes occurred in the air transportation industry: (a) the development of helicopters, better general aviation airplanes, and larger, longer-range, and faster commercial airplanes; (b) the resolution of contradictory political attitudes toward the development of international air transportation services; (c) the expansion of U.S. airlines; (d) the large-scale development of airports; and (e) the expansion of existing national airlines and the emergence of national airlines from newly independent nations.

With respect to the first development, airplanes, the Brabazon Committee in England was established in December 1942 to examine the need for postwar transport airplanes. The committee recommended the development of a turbojet airplane capable of operating transatlantic flights and a turboprop airplane to operate on short-haul routes. These recommendations ultimately led to the development of the de Havilland Comet (figure 1–2), the first turbojet, and the Vickers Viscount (figure 1–3), the first turboprop airplane. In the United States, manufacturers began to incorporate into commercial designs the technological advances that had been developed for military airplanes. For example, the experience gained from the C-54 Skymaster (the military version of the DC-4) was used to develop the DC-6, which, along with its arch-rival, the Lockheed Constellation, represented a giant step forward in commercial air transportation. Powered by four engines, these economical airplanes were capable of carrying up to fifty passengers at cruise speeds exceeding 300 miles per hour. The cabin pressurization feature of these airplanes greatly enhanced passenger comfort. Subsequently, their payload and range capabilities were improved so that the airlines could begin providing nonstop flights across the United States and the North Atlantic. Later models, such as the DC-7, the Lockheed Super Constellation, and the Boeing Stratocruiser, were all capable of carrying a hundred passengers across the Atlantic, nonstop, at about 300 miles per hour.

Air transportation also improved in ultra-short-haul markets as a result of helicopters, which were not fully developed until after World War II. Although designers—such as Igor Sikorsky from Russia and Theodore von

Figure 1–2. de Havilland Comet 1

Photo Courtesy of British Aerospace

Figure 1–3. Vickers Viscount

Photo Courtesy of British Aerospace

Karman of Hungary, both of whom had been working on helicopter designs since the early 1900s—had not found a solution to the basic problem of controlling the helicopter while hovering, it was not until the 1920s that Don Juan de la Cierva of Spain solved the control problem by hinging the rotor blades at a hub, which allowed the blades to respond individually to aerodynamic and centrifugal forces. Later, in September 1939, Sikorsky, under the sponsorship of United Aircraft Corporation, developed and flew the VS-300, various derivatives of which were placed in service by the U.S. military during the next five years. The commercial version, the S-51, which received its civil certification in 1946, was placed in scheduled service by Los Angeles Airways; subsequently, helicopter service became available in New York, Chicago, and San Francisco and in England and Belgium. Although helicopters clearly provided operational advantages for airlines—for example, by eliminating the need for long runways—the economics of their operations were poor because of their small size, slow speed, and low utilization.[19] Nonetheless, in civilian use helicopters served an important role in agricultural crop spraying, law enforcement, surveying, and fire fighting.

Activity also increased in the use of light airplanes. Not only did military-surplus airplanes become available to provide commercial air service, but hundreds of surplus military airports were turned over to local civil authorities, providing a greater number of landing facilities for general aviation aircraft. Moreover, hundreds of flight training schools were established throughout the United States. These developments led the manufacturers of light airplanes to produce dozens of new models, a number of which were successful, such as the single-engine, low-wing, V-tail Beech Bonanza and the single-engine, high-wing Stinson Voyager. The highly optimistic forecasts of the demand for new light airplanes did not, however, materialize, for reasons such as the greater utility of the automobile, the availability of cheaper war-surplus airplanes, and the public's reluctance to spend money on private flying in light of potential international conflicts on the horizon.[20] Consequently, a number of manufacturers of light airplanes were forced to leave the marketplace.

The second postwar development involved the regulation of commercial air rights. In the international arena, many nations were interested in formulating a universal air transport policy that would regulate commercial air rights and establish rules governing technical and navigational aspects. In 1944, at the invitation of the United States, fifty-four nations sent representatives to the Chicago Conference to establish an international convention whose objective was to set out general rules under which international air transport services could be operated. But because of the conflicting interests of the various nations present at the conference, agreement could not be reached on a means for exchanging commercial rights to fly in and out of foreign nations. Basically, there were two conflicting views: Whereas the United States sought relatively complete competitive freedom, the United Kingdom, in contrast, supported rather heavily regulated operations. The

British wanted to set up an international agency to control capacities, frequencies, and fares; under the British system, routes would be assigned through bilateral agreements. The United States was against the policy of regulating capacities and fares and suggested that control be limited to the technical side of air transportation.

Despite the impasse that characterized the Chicago Conference, the proceedings did lead to the establishment of both the International Air Services Transit Agreement and the Provisional International Civil Aviation Organization (PICAO)—a multigovernment body superseding the International Commission for Air Navigation established by the Paris Convention of 1919. The International Air Services Transit Agreement allowed civil aircraft of the signatories to fly across another signatory's national borders without landing and to land for noncommercial purposes when necessary. Although PICAO was responsible for the technical, operational, and legal framework for operating international air transport services, it did not possess any economic powers that could be applied to the international air transport industry, such as those affecting passenger fares and cargo rates.

Since the Chicago Conference failed to produce general agreement as to the manner in which international fares and rates could be established, international airlines subsequently met and agreed to organize a committee to draft articles of association for determining international fares and rates, subject to government approval. In 1945 the International Air Transport Association (IATA) was formally established by the airlines through a special act of the Canadian Parliament. This organization superseded the original one formed in Europe in 1919 to standardize air travel to foreign countries. Unlike the old organization, the new IATA had as its principal function the establishment of a traffic conference forum for international airlines to negotiate fares, rates, and conditions of carriage. (See chapter 6.)

Similarly, since the Chicago Conference failed to produce an agreement regarding the exchange of commercial rights, representatives from Great Britain and the United States met again in Bermuda in 1946 to exchange operating rights between the two nations. The Bermuda Agreement resulted in the "five freedoms" of the air. The first two freedoms were essentially those provisions agreed to at the Chicago Conference—specifically, the right to fly across another nation's territory and the right to land for noncommercial, emergency purposes. The remaining freedoms were the rights to (a) disembark in a foreign country passengers and cargo that had originated in the carrier's home country, (b) pick up from a foreign country passengers and cargo destined for the carrier's home country, and (c) transport passengers and cargo from one foreign country to another.

The national and international expansion of U.S. airlines was the third key development after the war. The Civil Aeronautics Board (CAB) approved the start-up of *local-service carriers* to operate "feeder" routes between major metropolitan areas and smaller communities, *supplemental carriers* to provide charter services, *air-taxi operators* to provide on-demand service, and *commuter carriers* to provide scheduled service in markets with very low density passenger traffic. The larger trunk-line carriers and local-service carriers received federal subsidies (which lasted until the early 1950s and early 1980s, respectively). Although, a number of U.S. airlines expanded their international operations, Pan American was clearly the preeminent world airline offering service to five continents and, as of 1947, the first single-carrier, around-the-world service.

The fourth major postwar development was the large-scale, worldwide construction of airports. In the United States, Congress had appropriated funds during the war years to construct and improve airports considered vital to national defense. After the war, the Federal Airport Act of 1946 increased the size of the airports program by providing investment capital totaling $500 million over a seven-year period. Recipients of these federal funds were required to comply with new construction standards established for airports—covering site location, airport layout, lighting, and the safety of approaches.[21]

The fifth postwar development was the expansion of existing national airlines and the emergence of national airlines from newly independent nations; examples included El Al Israel Airlines, founded in 1948, and Garuda Indonesia, founded in 1950. Similar developments occurred in Africa from the mid-1950s to the mid-1960s. The Gold Coast, which was renamed Ghana in 1957, formed Ghana Airways in 1958, and Nigeria, which became an independent African nation in 1960, established Nigeria Airways as a wholly owned government airline in 1961. This trend continued even in later years, when, for example, newly independent Brunei founded Royal Brunei Airlines in 1974.

As new airlines formed, aircraft continued to improve. The British introduced both turbojet and turboprop aircraft into commercial service. BOAC (the predecessor of British Airways) introduced the first turbojet service in 1952, with the de Havilland Comet flying London-Johannesburg (via Rome, Beirut, Khartoum, Entebbe, and Livingstone). The Comet cruised at 500 miles per hour, completing the 6,700-mile trip in just under twenty-four hours; the thirty-six-passenger cabin was pressurized for operations up to 40,000 feet. Unfortunately, however, fatigue failures in cabin pressure caused several tragic accidents, leading to the temporary removal of this airplane from commercial service. In 1956, Aeroflot introduced the TU-104 on the Moscow-Omsk-Irkutsk route.[22] The TU-104, with a capacity of fifty seats, reduced the travel time on this route from about fifteen to seven hours. Turboprops were introduced in 1953, when BEA (now part of British Airways) started service with the Vickers Viscount V-700 on the London-Rome-Athens-Nicosia route. This airplane had four Rolls-Royce Dart turbines driving four-blade propellers, could accommodate forty-seven passengers in a five-abreast configuration, and in short-haul operations was more economical than turbojets.

Unfortunately, the development of the aviation infrastructure did not keep pace with the development of the airplane. Although some improvements were made to the air traffic control system—such as the use of radars for monitoring airplane progress and precision landing systems at busy airports—they were not enough so as to prevent numerous delays and accidents. For example, on "Black Wednesday" in September 1954, forty-five thousand passengers in the New York region were delayed for hours, and on June 30, 1956, a TWA Super Constellation and a United DC-7 collided over the Grand Canyon, killing all passengers. Such incidents forced the government to attempt to upgrade the air traffic control system and elevate the stature of air traffic control issues. One important result of these efforts was the establishment, on July 1, 1953, of the new Office of Air Traffic Control.[23]

Developments between 1958 and 1978

The government's regulatory responsibilities under the Civil Aeronautics Act of 1938 increased to the point that additional regulatory policies and procedures were needed to enable the CAB to deal effectively with complex problems. It was necessary, for example, to develop, administer, develop and control the various components of a rapidly expanding national airspace system and to harmonize civil and military aviation interests. Safety was a major issue. Less than two years after the disaster over the Grand Canyon, there was a midair collision near Las Vegas involving a military jet and a commercial airline's DC-7. Less than a month after the Las Vegas accident, there was another midair collision between an Air Guard T-33 and a Capital (now part of United) Viscount near Brunswick, Maryland.[24]

To make the national airspace system safer and more efficient, Congress enacted the Federal Aviation Act of 1958, which amended and replaced the Civil Aeronautics Act of 1938. This new act established the Federal Aviation Agency (FAA) as a separate government agency, as of November 1, 1958. The FAA's mission was to regulate airspace; acquire, develop, and operate air navigation facilities; and prescribe air traffic rules for all aircraft. FAA safety regulations became known as the Federal Aviation Regulations (FARs). The FAA was also charged with carrying out research and development on matters related to the FARs and with certifying pilots, maintenance facilities, and maintenance personnel. Among the FAA's first major undertakings were efforts to upgrade the outmoded air traffic control radar inherited from the U.S. armed forces and to establish an air traffic control system capable of monitoring airline transport airplanes from takeoff to landing. Although regulation of safety was under the jurisdiction of the FAA, responsibility for investigating civil aircraft accidents was retained by the CAB. Economic regulatory authority over airlines also remained with the CAB.

From a global perspective, the most significant development in 1958 was the introduction of the American jet airplane—the Boeing 707—into commercial service. (See figure 1–4.) Although the jet airplane had flown during the war and had been in commercial service with BOAC since 1952 and with Aeroflot since 1956, 1958 is referred to as the year of the jet revolution. The American jets (the Boeing 707 and later the DC-8), which because of their

Figure 1–4. Boeing 707

Photo Courtesy of Boeing Commercial Airplanes

larger size were more economical than the de Havilland Comet, redrew the airmap of the world and served as the catalyst for mass tourism. Moreover, the acquisition of these jet airplanes by larger airlines produced a glut of used propeller airplanes that were acquired by charter airlines and thereby also contributed to the growth of tourism. Additionally, the jet age unfolded at about the same time that a number of states in Asia and Africa were gaining independence. These emerging independent states expanded the number of national sovereign airlines, facilitated in many cases by the availability of very inexpensive used propeller airplanes.[25]

In Europe, France and Britain each developed a jet for short- to medium-range operations. The French Sud-Aviation (now known as Aerospatiale) Caravelle, introduced in 1959, was powered by two Rolls-Royce Avon turbojet engines mounted near the tail and had a capacity of up to eighty passengers, a cruise speed of about 450 miles per hour, and range of 1,000 miles. In England, Hawker Siddeley, which bought de Havilland, introduced the three-engine Trident jet.

Airlines and their passengers were not the only segments of the aviation industry to benefit from the introduction of jet airplanes. After 1958, corporate executives began to enjoy the benefits of company-owned business jets. Grumman Aircraft introduced the Gulfstream 1, which was powered by two Rolls-Royce Dart turboprops and had a capacity of nineteen passengers, a range exceeding 2,500 miles, and a cruise speed of 350 miles per hour. Lockheed introduced its JetStar, powered by four turbojet engines. North American (now Rockwell International) introduced the two-turbojet-engine Sabreliner, and William Lear, an entrepreneur, introduced the prototype Learjet in 1963. In Europe, British Aerospace introduced the eight-passenger BAe-125 jet and French manufacturer Dassault-Breguet brought out the Falcon-20. The performance of these airplanes offered a wide spectrum of options for the corporate operator.

The introduction of jets did, however, present three new challenges for airports and airlines. First, airports found themselves with inadequate facilities to accommodate jets, particularly larger ones. The length of runways, the width of taxiways, and the capacity of fuel storage systems were insufficient to meet the requirements of many jet operations. Second, inasmuch as the earlier jets were noisy, people living near airports complained bitterly about the sudden intrusion of roaring engines. Third, a number of foreign airlines, heavily subsidized by their governments, posed a significant competitive threat to U.S. airlines on North Atlantic and Pacific routes. This intense competition, however, ultimately led to improvements in the services offered to the public. It also led to greater cooperation among some airlines in certain technical/operational areas—for example, multicarrier pooling of spare parts to reduce inventory carrying costs.

The introduction of jets in both commercial and military service brought into focus the need to modernize airport and airway systems. Underscoring the continued shortcomings of the air traffic control system was a midair collision in December 1960 between a United DC-8 descending into New York's Idlewild (now Kennedy) Airport and a TWA Super Constellation on approach to La Guardia.[26] Both airplanes had been under radar surveillance. Following this catastrophe, attention once again turned to the need to strengthen the air traffic control system. Steps taken by the FAA at this juncture included the development of additional airways (prescribed intercity routes), the establishment of more stringent airspace restrictions around busy airports, and—an effort known as Project Beacon—the installation of more sophisticated radar surveillance systems to help air traffic controllers identify and manage the growing number and diverse mix of commercial aircraft. The capacity of the national airspace system was also increased through such procedures as parallel precision approaches at busy airports, like Chicago's O'Hare.

The 1960s represented a watershed for international commercial aviation. Broad passenger acceptance of the Boeing 707 and the DC-8 is widely regarded as one of aviation's most significant developments. Moreover, even as the Boeing 707 and DC-8 were being placed into service, worldwide attention began to focus on the potential of supersonic transport (SST) airplanes. In 1962, France and Britain signed an agreement to jointly develop the Concorde (see figure 1– 5), an airplane capable of cruising at an altitude of 50,000 feet and a speed of Mach 2.2—twice the speed of sound, or almost 1,500 miles per hour. Designers envisioned that the Concorde would have a delta-shaped wing and four Olympus turbojet engines, producing twice as much thrust as the engines on the Boeing 707. The Soviets were developing a similar airplane, the Tupolev TU- 144, the prototype of which made its first flight on December 31, 1968, and became the first SST to fly in commercially scheduled service. In the United States, two airframe manufacturers and two engine manufacturers undertook design studies of a U.S. SST for the FAA; the government was expected to assume 75 percent of the development costs, estimated at $1.5 billion. But although the Boeing Airplane Company and General Electric were selected to design the U.S. SST, in 1971 the project was abandoned for political, environmental, and socioeconomic reasons, as well as lack of both funds and customer interest.

The Concorde did make it through the certification process and entered into scheduled service, but not until 1976. The lengthy delay stemmed primarily from environmental protests over the airplane's excessively noisy engines. The British operated the Concorde on the London-Bahrain route over the Persian Gulf, while the French operated it on the Paris–Dakar–Buenos Aires route. When British Airways and Air France applied for permission to offer scheduled service to the United States, public hearings were held in the United States to determine the effect of Concorde operations on the environment and on residents living within the takeoff/landing "noise footprint" of the aircraft. Despite strong opposition, the two airlines were permitted to operate the Concorde to New York and Washington, D.C., for a trial period of sixteen months. But even with its great promise, the Concorde proved to be a financial nightmare, although in recent years British Airways has been able to generate modest earnings from charter flights, which now account for a substantial portion of

900 miles. This airplane generated modest support among foreign airlines and some U.S. carriers.

Next came the wide-body airplanes, so called because of their twin aisles and up-to-ten-abreast seating in the coach section. The wide-body concept can be traced back to the U.S. Air Force's requirements for a large military freighter and American Airlines' call for an airplane to overcome forecasted airport congestion problems. Having decided not to stretch its 707 and having lost an expensive Air Force large-freighter design competition to Lockheed's C-5A, Boeing sought to recoup its research and development costs by altering the large freighter's design in such a way as to make it suitable for use as a commercial transport airplane. The resulting end product was the 747. Powered by four high-bypass-ratio turbofan engines, the Boeing 747 was a long-range airplane with a capacity of 365 passengers in mixed-class seating. (See figure 1–6.) Douglas and Lockheed designed the three-engine, wide-body DC-10 and the L-1011, respectively, to meet the needs of domestic carriers. The market for wide-body airplanes, however, was just not big enough to support the combined capacity of three U.S. manufacturers. For Lockheed, sales of its L-1011 were never sufficient to offset its enormous development costs and so the company was driven out of the commercial jet airplane business.

Europeans were deeply concerned about the new airplanes being developed in the United States. Although Britain's de Havilland Comet and France's Caravelle were among the first commercial jet aircraft, the Comet proved to be a commercial failure and the Caravelle was only marginally successful. The European manufacturers were eager to weaken the dominant position enjoyed by American manufacturers. With the Americans actively engaged in the development of new airplanes, the British government in 1964 appointed Lord Plowden to chair a committee to examine its aircraft industry. The Plowden Committee recommended that because of the limited size of the local markets in even the largest European countries, the aircraft manufacturers of major European countries (for example, England, France, and Germany) combine forces to compete with the U.S. aircraft industry. The committee's efforts led in turn to the formation of the Airbus Industrie in the late 1960s. In 1969, Britain withdrew from the Airbus program over a disagreement involving the choice of an engine manufacturer for Airbus Industrie's products; however, Britain later rejoined the program after Airbus Industrie launched the A-310 to compete with the Boeing 767/757.

In 1970, the Boeing 747 was introduced on the New York–London route, and in 1971 the DC-10 began service on the Chicago–Los Angeles route. The L-1011 was placed in scheduled service the following year. In Europe, Airbus Industrie introduced the A-300, a twin-engine, 250-passenger, wide-body airplane best suited for shorter-range markets. In the United States, the A-300 was operated by Eastern Airlines.

The high-bypass-ratio engines on these wide-body airplanes provided substantial reductions in direct operating costs and lower noise levels. In these engines, large fans accelerated additional air around the outside of the engine

Figure 1–6. Boeing 747

Photo Courtesy of Saudi Arabian Airlines

to produce a larger, slower-moving exhaust that was more efficient at subsonic speeds. The large size of the airplanes also helped alleviate problems of airport congestion (although the resulting reduction in flight frequency also limited the choice of flight times for some passengers). Moreover, the large lower-hold capacity of wide-body airplanes enabled airlines to carry all their passengers' baggage plus large amounts of freight, which in turn led to a reduction in the demand for airplanes dedicated solely to carrying freight.

During this period, developments in airplane technology once again outpaced advances in other areas of the air transportation system. An increase in traffic delays, safety problems resulting from mixing flight patterns of jet airplanes and general aviation airplanes, and environmental concerns highlighted the persistent inadequacy of the existing infrastructure. In response to environmental concerns, the National Environmental Policy Act of 1969 was passed, requiring the integration of national environmental objectives into existing civil aviation policies.

Also in 1969, the FAA established noise standards and regulations for the certification of turbojet airplanes of new design (FAR part 36). These regulations were similar to those established by the International Civil Aviation Organization (ICAO) and contained in its annex 16. Chapters 1–3 of the ICAO annex show the format of compliance by type of aircraft and the date of compliance.

In 1970, the Airport and Airway Development Act and the Airport and Airway Revenue Act were passed to allow for the expansion, improvement, and funding of airways and airport systems. This legislation authorized a $5.4 billion federal expenditure for the improvement of the national aviation system during the 1970s. The Airport Development Aid Program (ADAP), part of the Airport and Airway Development Act, authorized an expenditure of $2.5 billion for the improvement of existing airport facilities and the construction of new airports. To receive federal monies, state and local agencies were required to provide matching funds. Under the Airport and Airway Revenue Act, the Airport and Airway Trust Fund was established with money collected from the users of the system (via taxes on passenger tickets and aircraft fuel). Subsequently, vast sums in this fund have been used to help balance the federal budget deficits rather than to improve or construct airports.

During the mid-1970s, in an effort to tackle the problems of high inflation and a slow-growing economy, President Gerald Ford created the National Commission on Regulatory Reform to examine federal regulatory agencies and regulations in order to see whether the attendant costs of these regulations to consumers could be reduced. Senator Edward Kennedy increased the effort's momentum by selecting the CAB as an example of a federal regulatory agency that was ripe for reform. Although many economists had been long-standing critics of the CAB's regulatory control, some politicians now joined forces with the economists to introduce regulatory reform in the airline industry. The airline industry was targeted for a number of reasons, including the growing criticism from economists; the remarkable accomplishments of a few intrastate carriers, such as California-based PSA and Texas-based Southwest Airlines; the significance of the data that the airlines were required to report to the CAB; and the industry's high visibility. Extensive media coverage also provided a strong boost to the push for regulatory reform.

It is important to note that the government's initial objective was to introduce regulatory reform, not total deregulation. For example, the DOT's proposal to Congress in 1975 was to reduce the CAB's control over pricing and market entry—not to eliminate it. The CAB, however, advocated total deregulation—phased in over time—as opposed to regulatory reform. The goal of total deregulation became firmly rooted with the appointment of Alfred Kahn as chairman of the CAB.

During the regulatory reform debate, not only did the CAB begin to relax its control over economic regulations but some major carriers began to change their positions. United began to favor deregulation, presumably because it was a means to future expansion. Pan American also became an advocate of deregulation, primarily because it provided a means for obtaining domestic route authority. For its part, the CAB liberalized the implementation of numerous discount fares and authorized new routes, particularly when a route proposal included lower fares. In the international arena, the government approved the application of a British airline, Laker Airways, to provide low-fare transatlantic service.

Passage of the Airline Deregulation Act (ADA) of 1978 was facilitated by two occurrences. First, most major U.S. airlines eventually came to support deregulation. Second, during 1978 the industry posted substantial profits and the public had access to a wide variety of discount fares. Politicians thus faced little risk of an outcry from either the industry or the public. Concerns about loss of service to small communities were relieved by providing a ten-year Essential Air Service (EAS) program. Similarly, concerns of unions were assuaged by providing employee protective measures for dislocated workers; that is, airline employees were to receive federal assistance payments if they lost their jobs as a result of deregulation.

Deregulation of the airline industry was achieved in two phases, each consisting of a number of steps that gradually removed various forms of regulatory control. In November 1977, all-cargo airplane operations were deregulated, an action that was particularly important to Federal Express (a small package-delivery service) and to commuter airlines, which until that time had been restricted in the size of the airplanes they could operate. Passenger operations were deregulated in October 1978. The CAB itself went out of existence at the end of 1984, with any of its remaining responsibilities—such as authority for hearing international route cases and administration of the EAS program—being turned over to the DOT.

Developments after Deregulation

After passage of the ADA, the Aviation Safety and Noise Abatement Act (ASNA) of 1979 was passed to deal with noise and safety problems. In essence, this legislation called for the establishment of a single airport-noise measuring system and the identification of land uses that were compatible with airport development. Although local airport authorities still had responsibility for determining the most desirable land-use compatibility programs, the act required that they have their plans approved by the FAA, which in turn established standard procedures for measuring aircraft noise and for evaluating noise-compatibility programs. ASNA legislation also authorized the FAA to provide funding for noise-compatibility programs. Portions of Title I of the ASNA are included in FAR part 150.

Within the first three years of airline deregulation, two significant developments profoundly affected the traveling public's confidence in air transportation: the grounding of all DC-10 aircraft and the air traffic controllers' strike. In 1979, an American DC-10 taking off from Chicago's O'Hare airport crashed after an engine and supporting pylon dropped from the wing. This event put airplane manufacturers, airlines, and the FAA under intense pressure. Before the Chicago accident, there had been another accident involving a DC-10, when a rear cargo door blew out and the airplane crashed near Paris in 1974. These two DC-10 accidents raised so much public concern that the FAA not only grounded the DC-10 but also withdrew the DC-10's airworthiness certificate, an action that had not been taken against a commercial airliner since the end of World War II. After an intensive investigation, the FAA issued a series of airworthiness directives—which carry the force of law—mandating equipment modifications and changes in DC-10 maintenance procedures. As soon as the airlines were able to show compliance with the directives, their DC-10s were recertified and returned to service.

In an article tracing the history of the air traffic control system (and the FAA), James Loos, an air traffic control expert, noted the existence of two central issues: automation and labor-management relations.[27] Although the importance of both issues can be traced back at least forty years, in recent years related activities have increased significantly. The trend has been toward increased automation of decision making in airplane routing and separation, occurring against a backdrop of deteriorating labor-management relations.[28]

Labor-management problems reached their peak on August 5, 1981, when President Ronald Reagan fired more than eleven thousand striking air traffic controllers. Initially, this decision had a devastating impact on the aviation industry, dramatically reducing the air traffic control capacity of the system. In an effort to ease system demand by en route air traffic, the FAA imposed a quota system at the twenty-two large hub airports in the United States. But the quota system played havoc with the airline scheduling process, causing delays and creating enormous controversy over the process of allocating takeoff and landing slots. And although the quotas were eventually lifted as new air traffic controllers were added to the system, it was expected to take quite some time before the newly hired controllers could reach full-performance capabilities.

As the air transportation system struggled under the constraints imposed by the controllers' strike, a significant piece of legislation was enacted—the Airport and Airways Improvement Act of 1982 (AAIA). The existing national airspace system, including procedures and equipment, had evolved over the previous four decades through a series of piecemeal adjustments, using a mixture of equipment of varying technological generations. The FAA determined that the existing system had limited capability to expand and adapt to the changing requirements; moreover, the aged equipment was expensive to operate and maintain. The system's problems became even more evident after the strike by the Professional Air Traffic Controllers Organization (PATCO) in 1981. Developing a comprehensive plan to modernize air traffic control and the airway facilities system, the FAA in 1981 issued its National Airspace System Plan for Facilities, Equipment, and Associated Development. To implement this plan, Congress passed the AAIA in 1982, establishing an authorized level of funding for facilities, equipment, and airport grants. Also, given that the principal beneficiaries of the desired improvements were to be the users of the system, the AAIA set up a schedule of user fees similar to those levied by the ADAP in 1970 and consisting of a tax on (a) airline passengers and airfreight shippers and (b) fuel purchased by the general aviation community. As of 1989, the trust fund contained a surplus and was not being used for the purpose intended.

In the years following deregulation, free-market forces began to change the structure of the U.S. airline industry dramatically, primarily by fostering the emergence of many totally new airlines. The new entrants were homogeneous in neither the geographic scope of their route systems nor the services and prices they offered to the public. Although the spectrum of service/ price options offered by new entrants ranged from all-frills/high-price to no-frills/low-price, the new entrants as a group tended to have relatively low operating costs. Their lower costs were largely the result of a different type and level of service offered (that is, no frills) and higher productivity among employees (exemplified by the operations of People Express). Most new entrants remained small and had a high mortality rate. Nonetheless, low-cost carriers collectively have had an enormous impact on the rest of the airline industry, opening up air travel for people who previously might not have traveled or who might have traveled by other modes and stimulating the sharp competitive battles among various groups of airlines that have continued to produce winners and losers.

The major airlines, initially the losers, eventually assumed a superior competitive position because of the size of their route networks, the inherent benefits of their computer reservation systems, their more attractive mileage bonus programs, and their financial resources. In addition, many large incumbent carriers acquired smaller two-engine, two-pilot airplanes, and most negotiated wage concessions with their unionized labor force.

Among those airlines classified as commuter carriers, the number of commuters in operation has remained fairly constant since deregulation, but there has been substantial turnover. Furthermore, in exchange for various assistance incentives, many of the surviving commuter carriers have become exclusive feeder lines for individual large carriers (see chapter 5).

The growth and changes experienced by the U.S. airline industry following deregulation once again overburdened the infrastructure, leading to airport congestion and delays. The situation has led the government and industry to examine alternative methods of harmonizing the demand for air transportation services and the limited capacity of the airport and airway system. The alternatives being examined include an array of both technological solutions, such as simultaneous operations at closely spaced parallel runways, and economic solutions, such as implementation of differential pricing policies. (See chapter 4.)

Deregulation of the airline industry in the United States and the structural changes following it (such as the development of mega-carriers—the largest airlines with competitive advantages in market share, financial resources, operating leverage, and productive assets) have also had a significant impact on the airline industry in other parts of the world. A trend toward liberalization is clearly evident in Canada, Western Europe, Australia, and Japan. The development of mega-carriers in the United States has put considerable pressure on foreign airlines to consolidate their operations or to market services through joint marketing arrangements involving code-sharing agreements. Examples include the decisions of Pacific Western Airlines to acquire Canadian Pacific (both from Canada), of British Airways to acquire British Caledonian (both from Great Britain), and of SAS (from Scandinavia) to bid for SABENA (from Belgium), as well as the joint marketing agreement between British Airways and United Airlines. In addition, the marketing advantages enjoyed by the owners of three major computer reservation systems in the United States—United's Apollo, Continental/Eastern's System One, and TWA/Northwest's PARS—have led to the development of two primary European consortia, Amadeus and Galileo, and to one major consortium in the Far East, Abacus. Further, the desire to boost efficiency has increased the pace of privatization of government-owned airlines in most parts of the world.

Airline deregulation has also had a substantial impact on the manufacturers of commercial transport airplanes. As previously noted, Lockheed stopped producing commercial jet airplanes in 1981, and competition among Boeing, Douglas, and Airbus has correspondingly heightened. In the wake of two fuel crises and faced with increasing pressure from cost-conscious competitors, air carriers and manufacturers have been focusing on developing fuel-efficient airplanes. They have also been striving to build airplanes that are more comfortable, that alleviate noise problems, and that have greater range. Models introduced since 1980 include, for example, the twin-engine, 150- to 170-passenger DC-9-80 (now called the MD-80); the twin-engine, wide-body Boeing 767, which seats up to 280 passengers; and the twin-engine, 210- to 250-passenger A-310. A general trend in the industry continues to be the acquisition of two-engine, two-pilot, narrow-body airplanes for the domestic system and wide-body airplanes for the international system, with greater emphasis on nonstop sectors. A significant development in the international market was made possible by the FAA's relaxation of its rule that a two-engine airplane could be no more than one hour's flying time from an airport: Under the new rule and within certain guidelines, an airline can operate an airplane such as the twin-engine Boeing 767 across the Atlantic.

Despite expressions of interest by many airlines, the development of an entirely new 150-seat airplane has been a subject of great debate among airlines and manufacturers because of its high launching costs. It is estimated, for example, that the start-up costs for a new-generation commercial jet airplane can exceed $3 billion; engine development costs alone are almost $2 billion. Consequently, the large investment and the inherent risks have led manufacturers to stretch production runs of existing airplanes by offering different versions of such popular models as the Boeing 737 and the MD-80. In addition, airplane firms (both airframe and engine producers) have been developing international manufacturing partnerships. And in the case of the Airbus Industrie, the company has produced its A-320, a 150-passenger, twin-engine, narrow-body airplane with advanced technology features, particularly in terms of avionics. Figure 1–7 shows the various parts of the A-320 manufactured by each of the Airbus Industrie partners. (Figure 1–7 follows page 144.)

These new airplanes, in addition to having lower operating costs, should solve the aviation industry's most serious long-term problem—aircraft noise. The United States has already banned certain older four-engine jets, such as the unmodified Boeing 707 and DC-8, and most countries in Europe are about to do the same. The focus has now shifted to Stage 2 (the equivalent of ICAO annex 16, chapter 2) aircraft, such as Boeing 727-100 and some DC-9 models. The decision to ban Stage 2 aircraft is highly controversial, not only because it involves almost two-thirds of the airlines' fleet worldwide but also because it affects numerous other concerns, such as airline access to airports, airport capacity, and the value of used aircraft. Given the gravity of the decision, a number of different proposals are being examined to identify cost-effective ways of complying with Stage 2 and forthcoming Stage 3 requirements.

In the general aviation industry, the total number of active airplanes has remained at about the same level (210,000) since deregulation, but the number of new units shipped by manufacturers has been declining from a peak of 17,811 in 1978 to a low of 1,085 in 1987.[29] The decline in sales dollars, however, has not been as disappointing as the decline in units shipped, because of the production of more expensive corporate jets and turboprops. The reduction in the number of units sold has been the result of an increase in the price of airplanes and considerably higher operating costs. This trend has led to consolidation. There are now less than a dozen significant general aviation manufacturers in the United States, a number that is likely to decrease even further because of the increase in the level of foreign competition, particularly from foreign manufacturers that are supported by their governments (see chapter 8).

Despite its shaky beginnings, the multifaceted aviation industry has become an integral and dynamic component of the worldwide economy. Commercial aviation now provides reliable, convenient, and affordable domestic and international passenger service. In recent years, the aviation industry worldwide has been going through major structural and operational changes as a result of several factors, such as a rising global interest in the free enterprise system as a means of obtaining faster economic and social development; consumer demands in more mature markets for lower fares and broader price/service options; the privatization trend affecting many government-owned enterprises; limiting infrastructural constraints; and pending noise regulations. This changing environment worldwide has produced significant challenges for the aviation industry. Nevertheless, history makes it quite clear that the industry not only is accustomed to facing challenges but has repeatedly overcome and prospered from them.

Notes

1. M. Caidin, "Airplane," in *The World Book Encyclopedia* (Chicago: World Book, 1983), 200-229.

2. C. Solberg, *Conquest of the Skies: A History of Commercial Aviation in America* (Boston: Little, Brown, 1979), 4.

3. M. Caidin, "Airplane."

4. R.E.G. Davies, *A History of the World's Airlines* (London: Oxford University Press, 1964), 10.

5. Ibid., 39.

6. P.M. Bowers, *The DC-3: Fifty Years of Legendary Flight* (Blue Ridge Summit, Pa.: Tab Books, 1986), 1.

7. Ibid., 3.

8. Ibid., 4–5.

9. Ibid., 3.

10. Solberg, *Conquest of the Skies*, 38.

11. Davies, "*A History of the World's Airlines*", 56–57.

12. D. Mondey, ed., *The International Encyclopedia of Aviation* (New York: Crown, 1977), 291.

13. A.T. Wells, *Air Transportation: A Management Perspective* (Belmont, Calif.: Wadsworth, 1984), 80.

14. Jeppesen Sanderson, Inc., *Aviation Fundamentals* (Englewood, Colo.: Jeppesen Sanderson, 1983), 13–43.

15. J. Loos, "In the Beginning," *Journal of Air Traffic Control* 27, no. 3 (July-September 1985): 9–14.

16. Mondey, "*The International Encyclopedia of Aviation*," 250.

17. Solberg, *Conquest of the Skies*, 75.

18. Ibid., 76.

19. Davies, "*A History of the World's Airlines,*" 473.

20. A.T. Wells and B.D. Chadbourne, *General Aviation Marketing* (Malabar, Fla.: Krieger Publishing, 1987), 8–10.

21. H.P. Wolfe and D.A. NewMyer, *Aviation Industry Regulation* (Carbondale: Southern Illinois University Press, 1985), 26.

22. Mondey, "*The International Encyclopedia of Aviation,*" 283.

23. C.P. Burton, "Highlights of ATC History, 1945–1956," *Journal of Air Traffic Control* 27, no. 4 (October-December 1985): 25–29.

24. D.D. Thomas, "ATC in Transition, 1956–1963," *Journal of Air Traffic Control* 27, no.4 (October-December 1985): 30–38.

25. A. Sampson, *Empires of the Sky: The Politics, Contests, and Cartels of World Airlines* (New York: Random House, 1984), 115.

26. Thomas, "ATC in Transition, 1956–1963," 35.

27. J. Loos, "ATC History: The Modern Era, 1972–1985," *Journal of Air Traffic Control* 28, no. 2 (April-June 1986), 9.

28. Ibid., 10.

29. General Aviation Manufacturers Association (GAMA), *General Aviation Statistical Databook* (Washington, D.C.: GAMA, 1988), 4.

2

The Airplane: Evolution, Aerodynamics, Systems, and Design

his chapter, which examines powered flight from a number of viewpoints, begins with a brief history of airplane development. Basic airplane components, airplane movements and controls, and fundamental principles of aerodynamics are covered in the second section. The last section of the chapter provides an overview of airplane design.

It should be noted that although the words *airplane* and *aircraft* are often used interchangeably in the aviation industry, *aircraft* encompasses a broader definition. It includes both lighter-than-air and heavier-than-air vehicles; the lighter-than-air group including balloons and airships and the heavier-than-air group including fixed-wing airplanes, helicopters, and gliders. In this context, the word *airplane* usually refers to a vehicle that is power driven and has a fixed wing. It should also be noted that in the United States, the FAA, for the purpose of certifying pilots, classifies aircraft into four *categories:* lighter-than-air, rotorcraft, glider, and airplane. Within each category, aircraft with similar operating characteristics are grouped into *classes.* The airplane category consists of four classes: single-engine land, single-engine sea, multiengine land, and multiengine sea. Within each class, *types* specify particular makes or models of airplanes.

History and Development

Although the idea of flying has intrigued people for thousands of years, it was not until the latter part of the eighteenth century that significant progress occurred. Up to that time, efforts at human flight had generally focused on imitating birds, and inventors such as Leonardo da Vinci designed flying machines with flapping wings. In France in the late 1700s, however, the Montgolfier brothers began building and flying large paper balloons filled with hot air, and their balloon ascents are widely recognized as the first "flights" by humans.

Sir George Cayley (1773–1857) is considered the Father of the Airplane as we know it today. Cayley's ideas about a flying machine differed from those of Leonardo da Vinci. Moreover, they represented a great improvement over the Montgolfier brothers' balloon, which had little directional control. Cayley proposed an aircraft with a fixed wing for generating lift, a separate propeller for propulsion, and a horizontal and vertical tail system for stability. Other inventors and engineers, such as Otto Lilienthal in German and Octave Chanute and Samuel Langley in the United States, advanced Cayley's designs. This combined body of knowledge was the basis for designs by the Wright brothers, who are credited with being the first to build an airplane capable of sustained, controlled, and powered flight.

Once the basic principles of powered, fixed-wing flight were accepted, the development of the airplane began to move at a more rapid pace. During the first two decades of this century, the following events unfolded: Trajan Vuia, a Romanian inventor, built a full-size monoplane (single-wing plane) with the propeller mounted in front of the wing; a French company built an airplane with a monocoque (tubelike, single-shell) body, which made the airplane lighter; Igor Sikorsky, a Russian inventor, built an airplane with four engines; and Hugo Junkers, a German inventor, built the first airplane (the Junkers J-1) with an all-metal body and cantilever wings (a design that eliminates external wing-support struts), which allowed the airplane to fly at a higher speed.

World War I accelerated the development of the airplane and led to improvements that made it faster and more powerful. For example, the British developed the Vickers-Vimy bomber, which in 1919 allowed pilots Alcock and Brown to make the first nonstop transatlantic flight from Newfoundland to Ireland—a distance of some 2,000 miles—in about 16 hours. That same year, the Vickers-Vimy made an 11,000-mile trip from Hounslow, England, to Darwin, Australia, in about 125 hours. The improvements in airplane design during the decade of the 1920s were amply demonstrated by Charles Lindbergh's nonstop solo transatlantic flight in a Ryan monoplane, the *Spirit of St. Louis;* Lindbergh's 1927 flight from New York to Paris covered a distance of about 3,600 miles in less than 35 hours.

The pace of airplane development increased as well during the 1930s, as exemplified by the introduction of the Lockheed Vega monoplane. In 1933, Wiley Post flew his Vega, the *Winnie Mae,* around the world, his solo flight covering 16,000 miles in 115 hours. In the area of commercial transport, Douglas in 1936 introduced the DC-3, an airplane featuring such state-of-the-art technical innovations as stress-carrying skin that saved weight, variable-pitch propellers, wing flaps, and retractable landing gear. The DC-3 was popular with airlines because they could operate it at a profit, and it was popular with passengers because of its speed and comfort. With a maximum cruise speed of about 200 knots and a range at maximum payload of 300 nautical miles, the DC-3 could comfortably accommodate twenty-four passengers in a four-abreast seating configuration or carry sixteen sleeping berths—a feature that made it known as the Douglas Sleeper Transport. The success of the DC-3 led Douglas to introduce a whole series of more advanced airplanes that provided pressurization, larger capacity, greater speed, and longer range.

In 1939, airplane development took a giant step forward when the Germans flew the Heinkel 178, the world's first turbojet airplane. Engineers in the United Kingdom further refined the jet engine, which ultimately led to the development of a broad spectrum of commercial jet airplanes with higher productivity and eventually lower unit operating costs. For example, the British introduced into commercial service the de Havilland Comet in 1952, the French put their Caravelle into commercial service in 1958, and the Americans' Boeing 707 and DC-8 made their commercial flights in 1958 and 1959. Later, aircraft manufacturers introduced efficient short- and medium-haul jets, such as the DC-9 and the Boeing 727, and business jets, such as the Lockheed Jetstar, the North American (now Rockwell International) Sabreliner, and the Learjet. Subsequently, the development of more powerful, more economical, and quieter jet engines allowed the development of wide-body airplanes, such as the Boeing 747, DC-10, L-1011, and A-300.

The growth of the air transportation industry has been paced, to a large extent, by the increase in the productivity of the airplane. Airlines of the United States, for example, experienced a growth in passenger traffic of 15 percent during the 1950s and 13 percent during the 1960s. During both of these decades, airlines introduced airplanes that could fly at almost twice the speed of their predecessors (for example, the DC-7 relative to the DC-3, and the Boeing 707 versus the DC-7), with improved economics. Lower unit operating costs in turn allowed airlines to offer lower fares, which stimulated the personal and leisure travel markets.[1] These trends of increasing productivity and lower fares continued with the introduction of wide-body airplanes, even though those airplanes provided no increase in speed.

Based partly on the commercial success of the faster jet airplanes introduced in the 1950s and partly on the desire to leapfrog the Americans who had launched jet airplane programs offering improved economics, Britain and France independently decided to examine the feasibility of developing commercial supersonic transports (SSTs). The similarities of their two designs and the enormous anticipated development costs of each led both governments to decide, in the early 1960s, to pool their resources. The prototype flew in 1969, and production models entered airline service in May 1974.

The flag airlines of both Britain and France—that is, British Airways and Air France—had hoped that their SST, the Concorde, would attract significant traffic between their capitals and important cities such as Tokyo, Sydney, Johannesburg, and New York. The introduction of the Concorde was accompanied, however, by widespread environmentalist protests. In particular, the applications by British Airways and Air France to operate the Concorde to New York's John F. Kennedy Airport and Washington's Dulles Airport (from London and Paris, respectively) met with substantial public opposition. The U.S. secretary of transportation held hearings at which various parties involved in the issue of environmental impact had an opportunity to present their case. At the conclusion of the hearings, the Concorde was given permission to operate into Kennedy and Dulles airports for a trial period of sixteen months. The high projected operating costs (particularly for fuel), the environmental concerns, and the lateness of the Concorde program reduced other airlines' interest in the Concorde, resulting in a total production run of only sixteen airplanes.

During most of the first ten years of its operations, the Concorde was considered a commercial failure, primarily because of its high operating costs. An article published by *Air Transport World* in January 1986 provides the following explanation for the Concorde's inability to penetrate the North Atlantic market. First, for a typical transatlantic operation, the Concorde uses approximately the same amount of fuel as the Boeing 747, while it carries only about one-fourth the passengers. Second, maintenance costs for the Concorde are about four times as high as those for the Boeing 747. Third, annual utilization of the Concorde is less than one-third the utilization of subsonic transports—about 1,000 hours versus more than 3,000 hours per year. The result of the Concorde's higher operating costs was fares higher than those charged for travel on subsonic jets.[2] Unlike other new generations of airplanes, the Concorde did not offer improved economics and consequently did not penetrate the growing nonbusiness market.

An SST project in the United States was canceled in 1971 for political, economic, and environmental reasons; however, the idea has been kept alive by engineers at airframe manufacturing companies and at NASA. Further momentum was achieved in 1985, when the U.S. Office of Science, Technology, and Policy announced its National Aeronautical R&D Goals, focusing on the need to provide safe, efficient, and economical high-speed transportation and outlining as one of its goals to increase R&D activities aimed at developing technologies capable of providing transatmospheric flight by the twenty-first century. Such R&D activities are likely to concentrate on the National Aero-Space Plane (the X-30), an aircraft in the design stage that can take off and land on a conventional runway and undertake hypersonic, single-stage entry into space. The British version of the Aero-Space Plane is the HOTOL (horizontal takeoff and landing; see figure 2–1), currently being designed as a launch vehicle able to carry satellites into low orbit for a fraction of the cost for the Space Shuttle prior to the *Challenger* accident. As in the case of the United States, the British hope that the technology will be applicable to other vehicles, such as a hypersonic transport.

Although much of the interest and funding for the National Aero-Space Plane has come from the military, it is hoped that the development of the National Aero-Space Plane technology will also spur the development of a high-speed commercial transport (HSCT). Three reasons have been cited for the renewed interest in HSCT: (a) a growing concern that foreign competi-

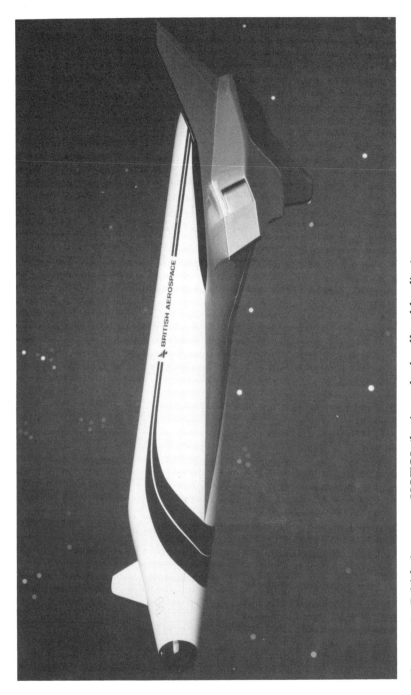

Figure 2–1. British Aerospace HOTOL (horizontal takeoff and landing)

Photo Courtesy of British Aerospace

tion is seriously challenging the U.S. lead in aeronautics technology; (b) a need to develop high-speed air links, now that the Pacific Rim countries have become the top trade partners of the United States; and (c) a belief in some circles that the technology is available to develop an economically feasible and environmentally acceptable second-generation commercial supersonic transport.

After the announcement in 1985 of the National Aeronautical R&D Goals, NASA sponsored studies to be conducted by Boeing Commercial Airplane Company and McDonnell Douglas to determine the viability of HSCT in the Mach 2 to 5 range (two to five times the speed of sound). Although at the time of this writing those studies have not been finalized, tentative findings are as follows: Beyond Mach 3, gains in productivity are marginal and technological challenges are enormous.[3] For example, at speeds greater than Mach 5, it is necessary to use cryogenic fuel, such as liquid methane or liquid hydrogen. This conclusion reduces the feasible speed limit on second-generation SSTs to less than Mach 3; however, even for a vehicle to travel at Mach 2, the technical challenges should not be underestimated. Those challenges can be appreciated by comparing the mission of the proposed HSCT with that of the Concorde: HSCT involves three times the payload (300 versus 100 passengers), twice the range (6,000 versus 3,000 nautical miles), Stage 3 noise limitations in subsonic flight, and perhaps most important, commercial viability at an average fare much lower than that for the Concorde, despite the fact that HSCT's development costs would be much higher than the Concorde's.[4]

Airplane Fundamentals

Four Forces of Flight

To understand how airplanes fly, it is necessary to have a basic understanding of aerodynamics—the study of air in motion and the forces that act on a surface when it moves through the air. An airplane in flight has two pairs of opposing forces: (a) lift and gravity (weight) and (b) thrust and drag. Lift, the upward force, counteracts gravity (the airplane's weight). Thrust, produced by the power plant, offsets drag, which is the air resistance to forward motion.

Lift is generated by the interaction of air rushing over the wing. This interaction is explained primarily by *Bernoulli's theorem*, which shows the relationship between speed and pressure in a fluid flow. Consider air flowing through a venturi tube (a tube with a restricted area of flow in the middle; see figure 2–2[a]. When air passes through the tube, its speed increases as it approaches the narrow part of the tube and its speed decreases after it has passed the narrow part of the tube. This process is analogous to the speed

(a) The Venturi Tube

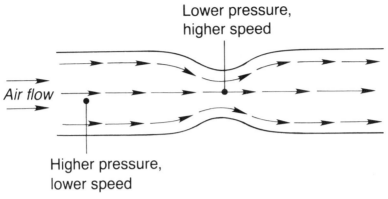

Lower pressure,
higher speed

Air flow

Higher pressure,
lower speed

(b) Generation of Lift

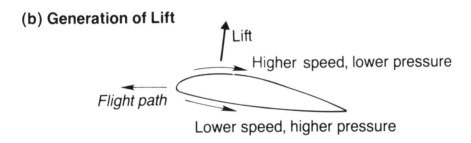

Lift

Higher speed, lower pressure

Flight path

Lower speed, higher pressure

(c) Four Forces of Flight

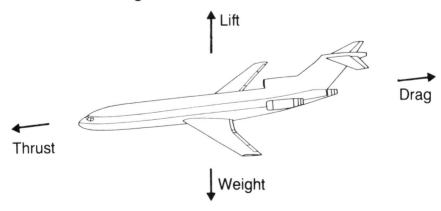

Lift

Drag

Thrust

Weight

Figure 2–2. Forces of Flight

of a river's current, which changes as the width of the channel changes; as the channel narrows, the current becomes swifter. Likewise, the speed of the air in the narrow part of a venturi tube increases relative to the wider part of the tube (the continuity principle). Energy is consumed in accelerating the air through the narrow part of the tube, and so there is less energy to exert pressure. Therefore, according to Bernoulli's theorem, as the speed of the air increases, its pressure decreases (other things being equal). As an airplane's wing moves through the air, the air moving over the curved upper surface of the wing increases in speed, resulting in a decrease in pressure. The air flowing over the flatter undersurface of the wing has a lower speed and a higher pressure relative to the air moving over the top of the wing. According to Bernoulli's theorem, this difference in pressure creates a net upward force—the lift (see figure 2–2[b]). The second part of lift can be explained by Newton's Third Law of Motion, which states that for every action there is an equal and opposite reaction. Notice in figure 2–2(b) that the wing is tilted slightly upward such that air moving over it is directed downward. The resulting downward force (the action) causes an equal reaction in the opposite direction—the lift on the wing.

Weight of an airplane is made up of three parts: the basic weight of the flying equipment and crew, commonly known as the operating empty weight (OEW); the weight of payload (passengers, baggage, and cargo); and fuel. The takeoff weight is the sum of all three parts. For jet airplanes in commercial service, the maximum takeoff weight ranges from about 90,000 pounds for the British Aerospace 146-200 to 870,000 pounds for the Boeing 747-400. Typically, the OEW accounts for about one-half the total takeoff weight; the payload and fuel together account for the remainder. From the standpoint of aerodynamic forces, both the total weight and the distribution of the weight within the airplane are important. Abnormal longitudinal weight distribution can disrupt an airplane's balance, making it nose heavy or tail heavy—conditions that can affect the pilot's ability to safely control the airplane. In simple terms, this condition is not unlike having individuals of different weights on a teeter-totter.

Thrust, the forward-moving force, is produced by an engine propeller or by the reaction of the hot gases coming out of a turbine engine. A propeller is shaped in such a way that when it is rotated it produces a force that pulls or pushes the airplane through the air. A *turbojet engine* generates thrust by drawing air into the engine, compressing and heating the air, spraying the compressed hot air with fuel, and burning the mixture in a combustion chamber. The expanding gases, with the associated increased pressure generated by the combustion, then pass through the *turbine* (giving it rotational motion) and exit through the exhaust *nozzle*. The turbine drives the compressor, which brings in more air. The *exhaust* progresses through the engine at a very high speed, and the reactive forces thrust the engine and the attached airframe forward.

Drag, the resistance of airflow, is made up of two parts: induced drag and parasite drag. *Induced drag* results from the aerodynamic forces that produce lift and occurs only when lift is being developed. The lift produced is not perpendicular to the flight path; rather, it slants slightly backward (see figure 2—2[b]). If the lift vector (showing the magnitude and direction of lift) is decomposed into two parts (vertical and horizontal), the rearward component of the lift vector is called induced drag. *Parasite drag* is the part of total aerodynamic drag that is not lift-induced. There are several types of parasite drag, but the most significant are form drag and skin friction drag. Form drag is that part of parasite drag which is influenced by the shape or form of the airplane and that can be reduced by streamlining the airplane. Skin friction drag pertains to the air clinging to the skin of the airplane.

Induced drag *decreases* with an increase in airplane speed, whereas parasite drag *increases* with an increase in airplane speed. The relationship between total drag (induced drag plus parasite drag) and airplane speed is a U-shaped curve. The bottom of the U represents the speed at which parasite drag is equal to induced drag and the total drag is minimized. This minimum is a unique point; on either side of this point (represented by either an increase or a decrease in speed), the total drag increases. Consequently, a decrease in speed from the minimum drag point increases drag and requires additional power to increase speed. Cruising speed is therefore maintained above the point of minimum drag to provide the benefits of a slightly shorter trip time without significant extra cost.

An airplane is in a *steady-state flight condition* when it is flying at a constant airspeed along a steady, level path. In this condition, lift is equal to weight and thrust is equal to drag (see figure 2–2[c]). To maneuver the airplane, it is necessary to change the balance of one of these two pairs of forces. For example, to climb, lift must be increased relative to weight.

Primary Parts of an Airplane

An airplane has three basic parts: (a) the airframe; (b) the propulsion system; and (c) instruments. The *airframe* consists of the wing, the fuselage, the tail assembly, the landing gear, and various subsystems (electrical, hydraulic, pneumatic, and the auxiliary power unit). The *propulsion system* on most commercial airplanes is one of two types, piston engines or turbine engines. Turbine engines, in turn, can be divided into three groups: turbojets, turboprops, and turbofans. *Instruments* can be subdivided into flight, engine, navigation, communication, and auxiliary instruments.

The Airframe. The *wing* has an almost flat lower surface and a convex top surface—a shape that helps create lift. It has four basic planform parts: the root, the tip, the leading edge, and the trailing edge (see figure 2–3). On most large airplanes, the wings are joined at their roots to the lower part of

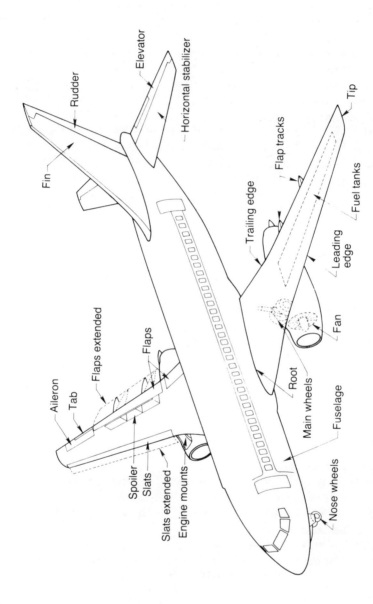

Figure 2–3. Primary Parts of an Airplane

the fuselage (*low-wing* design) and their tips are usually higher than their roots to provide stability (called a *dihedral* design). Lighter, slower airplanes tend to have a *straight-wing* design; that is, the leading edge of the wing is at a right angle to the fuselage. High-speed jets have a swept-wing design, with the wings slanting backward from the root to the tip. *Delta wings,* such as those incorporated in the design of the Concorde, provide advantages at supersonic speeds. The shape of the wing therefore depends on the type of the airplane and its basic flight mission.

Airplane wings have numerous devices that change the aerodynamic characteristics of the vehicle. These devices include flaps, slots, slats, spoilers, ailerons, and trim tabs. The *flaps* are located inboard (close to the fuselage) on the wing's trailing edge. When extended, they alter the shape and size of the wings (see figure 2–3). Flaps are lowered or extended a little during takeoff to increase the wing area, thereby creating more lift, which in turn decreases the runway length required for takeoff. (Wing chord—the distance from leading edge to trailing edge—and wingspan determine the wing area. Wing area determines lift capability and fuel capacity.) During landing, flaps are lowered by a greater amount to increase lift and drag, allowing an airplane to make a steeper approach and to land at a slower speed. A *slot* is a narrow gap at the leading edge of the wing that increases the amount of air flowing from the wing's lower surface to its upper surface. This increased airflow provides greater lift at lower airspeeds. A slot can be fixed or movable; if it is movable, it is called a *slat. Spoilers* are metal plates that are hinged on the upper part of the wings, and their purpose is to spoil the lift on the wing by disrupting the airflow on the upper surface (see figure 2–3). They act as airbrakes by creating drag when they are raised, helping the airplane increase the rate of descent during approach to landing. On landing, spoilers spoil the lift until the full weight of the airplane is taken up by the wheels, thereby increasing the braking capability. In this situation, spoilers assist in preventing the airplane from bouncing back into the air after landing, thus reducing the ground run after touchdown. It is also possible to bank (turn) an airplane by raising the spoiler on only one side. The *ailerons,* which are located outboard (away from the fuselage) on a wing's trailing edge, move up and down in opposite directions. They increase the lift on one side of the wing and decrease it on the other side, thus causing the airplane to roll. *Trimtabs* are secondary flight controls located on primary flight controls to exert pressure on control surfaces to which they are attached. Consequently, they are helpful in preventing pilot fatigue.

The *fuselage* is the main body of the airplane, extending from the nose to the tail. The fuselage on most commercial airplanes is tube-shaped and houses controls, crew, passengers, and cargo. In small single-engine airplanes, the engine is in front of the fuselage and the cabin can accommodate from one to six passengers, including the pilot. Large commercial transport airplanes have separate cabins for the crew and passengers. Commercial transport airplanes are further distinguished by cabin configuration: Narrow-body jet airplanes (10 to 12 feet in width) have one aisle, and wide-body jet airplanes (16 to 20 feet in width) have two aisles. In addition, passenger baggage and cargo are generally stored on a separate lower deck, although in a combi airplane—a modified combination commercial transport with a movable bulkhead—cargo is transported on the same deck as passengers. A convertible airplane is one that is designed to be used for passengers but can be "converted" to a freighter configuration. Quick-change airplanes—specialized versions of convertible models—are those with a fuselage that can be changed quickly from a passenger to a cargo configuration and vice versa. Although for a medium-size jet, such as the Boeing 727 the conversion time is short (about an hour), conversion is seldom done, because of the high cost of labor and the wear and tear on the airplane.

The *tail assembly* consists of a vertical stabilizer or fin and rudder, a horizontal stabilizer, and elevators (see figure 2-3). The *vertical stabilizer* keeps the rear of the airplane from swinging uncontrollably to the left or right; the *rudder,* which is hinged to the rear edge of the fin, enables the pilot to control the airplane's left-right movement. The *horizontal stabilizer* prevents uncontrollable upward and downward pitching of the tail. And the *elevators,* which are hinged to the rear of the horizontal stabilizer, allow the pilot to alter the plane's movement up and down (or, more accurately, to increase or decrease the angle of attack—the angle between the chord line and the relative wind). On some airplanes the entire horizontal surface moves as one solid unit; that kind of system is called a *stabilator* (a combination of *stabilizer* and *elevator*). As in the case of wings, tail assemblies also have a broad spectrum of arrangements. The horizontal stabilizer and the elevator can be located toward the bottom (for example, in the Boeing 737) or the top (for example, in the DC-9) of the vertical fin and the rudder. Some small airplanes, such as the Beech Bonanza, have a butterfly tail (V-shape), consisting of two fins with an elevator in each side.

The *landing gear,* or *undercarriage,* consists of struts, wheels, tires, and brakes that support the weight of the airplane on the ground and allow it to move on the ground. On light airplanes, the landing gear can be fixed or retractable. A fixed landing gear remains extended in flight, and although this system is simpler to make and maintain, it slows the speed of the airplane. When in flight, most transport airplanes are capable of retracting the main gear into either the wings or the fuselage, and the nose gear into the forward fuselage. Retracting the landing gear streamlines the airplane (reduces form drag), which allows the airplane to fly faster and farther.

The basic control systems in most airplanes include the control wheel (the yoke) and the rudder pedals. Whereas the control wheel operates the elevators and the ailerons, the rudder pedals operate the rudder. Subsystems—such as electrical, hydraulic, and pneumatic—assist the pilot to actuate the primary control surfaces (ailerons, elevators, and the rudder).

Primary control surfaces also have small, hinged sections called *trim tabs,* which are minicontrols that maintain the primary control surface in a deflected position aerodynamically, precluding the need for manual pressure. Thus, in a *trimmed* airplane, the pilot does not have to apply a force to keep a control surface in a deflected position. For instance, in a prolonged climb, the pilot can set the elevator trim tab to alleviate the need to continually pull back on the control wheel for the duration of the climb; then, upon reaching cruising altitude, the pilot can readjust the trim tab for straight and level flight.

Propulsion System. The power for flight comes from piston engines or turbine engines. A *piston-engine* airplane is propeller driven and powered by a reciprocating engine. The internal combustion reciprocating engine was the common propulsion system in airplanes through the 1940s and is still the most economical propulsion system in light airplanes that fly at speeds of less than 300 miles per hour. In this propulsion system, a mixture of air and gasoline is ignited inside the cylinders. The ignited mixture moves the pistons, which rotate the crankshaft; the crankshaft turns the propeller, which provides a thrust force in the forward direction. Thrust is provided by the *propeller,* which has blades that resemble the wing of an airplane. When the propeller is rotating, the pressure in front of the convex curved surface is less than the pressure at its flatter rear surface. This difference in pressure creates a net forward lift, or thrust, which causes the propeller to move forward—taking the airplane with it.

For high-speed airplanes and large commercial transports, the propulsion system is generally one of three types of gas *turbine* engines: turbojets, turboprops, or turbofans. Recently, engine manufacturers have been flight-testing a new type of propulsion system, the propfan, which is expected to produce substantial fuel savings relative to even the most fuel-efficient turbofan engines. A brief description of the propfan concept is provided later in this chapter. Figure 2–4 shows in schematic form the first three types of propulsion systems, while figure 2–5 shows the fourth type of propulsion system.

Jet propulsion developed commercially after World War II, and its availability enabled manufacturers to build airplanes that could fly higher and faster than their propeller-driven predecessors. Compared with internal combustion engines, jet engines are more efficient (having a higher thrust-to-weight ratio) and have less drag; they are also relatively free from vibration. The principle behind the *turbojet* is Newton's Third Law of Motion. Thrust is generated by the reaction to compressed, superheated gases blasting out of the nozzle at the rear of the engine. In a turbojet, all of the air flows through the combustion chamber and is expelled at a high speed. Because of the high speed of the jet exhaust moving through the nozzle, turbojet engines are noisy; efforts are now under way to develop a cost-effective hush

(a) Turbojet

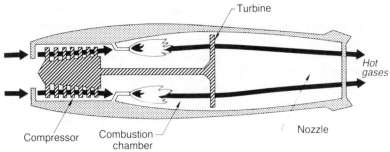

(b) Turbofan

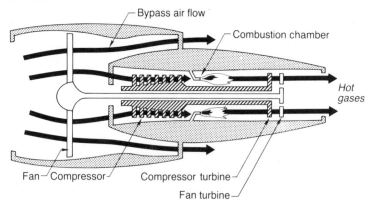

(c) Turboprop

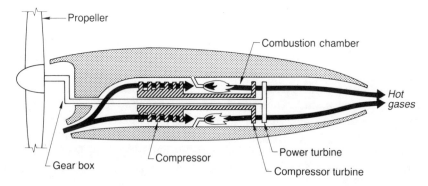

Figure 2–4. Propulsion Systems

Figure 2–5. General Electric Unducted Fan (UDF)

Photo Courtesy of Douglas Aircraft Company

kit for early model jet airplanes. In addition to being noisy, turbojets also have a high fuel consumption.

The *turboprop* engine, developed in the mid-1950s, is a gas turbine engine in which one turbine (the *compressor turbine*) drives the compressor and another turbine (the *power turbine*) drives the propeller via a shaft and a set of gears (see figure 2–4). Most of the turboprop's thrust (about 85 percent) is provided by the propeller, but a small amount (about 15 percent) is generated by the reaction of the hot gases escaping from the engine. Although turboprops are very efficient for airplanes flying in the range of 300 to 400 miles per hour, it is not feasible to use them for higher-speed airplanes, because of the compressibility problem that occurs when the tip speed of the propeller approaches the speed of sound.

The *turbofan* works like a turbojet engine, but it has a very large ducted (enclosed) fan mounted on a shaft in front of the compressor (see figure 2–4). The large fan acts as a first-stage compressor accelerating a large amount of air; however, only part of the total air drawn in by the fan passes through the turbojet and is burned with the fuel. The rest of the air bypasses the combustion chamber, thereby supplementing the thrust produced from the exhaust gases going through the nozzle. Accordingly, the total thrust produced is a combination of the thrust produced by the fan blades and that produced by the high-speed jet exhaust moving through the nozzle. Turbofans have two turbines, one driving the compressor and the other driving the fan. The *bypass ratio* is the ratio of the weight of air flowing through the fan (but bypassing the compressor and the burners) to the weight of air flowing through the compressor and the burners. Whereas the earliest turbofan engines had bypass ratios of between 0.3 and 1.4, later generation turbofans—those used on wide-body airplanes—have bypass ratios of between 5 and 6, hence the name *high-bypass-ratio* engines.[5] In turbofan-powered airplanes, the fan produces about two-thirds of the total thrust, which makes such engines more fuel efficient and less noisy than conventional turbojets.

The unducted (open) fan (UDF) engine is even more fuel efficient than the turbofan engine. (See figure 2–5.) It has a bypass ratio of 35 or even higher.[6] Consequently, this type of propulsion is also referred to as the *ultra-high-bypass* (UHB) engine. Additionally, the high, swept-back propfan blades are designed to delay the compressibility effects, allowing the airplane to reach significantly higher speeds in comparison with traditional turboprop engines. Two fans located at the *back* of the core engine rotate in opposite directions, their power coming from the power turbine. This type of propulsion system has been undergoing tests in actual flight conditions since 1986. The UDF/UHB concept could prove to be an important development for the next generation of transports, particularly if the price of fuel approaches the high levels which occurred during the early 1980s.

In vertical takeoff and landing vehicles, such as helicopters, the upward thrust is obtained by deflecting downward a part of the airstream from jets or propellers. The helicopter, for example, derives its lift and its forward propulsion from a system of long, slender rotating blades connected to a hub. For tilt-rotor aircraft, which are one type of short-takeoff and landing (STOL) vehicles, it is possible to tilt the rotor so that it functions as a propeller during the cruise portion of the flight. This configuration enables the vehicle to get off the ground quickly into steep or even vertical climbs, making the vehicle particularly useful for operating to and from congested areas. After lifting off the ground, safely clearing all obstacles, and reaching a cruising altitude, the vehicle looks and behaves more like a conventional propeller-driven vehicle (but with large-diameter, slow-turning propellers). The series of photographs shown in figure 2–6 depict the XV-15 in the helicopter mode, partially converted, and in the airplane mode. A civil version of the XV-15 has a strong market potential if it can achieve operating costs below those of the equivalent helicopters, fares competitive with short-haul airplane travel, and acceptable noise levels.

Instruments. The complexity of airplane instruments varies according to the performance capability of the airplane. In the cockpit of a modern large transport are five groups of instruments: flight, engine, navigation, communication, and auxiliary instruments. These instruments, coupled with the controls described earlier, enable the pilot to fly the airplane safely and efficiently in accordance with the flight plan. The instruments provide the pilot with information about the airplane and its subsystems; enable the pilot to obtain the necessary information to operate in the environment and communicate with other components of the aviation system (such as air traffic control); and provide vital information to the maintenance staff.

The most basic *flight* instruments common to all airplanes are an airspeed indicator, which informs the pilot about the speed of air flowing past the airplane; an altimeter, which indicates the height above sea level or the ground; and a turn-and-bank indicator, which provides data on the airplane's direction and rate of turn. More advanced aircraft, however, have many more flight instruments, such as a rate-of-climb indicator, which indicates vertical speed, and an attitude gyro, which shows the position of the airplane in relation to an artificial horizon.

Engine instruments measure performance and indicate how the engine is functioning. In the case of a single-engine, piston-driven airplane, the basic set of engine instruments includes an engine tachometer, oil pressure and temperature gauges, and a fuel quantity indicator. Large transports, of course, have many more instruments to monitor various temperatures and pressures, engine speeds, and fuel flows.

While the basic *navigation* instrument is the magnetic compass, airplanes—particularly those with the capability of flying in poor-visibility conditions—have much more complex instrumentation. Standard navigation

(a) Helicopter Mode.

(b) Partially Converted.

(c) Airplane Mode.

Figure 2–6. Bell Helicopter Textron X-V15

Photo Courtesy of Bell Helicopter Textron

equipment includes a very high frequency omnidirectional range (VOR) receiver that provides electromagnetic guidance along a selected course; a distance-measuring equipment (DME) receiver that shows the distance to VORs; and an instrument landing system (ILS) that shows the vertical and lateral deviation from a glide-path signal for landings at appropriately equipped airports. Airplanes with higher performance capability have additional sophisticated navigation equipment, such as RNAV (area navigation, discussed in chapter 3). An example of RNAV equipment is the inertial navigation system (INS), a very accurate, self-contained unit that provides information on the position of the airplane relative to specific points on the earth.

The basic *communication* instrument is a two-way radio that can be tuned to a variety of frequencies. This type of radio enables pilots to communicate with outsiders on different radio frequencies. Pilots communicate with air traffic control personnel, fixed-base operators (see chapter 8), weather stations, pilots in other airplanes, company staff, and the cabin crew. Larger airplanes have more than one radio for redundancy, using one unit for receiving information and the other for sending information or using the radios for two crew members to communicate with two outside parties at the same time. In addition, all commercial airplanes are equipped with transponders (see chapter 3), which automatically send coded replies to interrogations by air traffic control radar.

Finally, *auxiliary* instruments consist of a variety of instruments and controls for auxiliary systems. These instruments show the status of various kinds of electrical, hydraulic, and mechanical systems—for example, the position of landing gear and the status of cabin pressure and temperature. This group of instruments also includes fire detection and warning systems, flight data recorders, and cockpit voice recorders. It is also possible to have built-in test equipment to evaluate the response of particular subsystems. On many transports, equipment is used to record the performance of power plants and aircraft systems; these data are then evaluated by maintenance personnel to determine any need for adjustment, repair, or replacement of the monitored component.

Airplane Movements, Airplane Performance, and Airplane Stability and Control

Unlike surface vehicles that move in only two dimensions (right-left and front-back), an airplane moves in three dimensions. Rotational movements by airplanes around the three dimensions are called pitch, roll, and yaw. (See figure 2–7.) When the nose of an airplane moves up or down about the lateral axis (pivots on an imaginary line drawn from wingtip to wingtip), the movement is called pitch. This movement is achieved by moving the control wheel (yoke) forward or backward. A forward movement of the

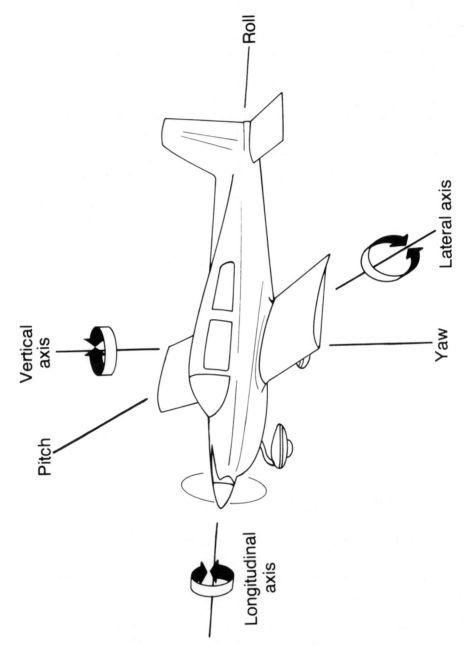

Figure 2–7. Axes of Rotation and Movements

control wheel lowers the elevator and makes the nose of the airplane move downward; pulling the control wheel backward raises the elevator and makes the nose move up.

When an airplane's wingtips move up or down about the longitudinal axis (pivoting on an imaginary line drawn from nose to tail), the movement is called roll. It is achieved by turning the control wheel from side to side, which operates the *ailerons*. The ailerons are connected (rigged) to the control wheel in such a way that they both move when the control wheel is turned, but they move in opposite directions. Turning the control wheel to the right causes the aileron on the right wing to be deflected upward and the aileron on the left wing to be deflected downward; this causes the left wing to rise and the right wing to dip, making the airplane roll to the right. The opposite movement takes place when the control wheel is turned to the left.

When an airplane's nose turns in either direction about its vertical axis (pivots on an imaginary line drawn from top to bottom), the movement is called yaw. The yaw movement is achieved by pushing the left or right rudder pedal, which moves the rudder. Depressing the left pedal swings the rudder to the left, causing the nose to swing to the left; the opposite movement takes place when the right pedal is depressed. It is necessary to keep in mind that because movements along the three axes are not independent, they must be controlled by coordinated use of the appropriate control surfaces. A deflection of ailerons, for example, will result in yaw as well as roll. To maintain a coordinated turn, it is therefore necessary to use more than one control surface to achieve a desired movement. If the four forces of flight (lift, weight, thrust, and drag) are out of balance, an uncoordinated turn will result.

The previous discussion of aerodynamic principles was limited to a simple explanation of the four basic forces of flight. Flight dynamics is a part of aeronautical engineering that deals with airplane performance and airplane stability and control. Airplane *performance* relates to the technical capabilities and limitations of an airplane in different phases of flight, the effect of forces such as drag and thrust, and the associated motion of an airplane in response to these forces. Performance measures of an airplane with respect to takeoff, climb, cruise speed, fuel efficiency, range, endurance, descent, glide, and landing characteristics are derived from well-defined formulas and manufacturer-supplied charts and tables.

The computation of each performance characteristic requires a consideration of numerous factors. For example, range—the distance an airplane can fly—is a function of, among other factors, payload. The payload-range diagram in figure 2–8 shows the relationship between payload and range for selected Boeing airplanes. The horizontal part of the line for each profiled aircraft shows the longest distance the airplane can fly with a maximum payload (the first breakpoint at the right-hand end). The corresponding weight

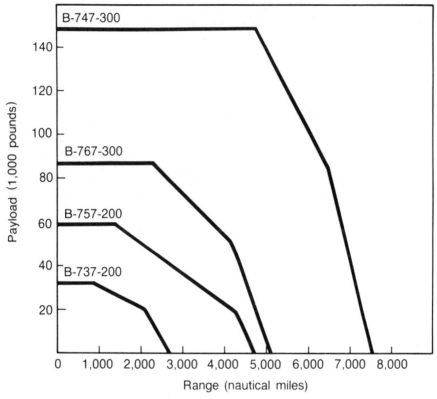

Figure 2–8. Typical Payload-Range Curves

Source: Boeing Commercial Airplanes
Note: The diagram is for illustrative purposes only.

is the maximum structural takeoff weight, which is usually less than the sum of the weights of a full passenger load and full fuel tanks. The second break-point shows the longest distance the airplane can fly with full tanks. To fly this distance, the airplane would still take off within its maximum structural weight, but to accommodate the added weight of full fuel tanks, some pay-load (passengers and/or cargo) would have to be sacrificed. For instance, the Boeing 747-200's maximum takeoff weight is 833,000 pounds. That air-plane's operating weight is approximately 375,000 pounds, its maximum fuel capacity is about 360,000 pounds, and its maximum structural payload is about 150,000 pounds. Notice that the sum of these figures for operating weight, maximum fuel capacity, and maximum structural payload is 885,000 pounds, which is about 6 percent more than the maximum takeoff weight. There is an obvious trade-off that must be made between the maximum payload and the maximum range (range with full passenger payload is about 6,900 nautical miles, versus the maximum fuel range of about 7,900 nautical miles).

The payload-range relationship is influenced by a number of factors, including type of engine, speed, altitude, fuel, rules on fuel reserves and distance to alternate airports, and atmospheric conditions. Of course, airplanes can be flown distances less than their optimum design range, but economic penalties are incurred in such situations. Figure 2–9 shows the relationship between direct operating costs and range for selected Boeing airplanes. Direct operating costs decline as distance increases, because the costs of climbing to and descending from cruise altitude are spread over longer cruise distances.

As mentioned in the "History and Development" section of this chapter, some of the biggest challenges confronting the first airplane designers were stability and controllability. *Stability* is the general tendency of an airplane to remain in any flight condition selected by the pilot; that flight condition could, for example, be a level flight or a climb. A stable airplane is designed to return to its selected flight condition after it experiences an unplanned force such as turbulence. Airplanes are designed to be stable to varying

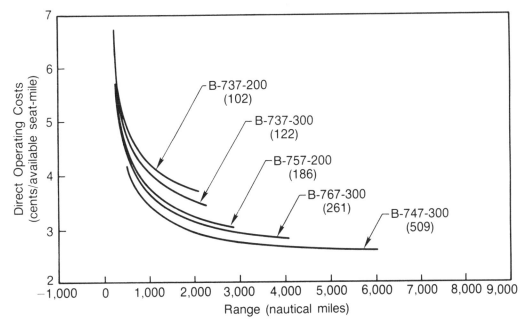

Figure 2–9. Typical Direct Operating Costs versus Range Curves

Source: Boeing Commercial Airplanes
Note: This diagram is for illustrative purposes only. Number of seats is given in parenthesis.

degrees—that is, they are designed to return, without pilot assistance, to their equilibrium position after they have been disturbed. At first, it would appear that an airplane should be designed to be as stable as possible. Yet, a pilot also needs to be able to maneuver the airplane quickly and without too much effort. Moreover, excessive stability can adversely affect the economy of the flight—for example, as a result of overdimensioned control surfaces. Consequently, airplane designers trade off a certain amount of stability for maneuverability and flight economics. The maneuverability trade-off is clearly evident, for example, in the designs of military airplanes (such as the F-16) versus airplanes used for commercial transportation. Stability is provided by the horizontal stabilizer, the vertical fin, and the wings. *Control* refers to the ability of the pilot to offset the influence of a disturbing force such as turbulence and to steer the airplane in a desired direction.

Airplane Design Considerations

As is the case for other segments of the aviation industry, airplane manufacturers must comply with government regulations. In the United States, aircraft manufacturers must comply with the FAA's Federal Aviation Regulations (FARs) encompassing design and certification requirements. In broad terms, the manufacturing industry works within the framework of FAR part 21, which spells out the certification process for new aircraft. Specific design requirements are contained in part 23 for small aircraft (with weight less than 12,500 pounds) and part 25 for larger aircraft (with weight more than 12,500 pounds). Airplanes must also meet noise standards contained in FAR part 36 ("Noise Standards: Aircraft Type and Airworthiness Certification"). These FARs deal with the processes that manufacturers must follow to introduce new airplanes into the marketplace. The overall certification process for a large transport airplane takes several years. The FAA's involvement begins during the design stage and continues through the development, production, and testing stages for each component (fuselage, wings, landing gear, power plants, and so forth). To gain an appreciation of what is involved in the airplane certification process, readers are referred to H.P. Wolfe and D.A. NewMyer's case study of the Boeing 767.[7] Readers interested in the certification process for general aviation airplanes are referred to chapter 17 of D.B. Thurston's *Design for Flying*.[8]

Designing a commercial airplane is a complex and economically risky process. It is complex because it involves selecting an optimal combination of cost-effective technologies and making numerous technical and economic trade-offs to produce an airplane that is safe, correctly sized, and launched at the right time to meet the current and future requirements of the marketplace. And the process is risky for at least two reasons. First, the time between the decision to launch an airplane type and the time it enters service is long—sometimes five years—and during this time, the needs of the marketplace can change drastically. During times when fuel prices are high, for example, customers are willing to pay a high acquisition price as long as the fuel component of the direct operating costs is low; during times when fuel prices are low, the opposite is true. The second part of the risk relates to the magnitude of the investment required to design, test, certify, and produce the airplane. At present, the investment required for a new large jet transport is estimated to be in excess of $3 billion.

The basic configuration of a commercial airplane is a function of a number of different (and often competing) considerations, such as payload requirements (number of passengers and amount of cargo), performance requirements (range, speed, runway capability), and marketing considerations (profitability of operations and passenger comfort). The payload-range performance dictates the takeoff weight for a given technology. The takeoff weight, combined with the desired approach and landing performance, dictates the wing area. The wing area, combined with aerodynamic considerations such as lift-induced drag, provides an input to wing characteristics, such as the aspect ratio (span squared, divided by area) and the sweep angle. Many trade-offs are made in selecting the ultimate shape and location of the wing; for example, a wing that is designed specifically for efficient high speed during cruise (low drag) will have poor lift characteristics at low speeds. Similarly, trade-offs are made for the location of wing, high or low. Factors considered include the aerodynamic performance (lift and drag characteristics), the impact on cargo space for low-wing design and the impact on headroom in the cabin for high-wing design, and ground clearance. Ultimately, the final wing design—at least in commercial airplanes—usually reflects a number of compromises.

The wing area and the required takeoff performance provide input to the required thrust-to-weight ratio and subsequently to the size of power plants required. Selection of a power plant is therefore a function of the thrust required, specific fuel consumption, and maintenance costs. Once again, the size of the power plant, the number of engines, and their location represent compromises. The number of engines represents a blended compromise of economics, the ability to deal with emergency situations such as engine failure, and operating performance. The current trend is to favor two engines, even for airplanes intended to operate on long-haul, overwater routes. The location of engines is a trade-off among many factors, such as noise, accessibility for engine maintenance, potential interference with flaps in the case of wing-mounted engines, and airplane performance. In propeller-driven airplanes with single engines, the engine is placed at the nose; two- or four-engine airplanes normally have the engines on the wings. Turbojets and turbofans can be placed above, on, below, or in the wings. They can also be placed at the back, on top, or on either side of the fuselage. There are no universal answers to the question of the optimal location of the power plant.[9]

Control of airplane noise has become an important consideration in airplane design. While part of the airplane noise-control problem can be handled by airport operators through effective land-use planning and through different ways of conducting operations, to a large extent noise is being reduced at the airplane design stage. Noise is most critical during the landing and takeoff phases of a flight. Federal governments around the world have established specific standards that must be met by both existing airplanes and new airplanes. In the United States, these standards are contained in the FAA's FAR parts 36 and 91. Part 36 contains three stages for controlling airplane noise. Stage 1, for example, which became effective in January 1985, prohibited certain types of airplanes (such as the Boeing 707 and the DC-8) from operating in the United States unless they received exemption or were modified. Part 91 deals with operating noise limits and shows the applicability of part 36. Although the precise time limit for Stage 2 has not yet been established, Stage 2 requirements when implemented would affect almost three-fourths of the U.S. domestic commercial fleet. New airplanes are being designed to meet the more stringent Stage 3 standards, which effectively reduce the noise to the ambient noise levels in the community. Airplane designers are able to achieve such low noise levels through the use of advanced technology.

Cabin design involves at least four kinds of considerations: safety, economics, comfort, and in-flight services. Safety considerations relate to such matters as the number and location of emergency exits and the ease with which passengers can get in and out of their seats. (A full aircraft evacuation is demonstrated during the certification process.) Economic considerations pertain to the ability of the user to make a profit. From this point of view, the objective is to squeeze the maximum number of seats into the airplane— a policy that has been followed by most charter airlines and some new low-fare scheduled airlines. Yet, the greater the number of seats in a given amount of space, the lower the level of comfort for passengers. Cabin design also takes into account freight operations, which can have a significant impact on airplane economics. And, cabin design is a function of the in-flight services offered. Long-haul flights, for example, require meal services, which in turn have an impact on the size, type, and location of galleys. In-flight entertainment, particularly in airplanes operating on long-haul routes, also has an impact on cabin design. Once again, as in the case of wing design and the selection and location of the power plant, cabin design is a compromise. Moreover, the process of resolving conflicting issues is often not subject to analytical analysis; rather, the compromise represents the designer's judgment.

The nature of such conflicting requirements dictates the need to examine several configurations in the preliminary design phase. Eventually a few general configurations are selected and scale models developed. Accurate scale models are then tested in the wind tunnel (which simulates conditions that the airplane will experience in actual flight) to determine whether the proposed design produces the desired performance. Specifically, wind-tunnel testing is undertaken to (a) verify design theories and assumptions; (b) analyze flying characteristics under various flight conditions for which there are no adequate theories; and (c) develop maximum or optimal parameters for flight performance. One of the general configurations is then examined in detailed design and subjected to more rigorous tests. Hundreds of thousands of person-hours are spent in analyzing the preliminary design. Each component of the structure is carefully tested, in great detail and many times over, before a final design can be accepted. High-speed computers have assisted in this process, for which the margins for error are very small.

Ultimately, a prototype is built to test the final design under actual conditions. The objectives of these tests are to demonstrate compliance with safety regulations and to verify expected performance. Initially, the prototype is used to conduct tests on the ground, such as running the engines at high speed and taxiing the plane at various speeds. Prototypes also need government approval before they can be test-flown. The flight-test stage is a long series of carefully planned test flights with a multitude of complicated instruments on board. Once the prototype satisfies all requirements, the design is released for production.

Airplane designers are constantly examining new technologies to improve airplane safety, economics, performance, and passenger service. Examples include the use of *composite materials* (nonmetallic materials made of two separate elements) to reduce weight, the proposed use of the propfan to reduce fuel costs, and the use of a flight management system in the cockpit to improve pilot-airplane interface. The decision to use advanced technologies in some areas (for example, composites) is a relatively straightforward analysis of costs and benefits. The decision to use advanced technologies in other areas, however, can be simple (as in using carbon disc brakes, which reduce weight) or complex (as in making improvements in the design of the cockpit). Improved cockpit and system design with computer technology has influenced the work load and pilot duties. For example, whereas the flight deck at one time had a crew that consisted of a captain, a copilot, a flight engineer, and a radio operator, the flight complement has now been reduced to three and on some jet transports to two pilots. Airplane designers must examine not only the availability and applicability of a particular technology (for example, sophisticated computers) but also various aspects of the human-machine interaction. Moreover, the decision to use a new technology becomes quite complex if it affects the role of the pilot. It is in this area that the research conducted by "human factors" specialists has been particularly helpful to airplane designers.

Human factors research (also known as the science of ergonomics) studies the relationship between people and the activities they perform. More precisely, human factors is a multidisciplinary approach—involving industrial engineering, psychology, computer science, and physiology—that seeks to study, explain, predict, and improve the behavior and performance of humans operating in complex environments. In contemporary literature, aviation human factors is also described as cockpit resource management or flight-deck resource management. The application of aviation-related human factors research deals with the efficient utilization and management of people, equipment, and information.

During World War II, a research group at Cambridge University in England built a flight-deck simulator and conducted experiments that led to the conclusion that the behavior of a skilled operator was affected by the design, layout, and interpretation of displays and controls.[10] Since World War II, the study of human factors has continued to play an important role in crew selection and training, the design of flight-deck controls and displays, and the development of flight simulators. It is now widely recognized that the ability to effectively and efficiently handle a pilot's work load depends on several factors, including the system design, amount and timing of the work load, training, decisional attributes and interpersonal behavior of the flight crew, and accurate conveyance of vital information.

Determining the amount of information a pilot can absorb in different situations, the most efficient form of displaying that information, and the type of information to be displayed to maximize performance and safety is the goal of human factors research. Researchers are studying, for example, the means by which different information should be displayed—visually, aurally, or tactually. Visual information, in turn, requires decisions relating to analog versus digital, exclusive panel versus shared panel, dial shape and size, scale graduations, and, in the case of alphanumeric displays, brightness, color, size, and legibility. Products of this research include the development of cathode ray tube (CRT) displays and *head-up displays* (HUD).

CRT displays are essentially small computer monitors that have replaced traditional mechanical flight and electrical navigation instruments. CRT displays incorporate the output of these many instruments into a few screens that give the pilot a clearer picture of the plane's status and progress. The HUD projects pertinent flight information onto a transparent screen by the windshield, allowing the pilot to monitor flight conditions outside the airplane while at the same time monitoring vital flight parameters. A HUD unit is particularly useful in an instrument approach during the low-visibility transition from instrument to ground navigation.

Another area of growing interest centers on warning, alerting, and advisory systems. Designers are particularly interested in systems that (a) provide timely information to the pilot on the occurrence of an unusual event and on the nature of the condition and then (b) supply the pilot with suggestions for appropriate corrective actions.

Just as the design of the displays depends on the type of information being sent to the pilot, the design of controls (buttons, switches, knobs, levers, and so forth) depends on the type of information being transmitted back to the system. In this case, designers are usually concerned with a control's location, sensitivity, direction of movement, resistance, and coding.[11] The development of automated flight-deck systems introduced keyboards, for data entry; however, that innovation brings into focus new issues, such as the accuracy of data entry and the detection of errors.

In recent years, airplane designers have been working toward increasing the level of automation on the flight deck. Advanced flight-deck designs now contain such advanced technologies as the fly-by-wire system, multifunction electronic displays, sophisticated computers to monitor system components, voice-interactive systems to communicate with computers, and innovative design features like the side-stick controller. (The *fly-by-wire* system is particularly noteworthy, in that it replaces the mechanical and hydraulic flight-control systems with electrical controls and provides an additional benefit in both weight savings and system maintenance.) A number of these technological advancements are included in the Airbus A-320 flight deck (see figure 2–10 following page 144). In addition, the development of *flight management systems* (FMSs) is another example of the movement toward increased flight automation.

There is some concern, however, that the movement toward increased automation is changing the primary roles of flight-deck personnel from pilots of airplanes to monitors of computer systems. On the other hand, automation has reduced the work load for individual pilots and has reduced the size of the flight-deck complement from three pilots to two on some airplanes. On the other hand, while additional automation will undoubtedly reduce operator work load and further improve flight performance, it does raise three critical issues. First, pilots could come to rely too heavily on automated flight systems, thereby neglecting fundamental piloting and navigating skills. Second, the automated systems may reduce pilot work load to the point that boredom and inattention become serious problems on long-haul flights. Third, automated flight systems may be designed according to existing technological capabilities but not necessarily according to the flight crew's needs or capabilities. Thus, with rapid advances in flight automation technology, the study of human factors continues to play an important role in examining the impact of the changing cockpit environment.

New plateaus in airplane design have represented more than just the frontier of technology. Not only have they had an enormous impact on the structure and operations of the entire civil aviation industry, but they have affected the economic, demographic, and social patterns of the world. Whereas the flights of the Wright brothers and Louis Bleriot opened a new age of possibility, the DC-3 proved that air transportation was safe, reliable, and economical. Whereas the jets redrew the airmap of the world, the wide-body airplanes made mass tourism possible. In the future, the high-speed commercial transport may well serve to further improve global mobility and contribute to the integration of a global economy.

Notes

1. M. E. Brenner, "Marketing Considerations for Future Supersonic Transports," in *High Speed Commercial Flight: The Coming Era*, ed. J.P. Loomis (Columbus, Ohio: Battelle Press, 1987), 79–90.

2. J.P. Woolsey, "British Airways Concorde Now Considered 'Flagship of the Fleet,' " *Air Transport World*, January 1986, 40–45.

3. J. Ott, "High-Speed Transport Study Focuses on Lower Mach Range," *Aviation Week and Space Technology*, February 29, 1988, 60–61.

4. J. Ott, "HSCT Research Defines Weight, Fuel Issues," *Aviation Week and Space Technology*, March 28, 1988, 88–90.

5. W. Green, G. Swanborough, and J. Mowinski, *Modern Commercial Aircraft* (New York: Crown Publishers, 1987), 32–34.

6. Ibid., 34.

7. H.P. Wolfe and D.A. NewMyer, *Aviation Industry Regulation* (Carbondale: Southern Illinois University Press, 1985), 123–27.

8. D.B. Thurston, *Design for Flying* (New York: McGraw-Hill, 1978), chap. 17.

9. R.S. Shevell, *Fundamentals of Flight* (Englewood Cliffs, N.J.: Prentice Hall, 1983), 348–54.

10. F.H. Hawkins, *Human Factors in Flight* (Brookfield, Vt.: Gower Technical Press, 1987), 16.

11. Ibid., 244–45.

3
Air Traffic Control and Navigation System

The preceding chapter described how an airplane flies and how it is designed. This chapter provides an introduction to how an airplane relies on air traffic control (ATC) services and various types of navigation systems to safely operate in domestic and international airspace. Together, these essential components of the aviation industry provide a safe, expeditious, and orderly flow of air traffic.

Using sophisticated equipment and well-defined rules and procedures, skilled air traffic controllers control the movement of an aircraft both on the ground and during a flight by allocating available resources (runways and airspace) among a large number of users. The controllers ensure safe separation among thousands of airplanes that share a common airspace. That safe separation requires efficient communication between pilots and ground-based air traffic controllers who monitor airspace.

Every airplane is equipped with some form of navigation equipment, which may range from a simple compass in a two-seat, single-engine airplane to an elaborate inertial navigation system in intercontinental transports. Regardless of its degree of sophistication, such equipment serves one purpose: safe and efficient guidance from one airport to another.

Although the objectives of most ATC systems and the principles of various navigation systems are essentially the same throughout the world, the equipment, airspace structure, and procedures for controlling air traffic vary from region to region. Because a single chapter or even an entire book cannot possibly cover all the unique characteristics of each country's ATC and navigation system, this chapter provides only a broad overview of general ATC and navigation principles applicable worldwide; however, from time to time, discussion focuses on one system in particular—the domestic air traffic control and navigation system in the United States.

The U.S. system is chosen for closer study for two reasons. First, it is one of the oldest air traffic control systems in the world and indeed has become the largest and most complex air traffic network in the world. Second, experience gained from the U.S. system, coupled with that of other leading nations (for example, the United Kingdom, France, and West Germany), has helped develop, through the International Civil Aviation Organization, international standards, practices, and procedures covering various aspects of air traffic control. Consequently, although subcomponents of individual systems may vary from nation to nation, an understanding of the U.S. system will provide insight into the fundamental principles of complex ATC and navigation systems.

Air traffic control and navigation systems around the world have evolved over the past seventy years in response to the growing and changing needs of users in general aviation, commercial aviation, and the military. User requirements are based on vastly different aircraft performance capabilities and on the experience levels and flying skills of the pilots using the system. In the United States, for example, the general aviation fleet numbers more than 220,000 aircraft, consisting of fixed-wing airplanes (ranging from simple, single-piston-engine airplanes to sophisticated, multiple-turbine-engine airplanes), helicopters, gliders, and lighter-than-air vehicles. The commercial airline fleet in the United States accounts for 4,500 more aircraft, about two-thirds of which are turbojets with 80 to 400 seats. Similarly, a broad range of experience exists among pilots using the U.S. airspace system. Of the 699,653 pilots certified in the United States as of the end of 1987, 21 percent were student pilots, 43 percent were private pilots, 21 percent were commercial pilots, and 13 percent were airline transport pilots. The remaining 2 percent held a variety of certificates involving helicopters, gliders, or lighter-than-air vehicles.[1]

The basic air traffic control and navigation system comprises three broad categories: (a) rules and procedures; (b) facilities and services; and (c) equipment, including that for surveillance, navigation, and communication. This chapter provides a brief description of each of these categories in the context of the U.S. system and, when appropriate, the worldwide system.

Rules and Procedures

Safe and efficient operation of aircraft both on the ground and in the air requires well-defined rules and procedures that must be followed by pilots and air traffic controllers. Worldwide, 158 nations have signed the Convention on International Civil Aviation, which at present has eighteen annexes, a number of them pertaining to the ATC and navigation system. For example, annex 2 ("Rules of the Air") deals with general rules as well as those relating to the conduct of visual and instrument flights, and annex 11 ("Air Traffic Services") defines air traffic services and specifies the worldwide standards and recommended practices (SARPs) applicable in the provision of those services. The International Civil Aviation Organization (ICAO) also formulates Procedures for Air Navigation Services (PANS), composed, for the most part, of operating practices and often amplifying the basic principles in the corresponding SARPs. While the ICAO is responsible for the international coordination of rules and procedures relating to the establishment and operation of air traffic control systems, each country has its own agency responsible for operating and maintaining its domestic air traffic control system and for promulgating a broad spectrum of rules, procedures, and standards for regulating the use of its national airspace system. In the United States, the Federal Aviation Administration (FAA) is responsible for this activity.

The rules by which government organizations control the use of their national airspace systems are codified in national government regulations— for example, the Federal Aviation Regulations (FARs) in the case of the United States. Many sections of the U.S. FAA FARs have in turn been organized into parts. Part 61, for instance, specifies the requirements for pilot certification; part 71 deals with the designation of federal airways, area low routes, controlled airspace, and reporting points; part 73 addresses special-use airspace (discussed below); and part 91 lists general operating and flight rules. Although a detailed discussion of the ATC rules, procedures, and standards relating to any one country, let alone to nations worldwide, is beyond the scope of this chapter, there are some general rules with which students of aviation should be familiar.

All civil flights fall into one of two categories: flights governed by visual flight rules (VFRs) and those governed by instrument flight rules (IFRs). VFRs are the less stringent of the two, in that airplane and pilot certification requirements governing VFR flights are comparatively fewer. The VFR pilot has to satisfy certain minimum requirements concerning visibility and cloud clearance. That the "see and be seen" concept of collision avoidance underlies all VFR flights has led governments to set forth strict weather minimums for VFR flight. Specifically, whenever forward visibility or the bottom of an obscuring cloud level (ceiling) deteriorates below the legal VFR minimums, instrument meteorological conditions prevail and VFR flights are prohibited. The least restrictive VFR minimums permit low-level flights in certain areas if the weather allows the pilot to stay clear of clouds and maintain one-mile visibility (1,500-meter visibility in ICAO standards).

To begin a flight in instrument meteorological conditions, the pilot must be IFR-certified—that is, trained and licensed to fly the airplane by referring only to the airplane's on-board instruments. In addition, the aircraft must be IFR-equipped with legally prescribed radio and flight instruments, and ATC must give the pilot clearance to operate the IFR flight. In instrument meteorological conditions, the pilot usually cannot see other airplanes and the safe separation between IFR aircraft becomes the responsibility of ATC personnel. Therefore, pilots must file IFR flight plans that specify, among other things, the desired route, altitude, and speed of the intended flight. Air traffic control personnel then issue a clearance that assigns a specific route and altitude and monitor the airplane's progress for the duration of the flight to maintain minimum separations between airplanes. Aircraft position is determined by the use of radar surveillance. Ground-based radars operate in conjunction with an airplane's transponder (the receiver-transmitter unit in the aircraft) to provide ATC controllers with information on aircraft altitude and identity. Some areas do not have radars to determine an aircraft's position; in these situations, controllers rely on pilot reports of position.

IFR-certified pilots in IFR-equipped airplanes can always file an IFR flight plan regardless of weather conditions. Moreover, flights above a certain altitude—18,000 feet in the United States—require an IFR flight plan regardless of weather minimums. This latter restriction ensures that all aircraft will be under the control of ATC personnel at the higher altitudes commonly used by commercial airplanes. Although strongly encouraged, flight plans for VFR operations are optional.

The world's airspace is divided into a series of contiguous flight information regions, within which different levels of flight services are provided. In some regions covering large oceanic areas with relatively low air traffic activity, only flight information and alerting services are provided; in regions such as the North Atlantic, by contrast, extensive communications are needed to maintain an orderly, safe flow of air traffic. Figure 3–1 depicts the communication and control boundaries for operations on the North Atlantic (New York, Gander, Sondrestrom, Reykjavík, Shanwick, and Santa Maria flight information regions). In flight information regions in which air traffic activity is heavy, large portions of the airspace are controlled and within these portions ATC separation service is provided in addition to flight information and alerting services; however, this type of service can be provided only when aircraft are within a 200- to 300-mile range of ground-based antennae. Consequently, even with sophisticated on-board navigation equipment the traffic over the North Atlantic is still limited to aircraft remaining ten minutes in trail of another aircraft on the same assigned track, direction, altitude, and speed.

In the United States, the FAA has prescribed certain restrictions on the use of common airspace, portions of which have been carefully designated as controlled airspace. Within the broad category of controlled airspace are various subsets, such as the continental control area, control areas, transition areas, and airport traffic areas (see figure 3–2). In controlled airspace, pilots are required to comply with certain restrictions.

The FAA's definition of parts of the domestic airspace as uncontrolled does not necessarily mean that air traffic services are unavailable, nor does it mean that certain minimum requirements do not apply. Rather, the division of airspace into controlled and uncontrolled portions is based on the need to control flights in and around high-traffic areas. Accordingly, division of the airspace is hierarchical related to the number of restrictions that apply while flying in that airspace and to the amount of control ATC must exert on operations within the airspace. The applicable weather minimums for

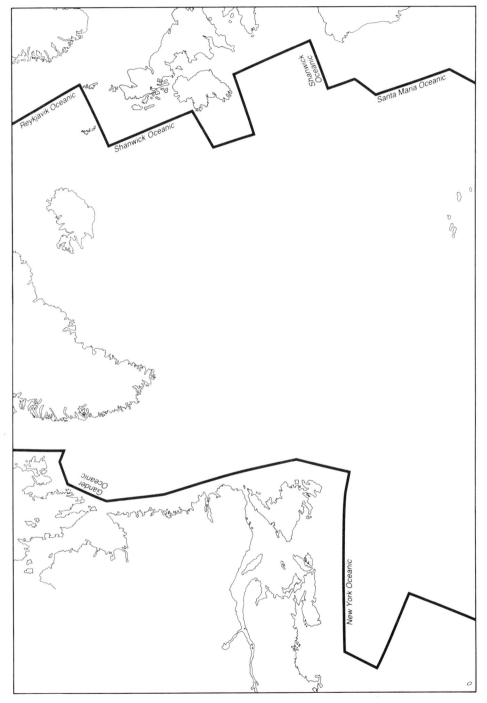

Figure 3–1. North Atlantic Communication and Control Boundaries

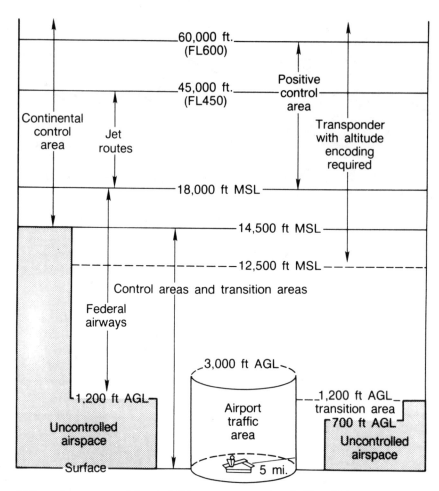

AGL—above ground level; MSL—mean sea level; FL—flight level.

Figure 3–2. U.S. Airspace Structure

Source: Federal Aviation Administration Administration

VFR flight, for example, depend upon an airplane's position in the national airspace.

In addition to the foregoing plethora of rules governing all flights is another subcategory of the ATC system: aircraft procedures, which can be classified as either terminal or en route. *Terminal* procedures involve aircraft departures from and arrivals at airports. Procedures for departures, for example, pertain to taxi and takeoff runway instructions and to specific aircraft routing requested by the pilot or assigned by ATC; similarly, there are established procedures for arrivals. The airspace surrounding busy airports, known as terminal control areas (TCAs in the United States and TMAs in the United Kingdom), is closely controlled by ATC personnel and contains complex restrictions. Although the exact design of individual TCAs is a function of the airport's needs, facilities, and capabilities, TCAs are generally drawn to resemble inverted wedding cakes, each vertical level having a larger diameter than the layer below it. To operate in a TCA, pilots must meet certain minimum certification requirements and their airplanes must have specific pieces of equipment. In addition, ATC approval is required before a pilot can enter a TCA.

When pilots are flying between two points, *en route* procedures enable them either to use the established airway system or to request alternate routes that may be more direct. En route procedures pertain to issuing or changing clearances, instructing pilots with respect to certain maneuvers, tracking a flight as it progresses through the area under the jurisdiction of the air traffic center monitoring the flight, and transferring control of the flight to an adjacent air traffic control facility.

The primary function of ATC is to maintain safe separation among the controlled traffic. To comply with this responsibility, the aviation community has established minimum separation limits between aircraft that are departing from or arriving at an airport or that are flying between two points. Separation standards vary, depending on such factors as phase of flight (departing, arriving, or en route), altitude, availability of and distance from surveillance (with or without radar coverage), and composition and pattern of traffic (for example, a light airplane following a heavy airplane). Separation standards are given in either time (minutes between aircraft) or distance (nautical miles between aircraft). For example, airplanes flying across the North Atlantic on the same track are separated by 2,000 feet vertically or ten minutes longitudinally (in trail) in time. Tracks are separated by 60 nautical miles laterally, which represents one minute of longitude in distance. Twice a day, ICAO and the controlling airspace countries determine the most reasonable tracks to be flown over the North Atlantic (NAT). A NAT track message (with all related coordinates of latitude and longitude) is then issued. As shown in figure 3–3, the tracks are sequenced alphabetically and positioned to take into consideration the jet stream eastbound and the headwind westbound. The NAT system shown in figure 3-3 consists of six tracks, and the airspace is controlled from 27,500 to 40,000 feet. This system does not, however, preclude a flight operating on routes, such as a polar flight en route from London to Los Angeles or from Tel Aviv to New York.

Facilities and Services

In the United States, air traffic control facilities are of three types: (a) en route air traffic control facilities, including the national flow control facility;

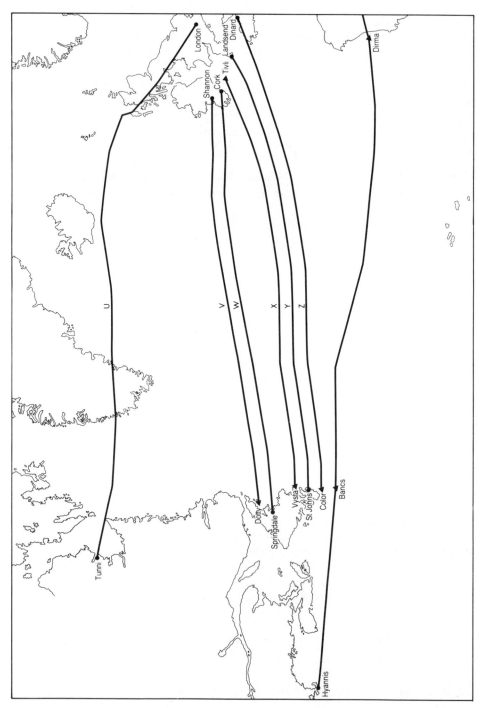

Figure 3–3. North Atlantic Tracks

(b) terminal air traffic control facilities; and (c) flight service stations. These facilities encompass specialized equipment and skilled workers and provide pilots with information and advice that enable them to use the national airspace system safely and efficiently.

En Route Air Traffic Control Facilities

In the United States, en route air traffic control is handled by twenty regional Air Route Traffic Control Centers (ARTCCs, commonly called centers) in the continental United States and four ARTCCs in Anchorage, Guam, Honolulu, and San Juan. By way of comparison, in the United Kingdom the ATC system has three centers. The London center, located at West Drayton in Middlesex, and a subcenter at Manchester are responsible for traffic over England and Wales up to the Scottish border. The Scottish and Oceanic control center has two separate operations rooms, one dealing with traffic in the Scottish flight information region and the other with traffic over the northeast corner of the Atlantic, where the United Kingdom ATC authorities work in conjunction with the American, Canadian, Portuguese, and Icelandic authorities to provide air traffic services to aircraft crossing the Atlantic Ocean. Another example of a busy center with sophisticated equipment is the Eurocontrol ATC center at Maastricht, located in the southeast corner of the Netherlands. This center is responsible for traffic in the upper airspace (usually above 20,000 feet, although the definition varies around the world) in Belgium, the Netherlands, Luxembourg, and northern West Germany, one of the busiest areas in Europe.

The primary responsibility of the ARTCCs in the United States is to separate aircraft as they fly under IFRs—at and above altitudes of 18,000 feet—between airports. Flight plans filed by pilots flying under IFRs are examined by an ARTCC to determine whether safe separation can be maintained along the requested route and altitude. Aircraft operating below 18,000 feet may also receive control service by filing an IFR flight plan; aircraft operating under VFRs can receive limited traffic advisory service if the controllers' work load permits it.

The centers separate traffic, provide traffic advisories to pilots, and occasionally are able to alert pilots to adverse weather while they are en route between airports. They also provide separation from terrain, obstacles, and severe weather to the extent that the necessary data are available. The centers are responsible only for the cross-country portion of each flight; at the departure and arrival airports, local traffic controllers provide separation and advisory services in a coordinated effort with the center controllers. Whereas at small airports responsibility for the aircraft is passed directly from the center air traffic controller to the local controller at the destination airport's tower, at large airports the center passes traffic to an intermediate facility, the approach control center. In the United States, this intermediate facility is known as terminal radar approach control (TRACON) and its controllers separate and sequence both arriving and departing flights.

A typical ARTCC in the United States monitors more than 100,000 square miles of airspace, using long-range radars and remote air-to-ground communication sites; the three centers in the United Kingdom, by contrast, collectively cover a total area of about 350,000 square miles. Each center's service is geographically divided into a number of sectors. Separation is a difficult task, complicated by the ever-changing mix of different aircraft speeds and sizes. Centers are equipped with powerful and sophisticated computers that provide controllers with digital radar displays. On these displays, each aircraft under control is identified with an alphanumeric tag, showing its altitude and identification; figure 3–4, following page 144, depicts an engineering model of an advanced automation system controller display. Computers also print and provide controllers with flight progress strips, items that in the future will be replaced with electronic tabular displays of flight data. In addition, computers supply information on conflict alert and minimum safe-altitude warning (discussed later in this chapter, in the section on surveillance).

The *Central Flow Control Facility* in the United States is an integral component of the en route system, its operations conducted at the FAA headquarters in Washington, D.C. The staff at this facility continually evaluate statistical and real-time information, nationwide, on traffic flow, weather conditions, and the current and forecast rates at which aircraft can be accepted at major airports around the country. All this information is first processed by computers located in the FAA Technical Center in Atlantic City, New Jersey, and then used to initiate systemwide flow control to relieve congestion at airports and in the airspace and to save fuel. Specifically, when the system becomes congested, departing flights are not given the necessary IFR clearance, resulting in a "gate hold" until the system can accommodate more flights.

Until recently, the en route centers in the United States depended on 1960s-vintage computers to process radar and flight data. The old ARTCC computer systems (IBM 9020s) have now been replaced with new systems (IBM 3083s) that have much greater capacity, processing speed, and reliability. Moreover, coupled with sophisticated software programs and advanced display systems (see figure 3–4), these new computers, known as host computers, will enable the consolidation of more than two hundred existing ARTCCs and TRACON facilities into twenty-three *area control facilities*. The use of advanced computer technology in these facilities will not only reduce maintenance, staffing, and supply requirements but also improve the human decision-making process by improving the timeliness and quality of information available to controllers and pilots. The goal of this particular program is to give controllers more time to manage their system resources by minimizing the routine, labor-intensive functions they must now perform.

The Central Flow computer complex at the FAA Technical Center is also being upgraded to provide greater coverage and enhanced forecasting capability. Nationwide management of air traffic flow achieved through these improvements will offer some relief to the airport congestion problem. Currently, when the level of traffic exceeds the level that the airport can handle efficiently, TRACON reduces the flow, either by asking pilots to reduce their speed or by stacking airplanes in holding patterns at designated points. Enhanced computer capabilities will allow controllers to "see" emerging problems hours earlier and thus take steps to prevent congestion and delays. With such tools for early detection, controllers in the Central Flow Control Facility will be able to direct traffic away from anticipated congested areas and thereby reduce delays, conserve fuel, and improve safety.

Terminal Air Traffic Control Facilities

Terminal air traffic control facilities include *airport traffic control towers* (commonly referred to simply as towers) and *terminal radar approach control* (TRACON). The controllers in an airport traffic control tower separate and sequence air traffic in the direct vicinity of the airport and on the airport's surfaces, and they provide clearance and weather information to pilots. At busy and complex airports, airport control is divided into an air control position and a ground movement position—for example, separate controllers for clearance delivery and surface movement. By contrast, TRACON controllers separate and sequence arriving and departing aircraft in the broader (within 50 miles) airspace surrounding the airport. TRACON facilities exist at airports with moderate- to high-density traffic.

In general, each TRACON is associated with one tower and is located in the same building as the tower; however, a TRACON can be situated in a remote location and coordinate its activities with more than one tower. The New York approach control facility, for example, serves the three major airports in the greater New York metropolitan area—Kennedy, LaGuardia, and Newark—as well as a number of the smaller airports in the area. At airports with low traffic activity, the TRACON facility is located in the tower cab of the airport, in which case TRACON is referred to as TRACAB (terminal radar approach control in tower cabs). At present, there are about five hundred towers and two hundred TRACONs and TRACABs in the United States.

Equipment and services available at terminal air traffic control facilities vary by airport. At busy airports, the facilities include radars and sophisticated controller display units. As in the case of centers, information received from radars, which work in conjunction with aircraft transponders, is made available to controllers with the use of automated radar terminal systems

(ARTS). These computer systems, as well as navigation systems used in the terminal area, are described later in this chapter.

Flight Service Stations

The network of flight service stations in the United States is an adjunct component of the domestic air traffic control system. Flight service stations provide an important link in air-to-ground communications and offer many valuable preflight and in-flight services, including acceptance of IFR flight plans (which are subsequently forwarded to the appropriate ATC en route and terminal facilities); preflight and in-flight weather briefings; en route progress reports from pilots on VFR flights; dissemination of special notices; accumulation and dissemination of pilot reports of conditions aloft; and assistance to pilots in distress. Since many of these facilities have direction-finding equipment, they are particularly useful in directing lost pilots. Their most important function, however, continues to be the dissemination of weather information to pilots and to other air traffic control personnel.

All *flight plans* are prepared on a standard preprinted form that the pilot hands or reads to the flight service specialist. This form indicates whether the flight will be under IFRs or VFRs and lists the aircraft identification number; aircraft type, equipment, speed, and fuel consumption; point and estimated time of departure; cruising altitude; estimated time en route; route of flight; passengers aboard; and pilot's name. A *VFR flight plan,* which is optional, is filed by a pilot who intends to fly according to visual flight rules. This type of flight plan acts as a form of insurance for the pilot and passengers. If the airplane does not arrive at the destination airport within a certain time after the estimated time of arrival, the nearest flight service station will initiate search-and-rescue procedures. An *IFR flight plan* is used for initiating the required ATC clearances for a flight according to instrument flying rules. Flight plans involving the use of foreign airspace take on added significance in terms of the quality of navigation services available as well as entry restrictions. Here, the international flight information manual is a particularly useful guide for planning flights into foreign airspace.

Pilots require accurate and timely preflight and en route information on weather and flight conditions. In the United States, the provision of weather service is a joint effort of the FAA, the National Weather Service (NWS), the military weather services, and other organizations, with more than fifty weather service forecasting offices producing and distributing hundreds of forecasts several times each day. The FAA provides weather information to pilots through its nationwide network of flight service stations; usually the stations furnish preflight weather briefings (custom-tailored to the pilot's qualifications, equipment, and route of flight), as well as in-flight weather information when the pilot is within radio range. NWS meteorologists at ARTCCs provide advisory services and short-term forecasts.

Since 1985, when there were more than three hundred flight service stations, the FAA has been consolidating facilities and introducing greater automation and improved communications into its stations. By the mid-1990s, the FAA plans to have sixty-one fully automated flight service stations in the United States. Increased automation and the replacement of aging communications equipment are targeted to improving information-processing capabilities and thus to providing more timely and accurate weather information. Greater automation, for example, will allow real-time processing of hazardous-weather data for air traffic control and improved user access to this information.

In addition to weather information, pilots also need a variety of other preflight and in-flight information, such as route maps and data on airport conditions, the status of navigational aids, and air traffic conditions. The International Civil Aviation Organization (ICAO), together with individual government agencies such as the FAA, publishes and disseminates continuously updated information relating to the regulations and procedures for efficient utilization of the international and national airspace systems. In addition, the aviation community worldwide publishes a series of aeronautical charts drawn to accepted ICAO standards, including general purpose charts, charts for visual navigation, charts for en route radio navigation, and detailed terminal area charts, as well as instrument approach charts to specific runways on major airports. Other important sources of aeronautical information are the automatic terminal information service (ATIS), which at most major airports provides a meteorological broadcast giving pilots information about local weather conditions and current operating procedures, and *Notices to Airmen* (NOTAM), which gives up-to-date information to pilots about almost anything that might affect flying—for example, closed runways or inoperative navigational aids.

Equipment

Governments operate a variety of equipment that enables pilots to communicate with facilities on the ground, navigate great distances, operate under air traffic control surveillance, and approach and land safely at the destination airport. Air traffic control equipment is of three general types: (a) surveillance, (b) navigation, and (c) communication.

Surveillance Systems

The essential purpose of the ATC system is to provide safe separation among aircraft using national and international airspace systems under IFR conditions. In the early days of aviation—the 1920s—the system was based on the use of radios and telephones. Pilots reported their time of arrival and altitude at designated points along the airways, as well as their estimated time of arrival over each upcoming checkpoint. Controllers used this information to keep track of airplanes by using markers on tabletop maps. In the 1950s, remote air-to-ground communication stations were established to send messages from pilots to controllers, who kept airplanes about fifteen minutes apart in their estimated arrival times at reporting points.[2]

Nowadays, surveillance information is provided by ATC radars—one of the most important developments in the aviation industry. Echoes from a primary, or search, radar signal provide information to the air traffic controller on the bearing and range of an aircraft relative to the radar facility and to other aircraft in the area. Primary echoes—blips—can be displayed on a map of the actual airway or airport area to show their positions in relation to runways, navigational aids, and any hazardous ground obstructions in the area.

Although a great advancement from earlier air traffic control techniques, primary radar is somewhat limited. Much more information is available to the controller from secondary surveillance radar (SSR), which transmits a signal that actuates the transponders of all equipped airplanes in the controller's surveillance area. Upon receiving an interrogating signal from a ground-based SSR, the transponder automatically transmits back to the SSR a signal containing enough information to allow the controller to make positive aircraft identification. Thus, whereas signals transmitted from primary radar are simply reflected or bounced back from the aircraft and displayed as blips on a screen, signals transmitted by SSR are in the form of interrogations to which a transponder in the aircraft responds by returning numerical data that are displayed on the controller's screen. These data include aircraft identification, altitude, and speed.

Information received from radars is presented to controllers on various display systems, each possessing a different level of sophistication. In the United States, ARTS III, an automated radar terminal system, is capable of detecting, tracking, and predicting the position of an aircraft in the terminal area. The system displays on the controller's radar scope such information as aircraft identification, altitude, ground speed, and flight plan data. Typically installed to serve medium- to high-density airports, ARTS III systems have two additional features. First, they contain minimum-safe-altitude warning features to alert controllers when a tracked airplane with altitude-reporting capability is either below or predicted to go below a minimum altitude. Second, ARTS III incorporates the feature of terminal conflict alert, which warns that airplanes will lose safe separation within two minutes unless there is a change in flight direction. Automated radar terminal systems such as ARTS III have simplified the establishment and maintenance of radar identification and have improved intra- and interfacility ATC coordination.

SSR represents one component of the *air traffic control radar beacon system* (ATCRBS); the other component of this system is the airborne transponder. At present, all aircraft operating in a busy TCA or flying above 10,000 feet are required to have airborne transponders with mode A and mode C capability—that is, the ability to provide information on airplane identity and altitude. It has been proposed that another mode, mode S, be incorporated, involving the transmittal of a digital message addressed to a specific recipient. Although the mode S data link is primarily an air-ground link, when used in conjunction with a traffic alert and collision avoidance system (TCAS) it involves air-air communications.

The FAA's modernization plan for surveillance equipment includes the following goals: (a) to expand the number of locations with radar coverage; (b) to upgrade existing old, maintenance-intensive technology terminal radars with new technology radars; (c) to increase the number of locations with airport surface detection equipment; and (d) to upgrade surface detection equipment at all locations. The implementation of mode S capability will involve air-to-air communications—an integral component of the airborne collision avoidance system being tested. A TCAS is being field-tested in several commercial airliners, with the most advanced version—TCAS III—providing vertical and horizontal maneuvering instructions to the pilot of a TCAS-equipped airplane.

At present, air traffic control personnel receive weather information from radars that have limited technological capability. The modernization plan also calls for the installation of sophisticated weather radar at terminals to detect hazardous weather. Such radar, known as Doppler radar, will provide timely information on severe conditions that threaten the safety of airport operations. The Terminal Doppler Weather Radar (TDWR) system will be particularly useful in detecting potentially hazardous weather, including microbursts; it will enable FAA facilities, for example, to provide timely windshear warnings to pilots flying near airports. (Wind shear is a meteorological phenomenon in which the winds being flown through change direction abruptly and can have dire consequences on aircraft performance.) In addition, enhanced central weather processors will gather weather data from multiple sources, including satellites, and process them into full-color meteorological charts and graphs on a video screen in a fraction of the time it now takes. National Weather Service meteorologists assigned to the FAA facilities will use the central weather processor to obtain updated information and advise controllers of significant weather patterns that might affect flight safety. Such advancements in providing weather information will not only increase safety but also improve traffic flow management and reduce weather-related delays.

Navigation Systems

Navigation aids allow a pilot to depart, navigate across country, approach, and land an airplane without external visual points of reference. In the 1920s, navigation systems generally consisted of ground-based beacon lights along a route that assisted pilots during the night and when visibility was poor. During the 1930s, ground beacons were replaced by nondirectional radio beacons that emitted continuous signals for pilots to follow using airborne direction finders. Then came the four-course radio station, which emitted a directional signal that formed four beacons, aligned relative to the compass and each defining a course. With this last system, a pilot used a radio receiver and followed radio beams from station to station.[3]

It should be noted that from the late 1930s to the early 1960s, pilots navigated long-range, overwater routes by the use of a gyroscopic compass system, while position was determined by a navigator using a sextant to obtain a position fix on the stars or the sun. This method was replaced—as were the navigator and the radio operator—in the early 1960s when the dual Doppler radio navigation system and loran-A became the mode of navigation performed by pilots.

In the 1950s, the low-frequency 4-course range was replaced with the *very high frequency omnidirectional range* (VOR)—another important development in the aviation industry. VORs, which are radio devices that provide azimuth guidance to pilots of suitably equipped airplanes, are used around the world as basic navigation systems. VOR stations transmit, along 360-course radials, continuous signals that can be picked up by VOR receivers in the airplane and displayed on a cockpit instrument known as the course deviation indicator (CDI). The pilot selects the desired VOR frequency and course, and the readings of the CDI needle show the location of the course relative to the location of the airplane. If the plane also has *distance-measuring equipment* (DME), a pilot can determine his or her distance from properly equipped VOR stations, which are marked on aeronautical charts to allow pilots to select a course from one VOR station to another. Designated radials between VOR stations are referred to as airways.

The corresponding navigation aid used by the U.S. military is ultra high frequency (UHF) *tactical air navigation* (TACAN). The FAA has been integrating TACAN with civilian VOR facilities, the integrated facilities being known as *VORTACs;* these stations also provide the use of DME. At the end of 1987, there were more than a thousand VOR and VORTAC facilities in the United States alone. Today, this system is the heart of the en route navigation system.

To organize the flow of high-speed, cross-country traffic, the FAA has defined an aerial network of preferred routings between navigational aids. Most IFR flights utilize one of three route systems: *VOR, Jet Route,* or *area navigation* (RNAV). An airway is a prescribed corridor, the centerline of which is defined by a line between adjacent radio navigation aids. The International Civil Aviation Organization marks airways by color and number. In the United Kingdom, airways are corridors of airspace 10 miles apart that extend up to 24,500 feet from the base. (See figure 3–5 following page 144, which shows the United Kingdom system of airways.) In the United States, the VOR airway system consists of two structures of airways. Below 18,000 feet—the low-altitude structure—the network is depicted on En Route Low-Altitude Charts, with airways identified by the letter *V* ("Victor"), followed by an airway number. Pilots fly between VOR stations by tuning into and tracking a signal on a discrete radio frequency. Routes between 18,000 and 45,000 feet—the high-altitude structure—are designated Jet Routes, identified on En Route High-Altitude Charts by the letter *J* ("Jet"), followed by the airway number. In international regions, airways located in the upper airspace (corresponding to the U.S. Jet Routes) are given the prefix *upper*.

Although most general aviation airplanes are equipped with VOR receivers, there is simpler navigation equipment—*non-directional beacons* (NDBs). NDBs are nothing more than radio stations that transmit signals in the low- and medium-frequency band in all directions (in fact, a standard AM-radio station can potentially become an NDB). The device in the airplane that receives the signal from the NDB is the *automatic directional finder* (ADF), termed *automatic* because it does not require the pilot to work out the transmitting station. The bearing to the NDB station is provided by the ADF unit, and the information is presented to the pilot on an indicator made up of a compass card with a pointer. Although this type of navigation system is less expensive, it is also less accurate and is more readily subject to atmospheric conditions and meteorological phenomena. At the end of 1987, there were more than twelve hundred nondirectional radio beacons in the United States.

VOR transmitters came into service in 1950. Although they have served the aviation community well since then, they have at least five limitations. First, because they are ground-based systems, they cannot provide coverage over oceanic routes. Second, because they are based on a line-of-sight system, their effectiveness is limited at low altitudes and in mountainous areas. Third, the concentration of mixed-speed traffic along popular routes can result in congestion and produce a potential for conflict at airway intersections. Fourth, navigation with the use of VORs frequently results in indirect routings between origin and destination because of ATC priority routings or the lack of sufficient equipment along the direct line between two points. And fifth, the maximum range of a VOR is limited to about 200 nautical miles and much less at lower altitudes.

Many of these navigational limitations can be overcome through the use of RNAV systems. A VOR/DME-based RNAV system utilizes an on-board device called a *course line computer* (CLC), which receives raw VOR/DME information (radial and distance) and performs geometric calculations to compute a straight-line course between two desired points that are within the range of VOR/DMEs in use. The pilot selects the destination point, termed an *imaginary waypoint*. The computer then takes in the information on that point with respect to the VOR/DME within range and to the position of the airplane and performs trigonometrical calculations to give the pilot the direct course between any two points.[4] Thus, a pilot is able to fly a direct route and avoid congestion along the airways between VORs.

In more sophisticated systems, such as Omega, loran, and the global positioning system (GPS), the RNAV calculations are based on information received from other navigational facilities and systems. Other systems, such as the inertial navigation system (INS), are self-contained. It should be noted that the cost of on-board equipment for advanced navigation systems—particularly the INS—puts most of these systems beyond the reach of many general aviation pilots.

The *INS*, unlike other systems, does not rely on external radio signals but instead is totally self-contained and therefore highly advantageous for international and overwater travel. It uses three gyroscopes, which indicate direction; three accelerometers, which measure changes in speed and direction; and a navigation computer to estimate an airplane's new position relative to its original position. The gyroscopes and the accelerometers simply keep track of the airplane's movement in all three dimensions, while the navigation computer uses that information, along with data on the airplane's original starting point, to compute the projected new position. Although the INS is extremely sophisticated, reliable, and accurate, it is, as noted above, quite expensive. Consequently, its use is limited to large commercial airplanes and the most advanced general aviation airplanes.

The *Omega* system is particularly useful for navigation over long-range oceanic routes and in remote parts of the world. Its eight powerful transmitters, located throughout the world, emit very low frequency (VLF) signals. The eight stations are located in the United States (one in Hawaii and one in North Dakota), Argentina, Liberia, La Reunion (in southeast Africa), Norway, Japan, and Australia. The low-frequency feature of Omega allows the signals to be received at distances of thousands of miles. Each station transmits a series of frequencies in well-defined patterns that are used by the receiver in the airplane to identify the station. In addition to Omega, which is a navigation system, are the U.S. Navy's seven *Naval Communication Stations* (NCSs), which also emit VLF signals for the purpose of communicating with submarines in different parts of the world. Although the navy's system was developed for communication purposes, the aviation industry does use it for navigation. Thus, the combined Omega/NCS systems provide fifteen VLF stations for airplane navigation, though inasmuch as the navy's VLF system is not dedicated to navigation, signal transmission is at the navy's discretion. And while all segments of the civil aviation industry can use the Omega navigation system, corporate aviation has found this system particularly useful.[5]

Loran-C—long-range navigation, version C—is a relatively new, low-cost navigation system, its low-cost feature making it well suited to the needs of the general aviation industry. Although version A of loran, primarily a marine system operating in the medium-frequency band, had been in existence for a long time, it had limited range and reliability and was difficult to use. Loran-C, by contrast, is a sophisticated long-range system that is much easier to use. Basically, it consists of a network of a master station and several slave stations. The master station transmits a signal in the low-frequency band that causes the slave stations to transmit similar signals. The receiver on the airplane receives all signals and decodes their source, that is, master versus slave, while keeping track of the time differences between when the master-transmitted and the slave-transmitted signals were received. This information enables the receiving unit to determine the airplane's line of position—that is, a line of various positions where the airplane could be located. A different line of position can be determined using the information from a second master-slave combination, and the intersection of the two lines of position determines the exact location of the airplane. Because of its relatively low cost, loran-C is expected to be particularly attractive to the general aviation community, though it does have one limitation: At present, loran-C does not cover certain parts of the world, including some parts of the United States.

GPS, or NAVSTAR, is a navigation system being developed by the U.S. Department of Defense, with additional plans under way to develop airplane receivers for civilian use. The system, based on the use of satellites, will enable an airplane to determine its exact position *in three dimensions* from the information received from four satellites (one for time). Whereas loran-C enables the receiving unit to "draw" two lines of position to determine the location of an airplane, the satellite-based system will enable the receiving unit to "draw" three lines of position to determine the location of an airplane in three dimensions—anywhere in the world. In this case, the line of position is more accurately termed a *surface of position.* Satellite-based navigation systems like GPS are expected to be extremely accurate, reasonably priced, and operationally efficient.[6]

The navigation aids described thus far pertain to en route navigation. As an aircraft nears its destination airport, it is guided by different navigation devices—landing aids—that are particularly useful during instrument meteorological conditions. There are two types of IFR approaches: nonprecision and precision. *Nonprecision approaches* utilize VOR or NDB transmitters that direct the pilot toward the airport but do not transmit a *glide slope* signal, which provides vertical guidance during approach. *Precision approaches* primarily utilize instrument landing systems (ILSs), almost a thousand of which were in service in the United States at the end of 1987. Because they use a more sensitive signal and provide glide slope guidance, precision approaches can be made in lower-weather minimums than nonprecision approaches can. For example, the FAA has set the following weather minimums for the decision height and runway visual range: For category 1, precision approaches are 200 feet ceiling and 2,400 feet visibility, respectively; for category 2, they are 100 and 1,200 feet; and for category 3-A, they are 50 and 700 feet.*

When weather conditions prevent the pilot from making a visual approach to landing at an airport, an ILS provides a precise path for the airplane during its approach (runway alignment and rate of descent). Directional signals from ground-based transmitters are picked up by a suitably equipped airplane and displayed by the glide slope and localizer needles of the airplane's ILS receiver.

Although an ILS is an affordable, proven, and precise navigation system, it does have certain limitations. First, an ILS restricts the approach to a single path, with a glide slope of typically 3 degrees. A single glide slope can be a limitation for airplanes able to use a steeper approach angle. Also, a single, straight-in approach can reduce runway utilization when approaching airplanes have different speeds and different sizes or when they approach from different directions. Second, the performance of the ILS equipment depends on the surrounding topography, the location of buildings, and the proximity of moving objects, such as taxiing airplanes, on the ground. Third, below altitudes of about 200 feet the glide slope may not be reliable. And fourth, the number of frequency channels available for the ILS are limited. To overcome most of these limitations, the *microwave landing system* (MLS) was developed. Consequently, this latter system has been adopted by the International Civil Aviation Organization as the standard instrument landing system as of January 1, 1998.

Figure 3–6, following page 144, shows a schematic diagram of an MLS. As its name implies, an MLS operates at microwave frequencies, permitting a greater number of transmission channels—about two hundred, compared with about forty for an ILS. Since an MLS uses a signal that scans a wider volume of airspace, the glide path and azimuth approach can be selected over a wide range of possible values within the coverage volume. Moreover, the approach can be along a curved path that intersects the runway centerline at any point.

An MLS is not as susceptible as an ILS to interference from terrain and airport ground traffic. Thus, not only is an MLS more efficient and reliable; it also provides much greater flexibility, particularly in poor weather conditions. The added flexibility allows an increase in runway utilization and an avoidance of flight paths over noise-sensitive areas. Moreover, an MLS can allow communication of such data as meteorological information and runway status. The airborne component of the MLS is relatively expensive,

---

*The *decision height* is the altitude at which, during an ILS approach, a decision must be made as to whether to continue to a landing or initiate a missed-approach procedure. The *runway visual range* is the visibility immediately adjacent to the runway—that is, the horizontal distance that a pilot should be able to see down the runway from the approach end.

however, and the system will not become available worldwide for a number of years.

Communication Systems

Pilots communicate their position to ground facilities either (a) passively, through the use of ATC radar, or (b) interactively, through the use of radio voice communications. For voice communications, civilian pilots use VHF bands and military pilots use UHF and VHF bands. In the United States, the FAA's modernization plan for ground-to-air communications includes improving the existing voice communications system and adding mode S, the new radar beacon system, to provide more accurate positional information and minimal interference in busy terminal areas. The addition of mode S will also provide a mechanism for transmitting data, including weather information, between the controller and the pilot or between TCAS-equipped aircraft.

The FAA is additionally responsible for a large and complex interfacility communications system that enables communications among all FAA facilities, including staffed facilities such as centers, towers, and flight service stations and remote facilities such as radar sites and ground-to-air radio sites. Whereas the existing interfacility system evolved piecemeal and is slow, expensive, and at times unreliable, the planned National Airspace Interfacility Communications System (NAICS) will combine the FAA's communication functions into a single integrated network that is fast, accurate, reliable, flexible, and economical. The NAICS is expected to provide voice and data communications among all components of the national airspace system.

Another component of the FAA's modernization plan in communications is establishment of the National Airspace Data Interchange Network (NADIN), which will provide greater flexibility and reliability by increasing routing capabilities—for example, to bypass failed or saturated areas—and by reducing operating costs. To achieve these goals, NADIN will take advantage of those lower-cost technologies in telecommunications which have resulted in part from increased competition in that field.

Future Challenges Facing the U.S. System

Tremendous improvements were made to the ATC system in the United States between 1930 and 1950 as a result of the development and sophistication of radio, radar, and the computer. By the beginning of the 1980s, the U.S. national aviation system had become the busiest and most complex in the world. Yet the domestic system was also plagued by a limited ability to expand and adapt to changing requirements. For example, the ATC terminal and en route computer systems were incompatible and had limited capacity;

the maintenance costs of the antiquated vacuum-tube equipment were high; and facilities and equipment in the field had overlapping coverage. To overcome these limitations, the FAA in 1982 initiated development of a comprehensive plan for modernizing the entire ATC system by the end of the century, with the goals of improving safety, increasing the system's capacity, making the system more responsive to the needs of users, and reducing the systems operating costs. Planned improvements to the ATC system have been highlighted in this chapter and are detailed in the FAA's *National Airspace Systems Plan.*[7]

Although most participants in the aviation industry applaud the FAA's modernization plan, some, particularly the Air Transport Association of America (ATA), whose members compose the majority of U.S. scheduled airlines, have expressed concern. The ATA fears that it will be increasingly difficult for the FAA to manage the ATC system effectively, a perspective that arises from the increasing complex political questions surrounding the FAA:

- During a period of closer scrutiny of the federal budget, can the FAA obtain the necessary financial resources to adequately operate and maintain the ATC system?
- Can the FAA continue to operate effectively under the bureaucratic control of the Department of Transportation?
- Can the FAA cope with significant involvement in its decision-making processes by other government bodies, such as the Office of Management and Budget and the General Accounting Office?
- Can the FAA realistically streamline the procurement process to expedite implementation of its national airspace system plan?

In light of these kinds of questions, there is, understandably, some support favoring separation of the FAA from the Department of Transportation.

According to the ATA, a more cost-effective ATC system will become a reality only if the government creates a national aviation authority. Such an authority, claims the ATA, should be an independent federal corporation, similar in structure to Amtrak and the U.S. Postal Service. As a result, the FAA would no longer be responsible for the management of either the ATC system or the airport grant system, although it would continue to be responsible for safety and regulatory functions and its budget would continue to come from existing user fees.

The intent of establishing the proposed national aviation authority is to partially privatize the ATC system. Presumably, the importance of a national ATC system to the national defense and to the general public welfare requires some degree of continued federal presence. The concept of a national authority recognizes the potential to have both a federal presence and a business orientation in the operation and management of the ATC system. The proponents of privatizing the ATC system, even if privatization is only partial, feel so strongly about the merits of the national aviation authority that they would like to broaden its responsibility to include the airport enhancement program. The theory presumably is that even if all three components of the air transportation system cannot operate in a free marketplace, then operation of the ATC system and the airport enhancement program should at least be conducted in a businesslike environment.

Notes

1. General Aviation Manufacturers Association (GAMA), *General Aviation Statistical Databook: 1988 Edition* (Washington, D.C.: GAMA, 1988), 14.
2. Office of Technology Assessment (OTA), *Airport and Air Traffic Control System* (Washington, D.C.: Government Printing Office, January 1982), 33–35.
3. Ibid., 28.
4. D.J. Clausing, *The Aviator's Guide to Modern Navigation* (Blue Ridge Summit, Pa.: Tab Books, 1987), 69–70.
5. Ibid., 127.
6. Ibid., chap. 12.
7. Federal Aviation Administration (FAA), *National Airspace System Plan* (Washington, D.C.: FAA, April 1987).

4
Airports: Development, Systems, Economics, and Challenges

S ince 1910, when the world's first airports were established in Germany, about fifteen thousand public-use and twenty thousand private-use airports have been developed around the world to meet the continuously changing demands of the aviation industry. During the past eighty years, airport development has had to keep pace with an increasing number of aircraft in service; technical advances in aircraft design; advances in other components of the aviation system, such as air traffic control; and other related issues, such as airport congestion, aircraft noise, and airport security. Today's airports are more than just places where airplanes land and take off. Airports are looked upon as resources that (a) provide their host communities with access to the national and international air transportation system and (b) make a large contribution to local, regional, and national economies by creating jobs, attracting new business investment, and promoting tourism. This chapter reviews various facets of airport development—its history, facilities, systems, and economics—and addresses the most important challenges facing airports around the world.

Historical Developments

The earliest airports were developed in Germany around 1910 to serve the zeppelins operated by the Delag Company, the predecessor of Deutsche Luft Hansa.[1] Through the end of World War I, Europe remained well ahead of the United States in the development of airports. During this time, airports typically consisted of grass areas for takeoff and landing and wooden hangars for airplanes. There was no equipment for radio communication between airports and pilots, nor were there any navigation systems to assist pilots in bad weather. The only form of air traffic control was a person waving a red flag as a signal for takeoff clearance. Such conditions confined flying to daylight hours. Immediately after the end of World War I, rudimentary advances in airport design were introduced in Europe just as a number of airlines began to offer scheduled passenger services. For example, London-

Paris service was made possible beginning in 1919 as a result of the development of Hounslow Airport near London and Le Bourget near Paris.

Airport development progressed steadily during the 1920s in both Europe and the United States. Lighting was installed for night operations; wireless telegraphy was developed, enabling communications between airports and airplanes; and vast improvements were made to terminals. Tempelhof Airport in Berlin exemplified these improvements. Built in the mid-1920s, Tempelhof was one of the largest airports in the world, with a terminal designed in such a way that large airplanes could taxi under a terminal canopy to load and unload passengers.[2] Certain areas in Europe—notably, parts of the Nordic countries—that experienced difficulty in building airports on land because of topographical problems posed by rocks, fjords, archipelagos, and so forth, began to focus on the development of seaplane terminals.[3] The Europeans' leadership role in the development of airports can be explained in part by the availability of government subsidies.[4] In addition, Europe was forced to develop better airports since airlines in Europe concentrated on the development of passenger transportation rather than mail.

At a time when an aircraft's effective range was less than 200 miles, many airports were built in distant parts of the world, such as Africa and the Middle East, as part of the development of major routes by European airlines. These government-owned airlines built air links between their respective mother countries and far-flung colonies, which required a safe network of airports and ground facilities. John Stroud, in his book *Famous Airports of the World,* attributes the development of several airports to exploration by Imperial Airways (the predecessor of British Airways) of its routes to India, via the Middle East, and eventually beyond, to Australia and South Africa. Other European airlines took similar initiatives; the Dutch airline KLM, for example, developed routes from Amsterdam to Indonesia, and the Belgian airline SABENA developed routes to the Congo.[5] Some U.S. airlines were also involved in the development of airports, particularly for their international operations, Pan American's survey flights of the Pacific during the 1930s being especially noteworthy in this regard. Airlines from the United States and Europe also contributed significantly to the development of major airports in South America, an area with a peculiar topography that presented unique problems in terms of not only airport construction but aircraft operations as well. At Bolivia's La Paz Airport, for example, located almost 14,000 feet above sea level, departing aircraft required either extra long runways or a reduction in their payload, that is, passengers and cargo.

World War II further stimulated the development of airports around the world. In the United States, where the federal government's view held that airports should be developed by local municipalities or the private sector, Congress ultimately decided to appropriate funds for the construction and improvement of some 250 airports—for reasons of national defense. The largest and best-equipped airports were taken over by the government, and facilities were significantly upgraded to accommodate heavier military airplane operations.

Federal aid to airports continued in the United States after World War II, when the Federal Airport Act of 1946 authorized expenditure funding for capital improvements. These funds were given directly to municipalities in the form of grants and matching funds. Moreover, most of the airports that had been constructed and operated for military purposes during the war were declared surplus and turned over to cities, counties, and states.

A significant postwar event was establishment of the International Civil Aviation Organization (ICAO), which played an important role in standardizing air traffic procedures and the design of international airports. ICAO standards and recommended procedures covered runway characteristics, airport lighting, and numerous other safety-related areas.

The widespread development of jet aircraft in the early 1960s increased the pressure on airports around the world to upgrade their facilities. First, advancing aircraft technology (faster, higher-gross-weight, and larger airplanes) required modification of airside components of airports, such as runways, taxiways, and airplane parking ramps. Second, the larger capacities of jet airplanes, coupled with the growth in passenger demand for air travel, presented a need for passenger terminals to be redesigned, upgraded, and expanded. As a result, large amounts of funds were needed to modify existing airports so that they could accommodate the new airplane technology.

In the United States, federal funds were limited and Congress was concerned about using general funds to support airport development. To increase the availability of funds and at the same time to silence critics of general fund appropriations, Congress enacted the Airport and Airway Development Act of 1970 and a concurrent bill to levy user charges. User charges were to be collected and placed in a trust fund, which was designed to provide airports with federal grants to supplement state and local funding. In addition, the FAA developed the *National Plan of Integrated Airport Systems* (NPIAS), listing more than three thousand airports deemed significant to the national system and therefore potentially eligible for federal funding under the Airport Improvement Program. This list was structured so that an "adequate" airport would be located within 20 miles of 97.3 percent of the U.S. population.[6] Under the FAA's plan, airports accepting federal assistance also assumed responsibility for complying with various requirements on their continued operation.

Airside (see the section on "Airport Systems," later in this chapter) improvements were not the only airport development activities arising from the growth in passenger and cargo traffic during the 1960s and 1970s. During this time, terminal design also went through significant change. Examples include the installation of passenger loading bridges, that is, covered telescopic corridors connecting the terminal and the airplane; people movers, that is, moving sidewalks and light-rail vehicles within expanded terminals; automated baggage-handling and -claim systems; and mobile lounges for transporting passengers between the terminal and remotely parked airplanes. In addition, many airports constructed new or expanded cargo-handling facilities and some airport authorities were granted "free-trade zone" status.

Unfortunately, the growth in aviation activity also aggravated the noise problem in the vicinity of many of the world's airports. The public outcry against airport noise led to a number of international meetings to examine such issues as procedures for describing and measuring airplane noise, human tolerance to airplane noise, airplane-noise certification, criteria for establishing airplane-noise-abatement operating procedures, and land-use control. These meetings prompted ICAO to develop its Standards and Recommended Practices for Aircraft Noise, which were adopted by the ICAO Council in 1971 and designated as annex 16 to the convention.[7] These standards have changed airport and airplane operating procedures (for example, the Potomac River approaches to Washington National Airport), altered the location of new airports (Mirabel in Montreal), and slowed the expansion of existing airports and the development of new airports around the world. Compliance with noise-related regulations has reduced the frequency of flights available at a number of existing airports. Specifically, such regulations typically restrict the type of airplanes that are allowed to use a particular airport, the times when aircraft operations are allowed, and the implementation of preferential runway rules. Nighttime restrictions can be particularly onerous for some airfreight operators, particularly those providing overnight service, and for some international airlines that must operate within tight time-zone parameters. At present, airplane noise is viewed as one of the most serious long-term problems facing the aviation industry. In addition to its effect on airport access and the construction of new facilities, implementation of Stage 3 (chapter 3, in international terminology) noise legislation will have an enormous impact on the composition of aircraft fleets worldwide and the financial position of airlines, since almost two-thirds of the world's commercial transport fleet do not meet Stage 3 standards.[8]

Facilities, Structure, and Operations

Airports around the world vary in size, structure, and method of operation. In 1987, there were about 36,000 civil airports located in the contracting states of the ICAO. About half the total private-use airports and more than a third of all airports open to public use are located in the United States.[9] At the end of 1987, there were 1,056 airports worldwide that served the needs of users operating international flights; more than half of these airports were open for regularly scheduled international air transport services (as opposed to being designated an alternate airport), and about 100 were available for nonscheduled international air transport services and about 200 for international general aviation operations. Table 4–1 shows the location of these different types of airports by region.

Table 4–2 shows a list of the 20 largest airports in the world in terms of passengers, cargo, and operations. The majority of these large airports

Table 4–1
Airports in the Air Navigation Plan, December 31, 1987

Region	International Scheduled Air Transport		International Nonscheduled Air Transport		International General Aviation		Total
	Regular	Alternate	Regular	Alternate	Regular	Alternate	
Africa-Indian Ocean	135	13	6	0	18	0	172
Caribbean/South American	120	17	16	0	48	0	201
European	203	21	48	0	114	0	386
Middle East/Asia	125	33	22	0	1	0	181
North Atlantic/North American/Pacific	62	43	1	0	10	0	116
Total	645	127	93	0	191	0	1056

Source: International Civil Aviation Organization (ICAO), *Bulletin* (Montreal: ICAO, July 1988), 55.

Table 4–2
The Top Twenty Commercial Airports in the World Ranked by Passengers, Cargo, and Operations, 1987

Airport	Total Passengers[a]
O'Hare International, Chicago	56,280,545
Hartsfield Atlanta International	47,649,470
Los Angeles International	44,873,113
Dallas/Ft. Worth International	41,875,444
Heathrow, London	34,742,100
Stapleton International, Denver	32,355,000
John F. Kennedy International, New York	30,192,477
Tokyo International (Haneda)	29,927,027
San Francisco International	29,812,440
La Guardia, New York	24,225,913
Miami International	24,036,104
Newark International, New Jersey	23,475,254
Boston/Logan International	23,283,047
Orly, Paris	20,427,446
Honolulu International	20,380,282
Lambert/St. Louis International	20,362,606
Frankfurt/Main	19,802,229
Detroit Metropolitan	19,746,992
Gatwick, London	19,372,600
Osaka International	19,291,209

Table 4–2
Continued

Airport	Total Cargo[b] (Tonnes)
John F. Kennedy International, New York	1,185,659
Los Angeles International	1,052,144
Frankfurt/Main	1,038,659
O'Hare International, Chicago	933,429
Heathrow, London	646,400
Hong Kong International	627,246
Miami International	618,756
Standiford Field, Louisville	583,311
Hartsfield Atlanta International	573,414
Charles de Gaulle, Paris	568,936
San Francisco International	550,562
Schiphol, Amsterdam	540,455
Tokyo International (Haneda)	487,558
Dallas/Ft. Worth International	469,612
Dayton International	446,227
Kimpo International, Seoul	433,491
Changi, Singapore	427,813
Osaka International	384,728
Chiang Kai-Shek International, Taipei	345,659
Newark International, New Jersey	341,306

Airport	Total Operations[c]
Hartsfield Atlanta International	796,939
O'Hare International, Chicago	788,791
Los Angeles International	667,200
Dallas/Ft. Worth International	624,760
Stapleton International, Denver	520,836
John Wayne, Santa Ana	512,959
San Francisco International	455,885
Phoenix Sky Harbor	438,439
Long Beach	434,993
Lambert/St. Louis International	419,234
Philadelphia International	417,941
Boston/Logan International	414,968
Detroit Metropolitan	404,632
Oakland International	396,036
Honolulu International	385,275
McCarran International, Las Vegas	384,526
Memphis International	380,911
Boeing Field, Seattle	377,361
Greater Pittsburgh International	373,802
Minneapolis/St. Paul International	373,660

Source: Airport Operators Council International (AOCI), *Worldwide Airport Traffic Report: Calendar Year 1987* (Washington, D.C.: AOCI, 1988).

[a]The total includes enplaned, deplaned, domestic, international and commuter. It does not include direct transit passengers.

[b]The total includes domestic freight, express and mail (enplaned plus deplaned).

[c]Total includes domestic, international, passenger, cargo, commuter, general aviation, and military operations.

are located in the United States: 14 out of 20 in terms of passenger volume, 10 out of 20 based on cargo tonnage, and 20 out of 20 in terms of airplane operations. This table also points out that an airport with a large passenger volume is not necessarily an equally large airport based on the amount of cargo handled or in terms of airplane operations. For example, John Wayne Airport, a general aviation airport near Los Angeles, is the world's sixth-largest airport in terms of airplane operations, because of its disproportionately large amount of general aviation activity. A number of other airports that rank high on the list—such as that in Long Beach, California—are in a similar situation. Nevertheless, some airports, such as Los Angeles International, rank high with respect to all three criteria.

Table 4–3 shows the distribution of passenger enplanements among the 30 largest U.S. airports in 1986; combined, these 30 airports accounted for more than two-thirds of total U.S. passenger enplanements in 1986. (The concentration of passengers at so few domestic airports underscores the severity of congestion problems.) Table 4–4 presents the number of flight operations for the 30 largest airports, which represented 22 percent of total U.S. operations during 1986.

Public-use airports are generally under public ownership—locally, regionally, or nationally—and their operating procedures and financial position vary by country. In the United States, airports handling scheduled airlines are required to obtain an operating certificate from the FAA under FAR part 139. These regulations require that airports establish minimum safety standards and that the standards be published in the airport certification manual and approved by the FAA prior to issuance of an operating certificate. The manual addresses various aspects of airport operations, including surface paving requirements, safety areas, marking and lighting, snow and ice control, rescue and fire fighting, handling and storage of hazardous substances and materials, airport emergency planning, operation of ground vehicles, and protection of navigational aids.

Most airports in the United States are owned and operated by states or municipal governments. At some airports, operations are conducted by semi-autonomous, usually multijurisdictional governmental authorities, such as the Port Authority of New York and New Jersey. As a result of governmental ownership, airports in the United States are under the control of state or local authorities; however, since airports receive federal grants, the federal government also specifies certain requirements. Consequently, airports comply with federal requirements relating to public rights and access. The option to end federal aid to large- and medium-size airports—defederalization—has been considered several times, and the issue continues to be controversial—in large part because defederalization would probably cause local airports to assess passenger service charges (head taxes) to meet their financial needs.

In other parts of the world, airports are also owned by local and national

Table 4–3
Top Thirty U.S. Airports Ranked by 1986 Total Passenger Enplanements

Airport	Total Enplanements[a] (thousands)	Percentage[b]	Cumulative Percentage
1. Chicago O'Hare	25,463	5.92	5.92
2. Atlanta	22,040	5.12	11.04
3. Los Angeles International	19,729	4.58	15.62
4. Dallas/Ft. Worth	19,682	4.57	20.19
5. Denver	15,694	3.65	23.84
6. Newark	15,361	3.57	27.41
7. San Francisco International	13,272	3.08	30.49
8. New York Kennedy	13,248	3.08	33.57
9. New York LaGuardia	10,774	2.50	36.07
10. Boston	10,628	2.47	38.54
11. Miami	10,438	2.42	40.96
12. St. Louis International	10,089	2.34	43.30
13. Honolulu	8,814	2.04	45.34
14. Detroit	8,611	2.00	47.34
15. Minneapolis/St. Paul	8,252	1.92	49.26
16. Pittsburgh	7,815	1.82	51.08
17. Phoenix	7,557	1.76	52.84
18. Houston Intercontinental	6,947	1.61	54.45
19. Washington National	6,937	1.61	56.06
20. Seattle-Tacoma	6,799	1.58	57.64
21. Philadelphia	6,009	1.40	59.04
22. Orlando	5,917	1.37	60.41
23. Charlotte	5,900	1.37	61.78
24. Las Vegas	5,772	1.34	63.12
25. Tampa	4,730	1.10	64.22
26. Salt Lake City	4,679	1.09	65.31
27. San Diego	4,480	1.04	66.35
28. Baltimore	4,296	0.99	67.34
29. Memphis	4,275	0.99	68.33
30. Washington Dulles	4,077	0.95	69.28

Source: Federal Aviation Administration (FAA), *FAA Aviation Forecasts: Fiscal Years 1988–1999* (Washington, D.C.: FAA, February 1988), 112.

[a]Includes U.S. certified route air carriers, foreign-flag carriers, supplementals, air commuters, and air taxis.

[b]Based on 430.461 million passenger enplanements.

governments and the form of ownership and of operating/management structure varies from one country to another. Examples of different entities responsible for operating and managing airports include government departments, quasi-governmental authorities, and concessionaires. As a result of such differences, the degree of control exercised by governments also varies from country to country. In some countries, for example, governments have established airport authorities but not given them financial autonomy. In other countries, airports are viewed more as commercial businesses than

Table 4–4
Top Thirty U.S. Airports Ranked by 1986 Total Aircraft Operations

Airport	Total Operations (thousands)	Percentage[a]	Cumulative Percentage
1. Chicago O'Hare	794.8	1.35	1.35
2. Atlanta	774.8	1.31	2.66
3. Dallas/Ft. Worth	575.2	.97	3.63
4. Los Angeles International	565.2	.96	4.59
5. Santa Ana	540.1	.92	5.51
6. Denver Stapleton	520.7	.88	6.39
7. Van Nuys	472.4	.80	7.19
8. St. Louis International	460.4	.78	7.97
9. San Francisco International	422.7	.72	8.69
10. Boston	420.1	.71	9.40
11. Newark	413.7	.70	10.10
12. Phoenix Sky Harbor	412.3	.70	10.80
13. Detroit Metro	406.0	.69	11.49
14. Minneapolis/St. Paul	401.8	.68	12.17
15. Seattle Boeing Field	400.7	.68	12.85
16. Long Beach	397.1	.67	13.52
17. Memphis	380.2	.64	14.16
18. Oakland	371.0	.63	14.79
19. Philadelphia	368.2	.62	15.41
20. Pittsburgh	365.6	.62	16.03
21. New York LaGuardia	365.2	.62	16.65
22. Pontiac	364.3	.62	17.27
23. Honolulu	363.9	.62	17.89
24. Denver Arapahoe	363.7	.62	18.51
25. Charlotte	361.2	.61	19.12
26. Las Vegas	352.2	.60	19.72
27. San Jose	348.8	.59	20.31
28. Miami International	345.2	.59	20.90
29. New York Kennedy	326.5	.55	21.45
30. Washington National	325.7	.55	22.00

Source: Federal Aviation Administration (FAA), *FAA Aviation Forecasts: Fiscal Years 1988–1999* (Washington, D.C.: FAA, February 1988), 113.

[a]Based on 58.956 million operations at 399 FAA-operated airport traffic control towers in Fiscal Year 1986.

as public utilities and are thus far more autonomous. With autonomy, however, comes the expectation that the airport should break even financially, earn a reasonable return on investment, and pay taxes.[10] Such a situation exists, for example, in the United Kingdom, where the government views airports as commercial enterprises and has privatized the British Airports Authority, which manages seven airports: Heathrow, Gatwick, Stansted, Edinburgh, Glasgow, Aberdeen, and Prestwick.

In the United States, large- and medium-size, publicly owned airports typically conduct their business in conjunction with privately owned airlines.

This public-private characteristic distinguishes the financial management and operation of these U.S. airports from those of organizations that are either exclusively publicly owned or exclusively privately owned. Examples of these differences include pricing policies and investment-planning practices that are negotiated but officially remain the responsibility and under the authority of airport operators. At some airports, the risks and responsibilities of airport operations are shared by the airport operator and the airlines that use the airport as long as the airlines continue to serve the airport. Terms and conditions of the relationship between the airport and airlines are contained in legal documents called airport-use agreements.

At the end of March 1986, there were 16,291 airports in the United States. About 6,000 of these airports were open to the public; 10,000 were private-use airports that were closed to the general public. Of the 6,000 or so airports open to the public, about 70 percent were publicly owned and about 30 percent privately owned. Figure 4–1 shows the structure of the U.S. airport system by ownership and use.

Figure 4–1 shows the number of airports in the NPIAS, disaggregated by three general classes: commercial service, reliever, and general aviation. Commercial service airports are defined as those with 2,500 or more passenger enplanements per year; within this class, airports having .01 percent or more of total U.S. enplanements are designated as primary airports. Relievers are general aviation airports in metropolitan areas that are intended to reduce congestion at nearby commercial service airports by providing general aviation pilots with alternative landing facilities. The bulk of civil aircraft operations is handled at general aviation airports.

In defining air service markets in the United States, the FAA utilizes various classifications of hub cities, which are quite different from an airline's definition of a hub. A large U.S. metropolitan center may have several major airports that serve as airline hubs, as well as several smaller airports. From the FAA's regulatory perspective, however, an air traffic hub is not a specific airport; it is a city and the surrounding Standard Metropolitan Statistical Area (SMSA), which may include more than one airport. For instance, a large air traffic hub such as New York or San Francisco has several major airports. Table 4–5 presents four classifications of hubs as defined by the FAA: large, medium, small, and nonhub. These classifications are determined by the percentage of total enplaned passengers represented by each SMSA. In 1986 there were 137 FAA-defined air traffic hubs, which accounted for 96.1 percent of total passenger enplanements.[11]

Airport Systems

Airports differ from other transportation terminals in two respects—land size and location. Because an airport includes a terminal and airside facilities,

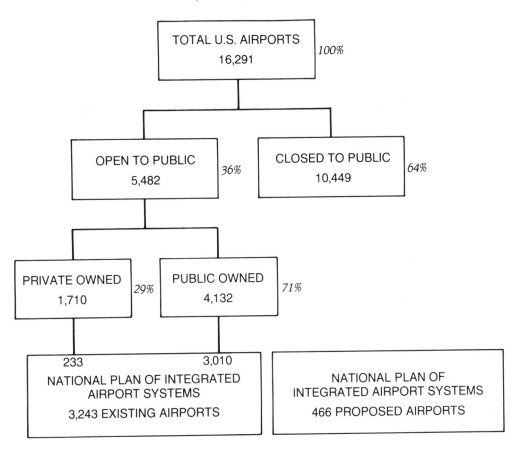

Figure 4–1. **Number of Airports by Ownership and Public Use,
March 31, 1986**

Source: Federal Aviation Administration (FAA), *National Plan of Integrated Airport Systems
(NPIAS) 1986–1995* (Washington, D.C.: FAA, November 1987), 2.

it requires much more land than either a bus terminal or a train depot does
for a comparable number of passengers. Specifically, to receive scheduled jet
service an airport must have an open flat space to accommodate one or more

Table 4–5
Hub Classification by the Percentage of Total Enplaned Passengers

Hub Classification	Enplaned Passengers	
	Percentage of Total	1986 Passengers
Large	1.00 or more	4,000,080 or more
Medium	0.25 to 0.999	1,000,020–4,000,079
Small	0.05 to 0.249	200,004–1,000,019
Nonhub	less than 0.05	less than 200,004

Source: Federal Aviation Administration (FAA), *FAA Aviation Forecasts: Fiscal Years 1988–1999* (Washington, D.C.: FAA, February 1988), 165.

long runways. It must also have adjoining taxiways and airplane parking space at the terminal. Dallas/Fort Worth International Airport, one of the largest U.S. airports, is located on some 18,000 acres of land, an area roughly equal to the size of the city of Newark, New Jersey. The need for a large landmass is explained by the operational requirements of modern jet aircraft, the need to physically separate airports from surrounding residential developments, and the need to accommodate future airport expansion. The location of the airport is determined not only by the amount of land required but also by the condition of the land; prevailing winds, altitude, and other weather conditions; relative locations of residential and industrial communities; availability of ground access by both passengers and cargo shippers; and availability of adequate utilities.

An airport serving large carriers is a complex system involving three components: (a) airside service, (b) terminal operations, and (c) landside facilities. The airside component encompasses the airfield surfaces on which an airplane moves; these surfaces include runways, taxiways, and terminal aprons, which are ramp areas surrounding the terminal where airplanes park to load and unload passengers. The terminal serves as an interchange between airside and landside facilities. The terminal building contains passenger loading and waiting areas, ticket counters, security checkpoints, baggage-handling facilities, car rental facilities, airline operations offices, and concessionaires such as shops and restaurants; international terminals also contain customs and immigration facilities. In contrast, the landside component of an airport comprises the roadways and fixed guideways (rails) leading to and from the airport, as well as auto parking facilities.

The Airside Component

Airside requirements—runways, taxiways, and apron—influence the amount of land area and the design required for an airport. Planning for this particular component is a function of the different types of aircraft using the airport, the location of the terminal and maintenance facilities, available land

(and trade-offs between size and accessibility), and the movement of ground service vehicles. Table 4–6 highlights various characteristics of selected transport airplanes that influence the planning of airside facilities. The mass of an aircraft, for example, is an important factor in determining the thickness, pavement surface, and underlying support of runways, taxiways, and apron areas. Similarly, taxiways and parking areas must be designed to provide adequate clearance for aircraft with different wingspans and fuselage lengths. Takeoff and landing mass influence the length of a runway. Presented in Table 4–7 are various characteristics of selected general aviation and commuter aircraft that, like their large jet counterparts, also influence the planning of airside facilities.

An airport can have a single runway, in which case its capacity is limited, particularly during IFR conditions. Moreover, a single runway has the disadvantage of closing the airport when anything happens to obstruct the runway. Multiple runways overcome many of these disadvantages; they increase the capacity of an airport and in many cases are designed to provide a cross-runway to reduce the number of crosswind landings. There are basically three configurations for multiple runway layouts: parallel, open V, and intersecting. The ideal layout maximizes capacity and wind coverage and minimizes crosswind potential, while maintaining required separation allowances between airplanes. Parallel runways require less land than diagonal cross-runways do, but conditions in certain areas mandate intersecting crosswind runways. Major airports have two or three runways—a long runway for commercial flights, a shorter runway for general aviation aircraft, and a crosswind runway. At busy airports such as Chicago O'Hare, it is possible to have triple parallel runways; Los Angeles International even has four parallel runways.

Runways vary in size and composition, from strips of mowed grass less than 3,000 feet long to paved runways 14,000 feet long. Length, width, and strength requirements are prescribed in FAA and ICAO planning documents. The graphical renderings of the documents depict in great detail variations in airport elevation, runway gradient, average temperatures, and gross takeoff and landing weights. Runway length influences not only the size and cost of an airport but also the type and size of airplane that can use it. Moreover, under certain conditions at some airports, particular airplanes may be forced to limit their payload, including their fuel load. For instance, because an airplane's takeoff performance deteriorates rapidly in hot, humid weather, an airline may need to reduce payload so that the airplane can become airborne. Runway orientation depends on local prevailing wind conditions, topography, height and position of obstructions in the area, size of the area available for runway construction, and noise considerations.

Taxiways allow an aircraft to get on and off runways, and they facilitate aircraft movement from one part of an airport to another. The design and layout of taxiways depend on the characteristics and mix of airplanes using

Table 4–6
Characteristics of Selected Transport Aircraft

Aircraft	Manufacturer	Wingspan (m)	Length (m)	Maximum Structural Takeoff Mass (kg)	Maximum Landing Mass (kg)	Number and Type of Engine[a]	Number of Seats[b]
A-300	Airbus Industrie	44.83	54.08	165,000	138,000	2TF	267–375
B707-320B	Boeing	43.41	46.61	151,318	67,132	4TF	141–189
B727-200	Boeing	32.92	46.69	76,657	68,039	2TF	134–163
B737-300	Boeing	28.88	32.18	61,220	51,700	2TF	122–149
B747-300	Boeing	59.64	69.80	340,100	255,800	4TF	522–624
B757-200	Boeing	38.06	46.97	100,800	89,800	2TF	178–217
B767-300	Boeing	47.57	54.94	159,210	136,070	2TF	254–312
BAe 146-100	BAe	26.34	26.19	37,308	32,817	4TF	82–93
Concorde	BAC Aerospatiale	25.55	61.65	176,447	108,862	4T	108–128
DC-10-30/4C	Douglas	50.39	55.35	251,744	182,798	3TF	270–345
DC-9-32	Douglas	28.44	36.37	48,988	44,906	2TF	115–127
DC-9-50	Douglas	28.44	40.23	54,431	49,895	2TF	130
F-27-500	Fokker	29.00	25.06	20,412	19,051	2TP	52–60
L-1011	Lockheed	47.35	53.75	195,045	162,386	3TF	256–330
MD 81	Douglas	32.87	45.06	63,503	58,060	2TF	115–172

Source: International Civil Aviation Organization (ICAO), *Airport Planning Manual, Part 1: Master Planning* (Montreal: ICAO, 1987), 1–51.
[a]T = turbojet; TF = turbofan; TP = turboprop.
[b]Approximate number of seats; depends on seating configuration and location of galleys.

Table 4–7
Characteristics of Selected General Aviation and Commuter Aircraft

Aircraft	Wingspan (m)	Length (m)	Maximum Takeoff Mass (kg)	Maximum Number of Seats[a]	Number and Type of Engine[b]	Runway Length[c] (m)
Beech V35-Bonanza	10.19	8.03	1,542.21	6	1P	400
Beech B200-Super King Air	16.61	13.34	5,670.00	15	2TP	867[d]
Cessna 172 Skyhawk	10.90	8.20	1,043.26	4	1P	465
Cessna T310	11.25	8.99	2,494.76	6	2P	545
Cessna Citation III	16.31	16.90	9,525.00	11	2TF	1,435
Dassault-Jet Falcon 20T	16.54	18.29	13,199.54	28	2TF	1,350
Gulfstream II	20.98	24.36	26,081.56	22	2TF	1,240
Lear Jet 25	10.85	14.50	6,803.89	8	2T	1,580
Lockheed Jet Star	16.59	18.42	19,050.88	12	4T	1,490
North American Sabreliner-60	13.54	14.73	9,071.85	12	2T	1,485
Piper PA-23-250 Aztec	11.33	9.22	2,358.68	6	2P	380
Piper Twin Comanche C	10.97	7.67	1,632.93	6	2P	570

Source: International Civil Aviation Organization (ICAO), *Airport Planning Manual, Part 1: Master Planning* (Montreal: ICAO, 1987), 1–52.

[a]Number of seats includes pilot.

[b]P = piston engine; T = turbojet; TF = turbofan; TP = turboprop.

[c]Maximum distance in nearest 5 m to reach height of 15 m for takeoff or land from height of 15 m.

[d]Landing length governs.

the airport and on the intended purpose of the taxiway, such as for entering or exiting a runway or accessing a hangar or apron. To minimize aircraft fuel expenses and takeoff/landing congestion, taxiing distances are kept as short as possible and runway occupancy time is minimized. The latter is achieved by using carefully located, angled exit taxiways that do not have sharp turns, thereby enabling landing and departing aircraft to taxi at higher speeds. The location of taxiways and the angle at which they intersect the runway are critical to runway occupancy time. When possible, taxiways parallel the runway(s). At smaller airports, the runway can also be used as a taxiway by providing room for turnarounds at the end of the runway.

Aprons, or gate areas, are conveniently located airplane parking places that facilitate loading and unloading passengers, baggage, and cargo. They also allow aircraft to be positioned for ground support services, such as galley and cabin cleaning, electrical ground power, fueling, and minor maintenance. The size and design of the apron depends on the number of gates in the terminal building; the number, size, and mix of airplanes to be accommodated; the positioning of aircraft around the terminal; airplane circulation and taxiing patterns; and the type, size, and number of ground service vehicles.

Because of the interrelationship between aprons and the terminal complex, these two elements are designed so as to be highly complementary. In broad terms, airports around the world employ four different apron-terminal concepts: linear, satellite, pier, and transporter. In the linear layout, airplanes are parked in a single line on one side of the terminal. Whereas in the satellite design airplanes are parked around a structure that is connected to the central part of the terminal by a corridor, in the pier concept they are parked in line on one or both sides of a corridor that is connected to the central part of the terminal. And in a transporter design, airplanes are parked at a remote location from the terminal and passengers are transported by mobile units.[12]

The Terminal

Terminal complexes of major commercial airports resemble small cities. They contain various combinations of passenger-ticketing and baggage-handling facilities, customs and immigration facilities, hotels, restaurants, bars, shops, banks, post offices, law enforcement offices, government agencies, ground transportation agencies, and chapels. Although not visible to passengers, numerous other offices exist, with many behind-the-scenes activities taking place—for example, in airline dispatch offices, briefing rooms, and communication centers.

For airports serving small carriers, general aviation aircraft, or both, terminal layout and facilities are less complex than for those serving major airlines. Nevertheless, in all cases the terminal's primary function is to provide a link between the landside and the airside facilities. As such, the terminal's design and operation can influence not only its own capacity but also that of the landside and airside components of an airport, as well as expansion capability.

The terminal must meet the needs of all users, not just primary users—that is, passengers and cargo shippers. Secondary users include airline, airport, and government employees; airport concessionaires; and well-wishers, meeters and greeters, sightseers, those attending meetings, and other visitors. Each user group has a different set of needs, and even within a user group, needs vary; for example, the needs of origin-destination passengers differ from those of connecting passengers.

Although variations in design have been many, terminal buildings normally have three main parts: the curb frontage, the central processing area, and the link(s) between the terminal and the aircraft. Airport designers attempt to maximize the efficiency with which users can enter and exit the terminal. Efficiency, as measured by the time and effort a passenger spends moving through the terminal, depends on the layout of the curb frontage and its relationship to other areas, such as parking lots, airport roadways, and pedestrian walkways. The central processing area encompasses ticket counters; passenger and baggage check-in positions; security inspection facilities, including customs, immigration, and health control for international operations; and baggage claim. The link between the terminal and aircraft on the ramp includes the concourse, the departure lounge, and public areas such as concessions. The overall design of this link can influence the efficiency of the terminal apron area in terms of the number and mix of aircraft accommodated and the time required to service those airplanes. Moreover, link areas are responsible for generating a significant portion of total airport revenues through concession sales. Passengers and the people accompanying them spend the majority of their time in this area of the terminal.

How passenger terminals are designed is largely a function of the configuration of available space and of existing terminals, average and peak-period traffic, type of passenger traffic expected to use the facility, number and type of airlines and aircraft serving the airport, and mode of surface access. Airports have selected different designs depending on whether traffic is predominately domestic or international, long-haul or short-haul, origin-destination or connecting, online or interline connecting, and scheduled or charter. Passengers connecting from one long-haul international flight to another long-haul international flight, for example, spend much more time in the terminal than passengers making domestic connections. With the exception of totally new terminals, most existing terminal complex designs have evolved over time, with expansion partially dictated by the availability of adjacent land, a compatibility with the existing layout, and the changing needs of users, both airlines and passengers. Lack of available adjacent land, for example, has forced some airports to use a transporter system. Airline needs have also changed, the trend toward the development of hubs having led more airlines to seek their own large and separate terminals.

Landside Facilities

Landside facilities include roads and rail links to the airport and to parking areas. At most airports in the United States, almost all passengers use private cars, taxis, rental cars, or hotel or motel courtesy vans to enter or exit an airport. At a typical airport in the United States, passenger traffic accounts for only about a third of the total traffic using landside facilities, the other two-thirds being made up of greeters and well-wishers, airport employees, delivery and service personnel, and visitors. Most of this nonpassenger traffic also use automobiles, hence automobile traffic, particularly at curbside and on airport access and circulation roads, is the primary source of landside congestion. In the United States, the development of this area of airports has lagged the development of airside services and terminal operations—perhaps because, with few exceptions, the FAA does not aid capital improvements for landside facilities. Responsibility for the bulk of such improvements rests with local and state agencies. While it is reasonable to expect some improvement in landside operations as a result of procedural changes—for example, the use of remote park-and-ride facilities—truly significant advancements will result only by finding a viable substitute for the automobile for travel to and from airports. The extension of underground train service directly to London's Heathrow Airport in 1977 demonstrates that such a concept is indeed feasible.

Airport Master-Planning

Continued growth of the air transport industry requires airports to period-ically upgrade their facilities and processing methods. The expansion and modification of existing airports and the development of new airports re-quire the preparation of a master plan, a document that outlines planners' concept of the long-term development of an airport. Generally, an airport master plan provides guidelines for cost-effective handling of anticipated passenger demand; at the same time, the plan must be responsive to the environmental and socioeconomic needs of the local community. The devel-opment of an airport master plan is a complex task, one that must comply with standards established by individual government agencies when govern-ment funding is involved. The FAA, for example, has published a document pertaining to the development of airport master plans,[13] and the ICAO has published a similar document to assist airport authorities around the world in preparing such plans.[14]

The first step recommended in the ICAO manual involves preplanning coordination. To increase the probability of acceptance and successful implementation of the plan's guidelines, it is necessary to coordinate the interests and seek the advice of private citizens and such groups as neighborhood associations, environmentalists, local government planning personnel, and users of airport facilities, including airlines, general aviation representatives, and concessionaires. The basic tasks to accomplish during this stage are to (a) define the airport's long- and short-term objectives; (b) identify sources of reliable and meaningful data; (c) produce preliminary estimates of the costs and benefits of proposed projects; (d) identify financing needs and sources; and (e) preliminarily determine the planning team, organization, and operating procedures.

If the preparers of the master plan successfully reconcile the oftentimes conflicting aims of the various interest groups, the heart of airport master-planning then becomes the forecasting process. Forecasts of aviation activity define the size, timing, and scope of the facilities required. Whereas anticipated aircraft movements determine the requirements for airside facilities, projections of passenger and cargo traffic influence the terminal and landside requirements. Annualized forecasts of aircraft movements and traffic volume are prepared for each year in the planning horizon, and most plans include estimates for hourly and daily peak periods. These estimates of peak activity are essential for determining facility requirements. Aggregate forecasts of aircraft movements are also disaggregated by type of aircraft (wide-body jet, narrow-body jet, commuter, general aviation), by type of user (airline, general aviation, military), and by mix of arrivals and departures. Similarly, aggregate forecasts of passengers are disaggregated by subgroups, such as domestic and international, scheduled and nonscheduled, and local and transit. In the case of cargo, forecasters separate the traffic moving in the bellies of passenger airplanes from the traffic moving in all-cargo airplanes. In the case of general aviation, the key forecasting variable is the number of aircraft based at the airport, by type of aircraft.

Once forecasts for demand have been produced, the next step is to analyze the capability of the existing airport to support that demand. The unconstrained forecasts of airside and landside demand are compared with the existing capacities of facilities to determine alternative strategies for accommodating the projected demand. In addition, attention is focused on balancing capacity among all components. In the event that existing airport facilities cannot be expanded to accommodate the projected demand, it may be necessary to undertake a site selection process for a new airport or to modify the role of existing airports in surrounding communities.

Airport site evaluation and selection are usually based on three sets of criteria: operational, social, and financial. Operational considerations include the required runways (number, length, and orientation), conflicting ATC requirements and patterns, natural and manmade obstacles, and weather. Social considerations include proximity to passenger demand, ground access, noise impacts, environmental effects, and compatibility of land use. And cost considerations include analyses of topography and soil, construction material, services, and land values.

One of the most critical aspects of airport planning is identifying the environmental implications of airport development alternatives. Prior to 1970, environmental feasibility studies were not a prime consideration in airport master-planning. Since then, they have become as important as, if not more so than, economic and engineering feasibility studies. Congress enacted the National Environmental Policy Act of 1969 to restore and maintain environmental quality. This legislation led to the requirement for an environmental analysis and impact statement if it is determined that the environment would be affected significantly by the expanded operation or construction of an airport.

Typically, the most significant environmental issue related to the development and operation of an airport is airplane noise, which affects people's ability to sleep and communicate. The severity of the airplane-noise problem is a function of numerous factors, including its magnitude, frequency, duration, and type. People's response to airplane noise is also a function of such factors as its level, time of day, the ambient level of noise, and land and building use. Forecast levels of noise are required to meet the government's land-use compatibility guidelines. The FAA's FAR part 150 contains a table ("Land-Use Compatibility with Yearly Day-Night Average Sound Levels") that identifies land uses that are "normally compatible" or "noncompatible" with various levels of noise exposure.[15] An airport's noise-exposure map and noise-compatibility program (the latter showing the noise-control and land-use planning strategies) are submitted to the FAA for review. The FAA, in turn, provides planning grants to study and produce noise-compatibility programs. In addition to noise, airport master plans must also consider other aspects of potential pollution, such as the impact on air quality, water, and soil.

Besides addressing various forms of pollution, airport development plans must also consider a number of social, ecological, and economic factors. Social factors involve potential changes in the use of land, not only in close proximity to the airport but also in more distant regions. Ecological factors pertain not only to the impact of airport development on wildlife habitats but also to the potential threat to airplane operations posed by bird strikes. And economic analyses must go beyond the obvious costs of airport construction and operation, revenues from operations, and benefits to users; such analyses must also examine the direct and indirect benefits to the entire community of increased economic activity in the region.[16] Indicative of the economic drawing power of a major airport is the recent rapid surge in development around Washington Dulles International Airport, which is about 20 miles from the District of Columbia area. In the final analysis, an airport must be compatible with its environs. Not only must airport location, size, and design be coordinated with various land-use patterns—residential, industrial, institutional, and so forth—but also consideration must be given to the effect of airport development on people, flora and fauna, the atmosphere, and water resources.

The next step in airport master-planning involves the development of airport layout and land-use plans, which are sets of drawings showing the airport boundary, landing area configuration, location of navigational facilities and clear zones, and areas for the passenger terminal complex, maintenance and cargo facilities, general aviation facilities, and other pertinent landside facilities. Besides being required by the government, the airport layout plan is a public document that serves as a reference for community deliberations on land-use proposals and budget and resource planning.

The final step in master planning involves the development of an implementation plan. This document shows schedules, costs, and sources of revenue to cover the capital improvement program, as well as operating and maintenance costs and financing during the construction stage. Since the planning horizon for an airport can extend up to twenty years, economic feasibility must be established for each stage of development.

Financial Operations

That airports around the world vary widely in their economic and financial operations is the result of numerous factors, including differences in airport size, organizational structure, scope of operations, and range of services provided. While some airports primarily handle general aviation operations, others handle commercial operations, and within the latter group is wide variation in the nature of the traffic accommodated. The degree of diversification also varies from airport to airport, with some having a stake in industrial parks located on their property and others having a stake in the activities of concessionaires. In addition, the degree of autonomy enjoyed by individual airports varies by locale. Differences also exist in the amount and form of subsidies provided by governments[17] and in the reasons subsidies are given. In addition to providing a community with access to the national and international air transportation systems, an airport is a community resource that has a strong impact on the local and regional economy, including direct and indirect employment, retention of existing industry, attraction of new industry, and expansion of tourism.

Because of differences in the basic structure of airports around the world, financial practices among airports vary widely as well. A number of airports in the United States, for example, have a relationship with carriers that allows airlines to share some of the airport's investment risk. In some cases, airlines agree to pay those costs of operating the airport or servicing its debt which are not recovered from other sources, such as automobile and terminal parking—an arrangement known as the residual-cost approach to pricing.

Here, a significant portion of the airport's financial risk is transferred to the airlines, since they agree to make up any operating deficit incurred by the airport. In exchange for assuming some of the financial risk under the residual-cost approach, airlines are able to exercise significant control over an airport's investment decisions. These powers are conferred in a "majority-in-interest" clause in airlines' use agreements; this clause provides airlines with the opportunity to review and approve or disapprove airport capital projects that could significantly raise the use charges incurred by carriers.

In other cases in the United States, the airport assumes the full financial risk of operations but sets airline fees at a level that will enable the airport to recover anticipated annual costs—an arrangement known as the compensatory approach to pricing. Although under this approach an airport attempts to ensure that it is fully compensated, there is no guarantee that rents and fees collected in any given year will be sufficient to meet the airport's operating and debt service requirements. Still, airports that use the compensatory approach employ standard principles of cost accounting to compute the total expense of each cost center and then assess the airlines a share of these costs based on the extent of their actual use of facilities and services within airfield and terminal cost centers.

Whether residual-cost or compensatory, the specific approach employed in the airport use agreement can influence an airport's credit rating and its ability to raise capital in the bond market. The choice of approach can also influence an airport's potential profitability. Under the residual approach, although an airport is assured of its ability to service its debt without resorting to supplemental local tax support, it is precluded from generating substantial earnings in excess of costs. Stated differently, although an airport using the residual approach is guaranteed by signatory carriers to break even, it will not garner excess profits, since the surplus revenues are used to reduce airline charges. Some lenders favor this approach from the viewpoint of debt service considerations. Under the compensatory approach, although there is no guarantee that an airport will break even, it can earn and retain substantial profits; moreover, airport management has greater flexibility and freedom to undertake capital improvements without direct approval from the airlines. In practice, however, airports do tend to consult with airlines about their long-term plans.

The size, structure, and distribution of airport operating revenues vary from airport to airport, depending on the type and size of the airport. At small airports, particularly general aviation airports, fuel flowage and hangar-use fees (instead of landing fees) are likely to be sufficient to pay for the use of airfield facilities. At airports serving large air carriers, the main sources of operating revenue include air carrier landing fees, commercial income from concession fees and parking, and charges for the use of terminal areas and hangars. Landing fees, usually based on aircraft gross landing weight, are normally set to cover the costs of operating airfield facilities and typically generate 20 to 25 percent of the airport's revenues. Concession contracts, which reimburse airports for the use of terminal areas, usually provide for either a percentage of a concessionaire's gross revenue or an annual minimum charge (whichever is greater), plus rent. For leased areas, such as ticket-counter space and hangars, airlines pay rent, usually based on the square footage utilized.

To gain further insight into the source and distribution of airport revenues, consider the financial operations of Toronto International Airport. During fiscal year 1985–86, total revenue from terminal-related activities amounted to CA$65 million, or 63 percent of aggregate revenues. Of this total, CA$20.5 million came from concessions, CA$15 million from auto parking facilities, CA$5.8 million from space rentals, CA$20.5 million from general terminal fees, and CA$3.2 million from other sources, such as bridge fees, security fees, and aircraft parking fees.[18] In the United States, large hubs obtain roughly 35 percent of their revenue from airlines and about 45 percent from concessions; medium hubs about 35 percent each from airlines and concessions; and small hubs about 30 percent from airlines and 25 percent from concessions.[19]

Airport expenses cannot be disaggregated as easily and precisely as airport revenue can, because of such factors as (a) the public/government nature of many airports; (b) the multipurpose, port-authority financial structure at some airports; and (c) the arbitrariness associated with allocating costs among different users of the system. Cost disaggregation may become difficult, for example, when certain services—police, fire protection, and so forth—are provided by the local government. Multipurpose port authorities may be responsible for operating a number of airports in a region, as well as other entities, such as harbors, tunnels, and bridges. And cost-allocation problems can arise in assigning costs to different users, such as air carriers, general aviation, and the military.

Notwithstanding these difficulties, an airport's expenses are divided into two main categories: operating and nonoperating. Operating expenses include such items as administration and staffing, maintenance of facilities (landing areas, terminals, hangars, and so forth) and ground equipment, utilities, insurance, security, and communications. Nonoperating expenses include debt service, that is, funds required to repay the principal and interest on outstanding debt, and depreciation. As in the case of revenue, the distribution of airport expenses varies among individual airports.

Airport construction, development, and improvement require large amounts of capital over and above the operating revenues generated by airports. Sources of financing vary throughout the world, ranging from aid provided by multigovernment entities to funds generated internally. In the United States, airports obtain funds for capital improvements from a number of sources, including the sale of bonds, state and federal grants, and private financing.

Airport bonds, essentially a U.S. phenomenon, are of three types: general obligation; revenue; and hybrid, such as self-liquidation general obligation bonds. *General obligation bonds* are issued by local governments and secured by the full faith and credit of the issuing body. The taxing authority of the government serves as security and allows these bonds to be sold at relatively low interest rates, resulting in a lower level of debt service charges. Yet because of the debt ceilings of the issuing agencies and the competing demand on local governments for other public projects, such as schools, streets, and water or sewage systems, there are limits on the amount of funds that can be raised from this source of financing. *Revenue bonds,* usually bearing slightly higher interest rates, are backed by the revenue generated by the facilities to be constructed. These particular bonds have become more common, partly because they do not depend on general tax funds. Although the airport remains responsible for repaying principal and interest on revenue bonds, it is the airlines which pledge that if the airport is unable to service its debt, they will allow the airport to raise landings fees to meet its debt obligations. The airlines that intend to use the airport therefore guarantee the facility's debt service obligation on the revenue bonds. *Hybrid bonds* combine the desirable features of both general obligation and revenue bonds. A self-liquidating bond, for example, like a general obligation bond, can be issued by a government body and bear a lower interest rate. It may not, however, reduce the general obligation borrowing capacity of the issuing body, since it is serviced from airport revenues generated from normal operations. The interest on these bonds is a function of the degree of financial risk involved—that is, the degree to which the general public is obligated if the airport is unable to generate sufficient revenue to service its debt.

Airports that are financially strong or have some inherent strength, such as a high level of origin-destination traffic relative to connecting traffic, are better able to compete in the bond market. In general, investors have significant confidence in airport bonds, both general obligation and revenue bonds. In the first case, the security is provided by the local community; in the second case, it is provided by the inherent viability of the airport's revenue flows, as determined by the strength of its market, and further guaranteed by the airlines. In addition, most municipal bonds are exempt from federal income tax, a feature sought by investors in high income tax brackets. In the past, revenue bonds and general obligation bonds have accounted for about 90 percent and 10 percent, respectively, of all airport financings. The larger the airport, the larger the share of capital raised through the sale of revenue bonds. General obligation bonds typically play a more significant role for smaller airports.

Federal, state, and local funds represent additional sources of financing for capital improvements. The FAA has estimated the needs for airport development eligible for federal aid between 1986 and 1995 to be $24.3 billion. More than half this amount is budgeted for increasing the operational capacity at existing large airports. The plan also includes the potential de-velopment of four new primary commercial service airports in Denver, Col-orado; Los Angeles, California; Austin, Texas; and Farmingdale, New Mexico. It is possible, however, that certain of these airports may not be built in the next ten years, because of lack of available funds, scarcity of acceptable sites, environmental considerations, and local resistance to large-scale construction in metropolitan areas; still, if a major new airport is de-veloped, the federal government is likely to pay up to 20 percent of the total costs.[20] Normally, commercial airports receive about 15 percent of their capital financing from the federal government; general aviation airports, about 40 percent.

In some cases, a third-party developer may finance, construct, and man-age an airport project. In these situations, the private developer must have access to the large private funding that is required. Moreover, an airport, before selecting a private developer, must be satisfied with the developer's expertise in airport design, construction, operation, and management; the developer of a terminal must not only coordinate and oversee its construc-tion but also have the knowledge and ability to deal with a broad spectrum of tenants. Third-party-developer financing is being used for the construction of Toronto International Airport's third terminal,[21] and the new London City Airport—a short-takeoff and -landing airport built among the disused docks of London's East End—was also financed and constructed with pri-vate capital.

Airline deregulation in the United States and the growing liberalization and privatization of airlines in other parts of the world have affected not only the management and operating practices of airports but airports' in-vestment practices as well. In the United States, for example, airlines and commercial airports once commonly signed long-term agreements in which the airlines assumed a significant portion of the financial risk of airport operations—an arrangement held in high regard by potential investors in airport revenue bonds. Under deregulation, airlines now prefer to remain flexible about the amount of service they provide at any given airport and consequently are interested in shorter-term agreements. Airports, too, are interested in shorter-term contracts, given the uneven fortunes of airlines. In turn, investors who once paid more attention to the strength of airport use agreements now examine more carefully an airport's local economic strength, this change in emphasis based on the assumption that a strong local economy will attract another carrier should an incumbent carrier leave the airport.

Airports in the United States are also moving toward compensatory ap-proaches to pricing and away from residual-cost approaches in airline use agreements. While this trend would seem to have detrimental effect on an airport's ability to access the capital markets, two other trends are bolstering airports' ability to raise capital. First, many airports have begun to strengthen and diversify their revenue bases through such strategies as vigorous exploitation of concession activities, more frequent adjustment of charges, and development of industrial parks.[22] Second, investors are beginning to realize that the need for an airport's services is a function more of the strength of local demand for air travel and the potential connecting traffic than of long-term airport use agreements.

The proliferation of liberalization policies in Europe is expanding the traffic base at affected airports. Consider the two airports in Ireland, Dublin and Shannon. Traffic growth at these two airports during the early 1980s was stagnant at best; in 1983, passenger traffic actually declined from its level in 1982. But the introduction of low-fare passenger service by a small Irish airline, Ryanair, coupled with the competitive responses of the two incumbent carriers, Aer Lingus and British Airways, led to a substantial growth in passenger traffic that in turn called for an expansion of airport facilities. According to airport officials, liberalization is also responsible for changes in other areas. In Ireland, for example, because a large percentage of the stimulated growth in traffic between the United Kingdom and Ireland represented first-time air travelers who required additional assistance, the airport authorities had to erect more signs and put more staff through customer service training.[23]

Finally, privatization—exemplified by the privatization of the British Airports Authority in the United Kingdom—is providing greater freedom to airport operators to manage their businesses. They can, for example, diversify into nonaviation activities; exploit new sources of capital, including equity participation by employees; and make other business decisions without the restrictions imposed by government bureaucracy. At the same time, the movement toward privatization could eventually bring additional regulation, reduce the possibility of monopolistic or predatory behavior, and ensure the existence of fair competition.[24] Moreover, the movement could alter the relationship between airports and airlines. Airlines, for example, could put pressure on airports to share profits through a variety of avenues, such as requiring a financial stake in airports or in certain sections of airports, such as duty-free shops.

The Airport Capacity Challenge

Airports around the world face a broad array of challenges, including an aging infrastructure, greater accountability on politically sensitive issues, terrorism, unlawful transportation of narcotic drugs, automation, and liability. But one of the most critical challenges facing major airports around the world is their basic inability to meet the rapidly increasing demand in passengers and airlines. During 1987, scheduled airlines belonging to the 158 contracting states of ICAO transported more than a billion passengers and some 16 million tons of freight. Even by conservative estimates, the volume of passenger traffic is expected to double by the end of this century, as a result of such factors as the growth in national economies, an increase in personal disposable incomes, rising educational levels, and lower fares attributable to a more competitive environment. Yet the major airports in most large cities around the world are already experiencing severe congestion problems—on the airside, in terminals, or on the roadways to and from the airport.

In the United States, where eighteen airports handling 42 percent of all passenger enplanements were considered severely congested in 1987, the number of seriously congested airports is expected to increase to fifty-eight by the year 2000. While it may appear that any problem involving just fifty-eight of the six thousand public-use airports in the United States cannot be too significant, it should be noted that those fifty-eight airports are expected to handle 76 percent of total U.S. enplanements by the year 2000.[25] And it should also be noted, of course, that the location of congestion—airside, terminal, or landside—varies among airports and that "fixing" one element may be futile if another element is almost as constraining. In Europe, the situation is similar. The number of congested airports is predicted to double by the end of this century, from about twelve to about twenty-five. The four largest European international airports—London Heathrow and Gatwick, Frankfurt Main, and Paris Charles de Gaulle—are already seriously congested.[26] Consequently, governments, airlines, and airports around the world are actively examining solutions to this pressing and highly complex problem. The following section provides an overview of the nature of the airport congestion problem and the various solutions that are being discussed.

In the United States, the seriousness of the airport capacity problem, together with the resulting congestion and flight delays, dates back to the late 1960s, when (a) the Port Authority of New York and New Jersey implemented a surcharge for general aviation aircraft landing during peak periods and (b) the FAA's "Special Air Traffic Rules for Designated High-Density Airports" established hourly quota limits on instrument flight rules (IFR) operations at five airports. Congestion problems persisted, and in 1974 the FAA established ad hoc working groups to identify specific capacity-related problems at eight airports and to assess potential improvements and implementation strategies.

The airports selected for study were Atlanta Hartsfield, Chicago O'Hare, Denver Stapleton, Kennedy and LaGuardia in New York, Los Angeles International, Miami International, and San Francisco International. The aim of the FAA studies was to review the causes and trends in airport delays and identify those projects and programs which could increase airport capacity and decrease delays. Prior to 1974, the problem had been manageable, in part because the airline industry was still regulated and in part because severe congestion problems had been limited to just a few major airports. The capacity shortage at most high-density airports was handled by the airlines themselves through scheduling committees that allocated available slots (takeoff and landing rights) among all carriers. Such otherwise collusive activity was tolerated during the regulatory regime by special permission of the government.

During the initial stages of deregulation, the slot-allocation system worked reasonably well. In 1980, however, New York Air, an upstart discount carrier, wanted to begin service to slot-controlled Washington National Airport. As a new entrant, New York Air had not been a party to the slot-allocation procedures agreed to by incumbent carriers at National Airport. Consequently, the FAA had to step in and require that existing airlines free up almost two dozen slots at Washington National Airport to accommodate New York Air. To do so, incumbent carriers had to surrender some of their takeoff and landing rights at National, which disrupted their entire route network. Reluctantly, the incumbents accommodated New York Air and other new entrants, presumably to keep the government out of the process of regulating slots.

After the strike by the Professional Air Traffic Controllers Organization in 1981, the slot-allocation process was extended to twenty-two major airports. During the following two years, the reduction in slots resulting from the strike did not have an unusually deleterious impact on the operations of most airlines, because of a coincidental jump in the price of fuel and the onset of a major recession. The operations of some airlines, however, were affected quite severely. After 1983, the U.S. economy entered a prolonged recovery and domestic carriers began to increase their operations, even though there was virtually no increase in the capacity of airports and the airway system. Ultimately, the congestion problem was aggravated by the proliferation of airline hubs, which put enormous strains on available airport capacity, both airside and terminal, during peak periods. Even nonhub airports that were not congested began to be affected because of the domino effect inherent in the structure of airline route systems. When airports became saturated, the air traffic control system mandated gate holds of inbound flights from originating spoke airports. The resultant delays completely disrupted the precise timing of incoming and departing flights needed for efficient operation of a hub-and-spoke network.

Another important aspect of hub development has been the proliferation of marketing agreements between large carriers and commuter carriers to provide passenger feed to each other at major hubs. Commuter carriers typically used turboprop airplanes with ten to forty seats to bring passengers into hubs from small cities. While the arrangement worked well for both the major carrier and the commuter carrier, it did consume a disproportionate amount of the capacity of the airport and airway system. For instance, because it required about a half-dozen commuter arrivals to fill one jet, it is not surprising that at some hubs commuter flights carried about 5 to 10 percent of passengers but consumed 30 to 40 percent of airport and airway system resources. Since the airside capacity of the airport and airway system is largely a function of the variety of airplanes using the airport (because of the wide separation required between approaching and departing airplanes of different speeds), mixing small commuter airplanes with large jet aircraft reduces the overall capacity of the system.

Over the past few years, the government has examined alternative ways of managing capacity. In April 1986, the Department of Transportation formally adopted and implemented the buy/sell plan, by which airlines could actually buy and sell airport operating slots from one another; however, there continued to be a shortfall in capacity relative to demand. The government's next step, taken in 1987, was to require that airlines begin reporting their on-time performance. In this, the Department of Transportation assumed that better-informed passengers and the competitive pressures arising from publicly disclosed performance statistics would motivate the airlines to initiate actions aimed at correcting the delay problem, at least in part.

The causes and extent of the airport capacity problem vary by country and indeed by airport. For some airports in Asia, for example, the causes of delays are curfew restrictions and congested airways. Consider an airline operating to an airport in Europe from an airport in Asia. Because the flight crosses so many time zones, the flexibility to move the flight to avoid a peak period at the arrival or departure airport is limited. Connecting flights arriving in Asia from Australia have to comply with curfews both in Australia and at the destination airport in Asia. Because of the substantial time-zone difference between Australia and Europe and the length of flight time, the departure "window"—that is, the number of hours during which a departure can take place—at the intermediate airport in Asia is quite small. The ability to move the departure time to avoid the peak is further limited by the relatively few airways that exist between some departure airports in Asia and arrival airports in Europe.[27] The clustering of airplane operations to comply with curfew restrictions at airports located on other continents also causes problems within passenger terminals, particularly in sections devoted to immigration and customs. Moreover, as has been the case with deregulation in the United States, the liberalization movement in Europe has greatly contributed to the diversity of the airport capacity problem: There is a growing shortage of runways, airspace, terminals, and airport access facilities.

The basic problem of airport capacity shortage is not the lack of capacity on a total systemwide or worldwide basis. Rather, the problem is that too much demand is being funneled through too few major airports. In the United States, for example, the top three commercial airports—Chicago O'Hare, Atlanta Hartsfield, and Los Angeles International—accounted for 16 percent of the total enplanements in 1986. In Europe, three airports—London Heathrow, Paris Charles de Gaulle, and Frankfurt Main—accounted for almost 40 percent of total European airport traffic.[28] Although other, unconstrained airports exist near some of the congested ones, users (airlines and/or general aviation) have been reluctant to use them to their fullest extent; examples include Midway in the vicinity of Chicago's O'Hare and Luton near London's Heathrow. Moreover, even at some of the congested airports, the shortage of capacity is really a problem only during peak periods. Almost all operations of international carriers at Bangkok, for example, take place between 10:00 and 12:00 P.M.; at Bombay, between midnight and 6:00 A.M. Although these airports may represent extreme cases, they illustrate the severity of the peak-period problem. In the United States, the FAA's analysis of aircraft operations during a random day, December 19, 1986, showed that there were thirty instances in which fifteen or more aircraft were scheduled to arrive at or depart from the same airport in the same minute.[29]

The lack of sufficient capacity to accommodate the growth in demand for air travel has been causing increasing levels of delays that are costly to airlines and their passengers as well as to users of general aviation airplanes. Table 4–8 shows that in the United States, the estimated cost of delays during 1985 at the top thirty airports was $1.85 billion, $1.15 billion to the airlines and almost $700 million to passengers. On a systemwide basis, the cost of delays is estimated at $2.9 billion.[30] Moreover, the public perceives, at least in the United States, that the inability of the airport/airway system to handle the growth in demand has eroded safety margins. Consequently, safety has become an integral part of the capacity issue.

While there is an extraordinary degree of consensus among passengers, government, industry, and the general public about the seriousness of the delay problem, there is no similar agreement about the causes of the problem or the optimal solution. In the United States, each group points the finger at other groups. The airlines are blamed for scheduling too many flights at peak hours; the FAA is blamed for being too conservative in implementing changes to the system; Congress is blamed for not providing sufficient funds to expand the capacity of airports and the airway system and for leaving the FAA under the control of the Department of Transportation; the Department of Transportation is blamed for creating institutional barriers and bureaucratic obstacles and for capitulating to special interest groups; airport owners and operators are blamed for neither expanding nor limiting access to their airports through such measures as curfews; the public is blamed for holding back the development of new airports and the expansion of existing major airports and for erecting barriers to the efficient use of existing airports; and passengers are blamed for showing intolerance to a deterioration in service as the inevitable trade-off for a lowering in fares.

It is the complexity of both the problem and the possible solutions that explains the apparent insolubility of the delay problem. The following five points further explain this complexity.

1. Measuring the capacity of an airport and the air traffic control system is a complicated process. Airport capacity is a function of the number

Table 4–8
1985 Air Carrier and Passenger Costs of Delay

Airport	Air Carrier Cost of Delay ($M)	Passenger Cost of Delay ($M)	Total Cost of Delay ($M)
Atlanta	$118.0	$67.9	$185.9
Boston	41.8	29.0	70.8
Baltimore Washington	11.3	5.9	17.2
Charleston AFB/Muni	2.1	.9	3.0
Cleveland Hopkins	9.9	5.2	15.1
Washington National	30.3	17.6	47.9
Denver Stapleton	55.4	34.3	89.7
Dallas/Ft. Worth	112.5	59.3	171.8
Detroit Metro	31.9	18.8	50.7
Newark	81.5	59.2	140.7
Washington Dulles	9.2	4.7	13.9
Houston Intercontinental	21.9	12.1	34.0
Indianapolis	5.7	4.1	9.8
Jacksonville	3.8	1.9	5.7
New York Kennedy	52.9	36.2	89.1
Los Angeles International	69.3	42.2	111.5
New York LaGuardia	63.2	37.3	100.5
Memphis	15.3	7.4	2.7
Miami	28.0	17.6	45.6
Minneapolis/St. Paul	26.4	29.2	55.6
New Orleans	6.8	4.0	10.8
Chicago O'Hare	140.2	77.5	217.7
Philadelphia	16.9	8.5	25.4
Phoenix Sky Harbor	32.2	14.8	47.0
Pittsburgh	20.5	13.8	34.3
Raleigh Durham	5.2	2.4	7.6
Seattle Tacoma	17.4	11.0	28.4
San Francisco	70.3	42.6	112.9
St. Louis Lambert	41.2	23.9	65.1
Tampa	12.2	6.2	18.4
Total	$1,153.4	$695.4	$1,848.8

Source: FAA Airport Activity Statistics, DOT Aircraft Operating and Performance Report, CAB form 41, schedules P–5.1 and P–5.2, and FAA Standardized Delay Reporting System.

and layout of runways and taxiways; of the characteristics of the terminal area airspace (geometry, natural obstacles, existence of other airports in the proximity); of prevailing meteorological conditions (wind, ceiling, and visibility); of ATC rules and procedures; of the mix of aircraft (size, performance characteristics, and pilot proficiency); of the proportion of arriving versus departing flights; and of local environmental constraints.

2. Capacity cannot be observed directly. Therefore, delays are often used as a surrogate measure of capacity under specific demand and operating conditions. Delays can occur, however, even when scheduled demand is less than capacity, because airplanes tend to arrive randomly rather than uniformly. Moreover, delays increase exponentially with an increase in demand.

3. An airport has three basic components: airside, terminal, and land-side. In different airports, different components are constrained.

4. The capacity of many airports has been reduced by noise-related restrictions. These restrictions have taken various forms, including limits on the number of operations allowed; curfews on operations during certain hours; bans on certain types of airplanes; and approach and departure paths that reduce the impact of noise on surrounding communities.

5. The framework of the U.S. air transportation system involves three components: the airlines, the ATC system, and airports. Whereas one component operates according to the rules of the marketplace (the airlines), the other two components continue to be under the regulatory jurisdiction of the federal government (the ATC system) and local governments (airports). Demand harmonization alternatives must therefore not only reflect the needs of the marketplace but also incorporate the goals of public policy and recognize the realities of politics. In addition, the availability of technology (for example, larger airplanes) and the supply and cost of capital must also be important considerations in any solutions.

Capacity can be increased in at least two ways: (a) by developing new airports and additional runways that minimize environmental impact and (b) by making optimal use of existing resources. The first option is not viable in the near term, because of public opposition and the enormous cost of building a new airport. Only two new major commercial airports in the world are currently under construction, one near Munich, Germany, and the other near Osaka, Japan. Eleven new airports around the world are, however, in the design stage, and the cost of developing them is estimated at $150 billion. These huge development costs reflect the higher costs of advanced-technology systems and the sheer scope of the work involved. Both these considerations are exemplified by the development in Japan of the Kansai International Airport, which is being built on a man-made island that will be connected to the mainland by a 4-kilometer, double-deck railroad bridge.[31] The cost of building new airports is, however, a relatively small concern compared with the issue of public opposition and with such controversial matters as the unwillingness of users to move to proposed new airports. The violent protests to the opening and subsequent expansion of Japan's Narita Airport is an example of how strong public resistance to airport development can become. Moreover, the major airlines are generally reluctant to move their operations to another facility.

The opposition to the development of a third airport in Chicago is an example of the concerns of parties other than the general public. To relieve congestion at O'Hare, a third commercial airport has been suggested for Chicago; however, opposition has come from both the city and the airlines serving O'Hare. Airlines are against the third airport, presumably because they have made large investments at the existing airport—for example, United's new terminal at O'Hare. To maintain market control and efficiency, these airlines would prefer to increase service at existing airports, not reduce or redeploy it to a nearby airport. Further, establishing a new airport with the objective of handling a large number of connecting passengers would not necessarily reduce flight frequency at existing airports, since hubs are beneficial only if they have large connecting complexes. It has been argued that airlines should develop pure connecting complexes at uncongested airports, an idea based on the premise that a coast-to-coast traveler could as easily make connections in a city like Columbus, Ohio, as in Chicago. But this argument overlooks the fact that mega-airline hubs are at cities with a large base of local origin-destination traffic, which the airline will continue to serve. Thus, some airlines are reluctant to transfer connecting traffic to another airport. Still another base of opposition to new airports is that they require vast expanses of land, likely to be located at great distances from city centers or in areas incapable of producing an adequate volume of origin-destination traffic. In addition, owners and sponsors of existing major airports are reluctant to have their major airlines relocate, since aviation activity, particularly hub operations, makes a substantial contribution to the local economy.

Optimizing the use of existing resources, the second option for increasing airport capacity, can be divided further into two parts: (a) extracting more capacity from the existing airport and airway system through the use of advanced technology and (b) implementing demand-management techniques. In terms of the first option, the FAA has been examining reductions in separation standards for aircraft on final approach, simultaneous operations on converging runways during IFR conditions and closely spaced parallel runways, the use of separate short runways for small airplanes, and the use of improved airport surveillance systems and vortex sensors. Wake vortex is a serious problem at airports having a broad mix of aircraft types; the turbulence caused by a large jet during its approach to landing can overwhelm smaller aircraft, and air traffic control procedures therefore prescribe time and physical separation limits between large and small aircraft operations, which can hinder airport capacity. The most attractive options for enhancing capacity appear to be related to the safe reduction of these separation standards. In addition, the complete segregation of slower and lighter airplanes from faster and heavier aircraft also promises to provide a significant increase in airport capacity.

The development of tilt-rotor aircraft is an example of advanced technology that could help increase the capacity of existing airports. On tilt-rotor aircraft, the engines tilt skyward, allowing the aircraft to act as a helicopter during takeoffs and landings; in the cruise phase of a flight, the engines revert to a standard fixed-wing position. Studies at NASA and Bell Helicopter Textron have demonstrated the feasibility of tilt-rotors aircraft that can operate with a capacity of forty or more seats, a cruise speed exceeding 300 miles per hour, and a range of about 500 miles. These performance levels cannot be matched by conventional helicopters. Tilt-rotor aircraft are also expected to be quieter than present-day helicopters, and they do not need a runway, which would alleviate airport congestion by allowing passengers to embark at downtown or suburban "vertiports." With this level of performance, tilt-rotor aircraft could provide a reasonable answer to the congestion problem, particularly in such areas as the crowded northeast corridor. Still, they are not expected to be available until 1995 and are likely to be very expensive in the early stages of production.

Opportunities for implementing demand-management techniques also fall into two groups: (a) the application of administrative procedures, such as the implementation of slots, nighttime curfews, and quotas and the enforcement of standards for airport noise, and (b) the implementation of market-oriented solutions, such as differential pricing policies and slot auctions. The first option, the application of administrative procedures, is quite controversial from the viewpoint of politics and public policy. Certain types of restrictions on general aviation access to busy airports are, for example, politically sensitive (and possibly even illegal), no matter how efficient they may be from an economic standpoint. The second option, management of demand through market-oriented solutions, is also plagued by numerous economic, political, operational, legal, and social considerations, yet it is in this area that the most progress is being made in coordinating capacity and demand. Evidence of such progress can be seen in the move by some airports to charge airlines higher landing and takeoff fees to operate during peak periods.

Another aspect of the use of free-market mechanisms to solve capacity problems is the provision of financial incentives. Although airlines already receive some incentives to harmonize airport/airway capacity and demand, they could be provided with additional incentives to schedule fewer flights during peak hours, utilize higher-capacity aircraft, or abate aircraft noise. Since environmental considerations are a major obstacle to airport development, Congress could provide economic incentives—investment tax credits, accelerated depreciation, and loan guarantees—to encourage the replacement of Stage 2 airplanes with Stage 3 aircraft to reduce noise. Providing airlines with financial incentives to acquire a fleet that is in compliance with the Stage 3 legislation could be an effective long-term solution to the problem of airplane noise, which is perhaps the most important challenge facing the aviation industry today.

Notes

1. D. Mondey, ed., *The International Encyclopedia of Aviation* (New York: Crown, 1977), 120.
2. Ibid.

3. J. Stroud, *Famous Airports of the World* (London: Frederick Muller, 1959), 57.

4. M. Greif, *The Airport Book* (New York: Mayflower Books, 1979), 57.

5. Stroud, *Famous Airports of the World.*

6. Federal Aviation Administration (FAA), *National Plan of Integrated Airport Systems, 1986–1995 (NPIAS)* (Washington, D.C.: FAA, November 1987), iii.

7. International Civil Aviation Organization (ICAO), *Environmental Protection, Volume 1: Aircraft Noise* (Montreal: ICAO, 1981).

8. J.W. Young, "The Stage 2 Ban: How, How Soon, How Much," *Avmark Aviation Economist,* September 1987, 14–16.

9. International Civil Aviation Organization (ICAO), *ICAO Bulletin* (Montreal: ICAO, July 1988), 56.

10. "The Limitation of 'Free Market' Solutions," *Avmark Aviation Economist,* September 1987, 8–11.

11. Federal Aviation Administration (FAA), *FAA Aviation Forecasts: Fiscal Years 1988–1999* (Washington, D.C.: FAA, February 1988), 114.

12. W. Hart, *The Airport Passenger Terminal* (New York: John Wiley, 1985)

13. Federal Aviation Administration (FAA), *Advisory Circular: Airport Master Plans,* AC no. 150/5070-6A (Washington, D.C.: FAA, June 1985).

14. International Civil Aviation Organization (ICAO), *Airport Planning Manual, Part 1: Master Planning,* document no. 9184-AN/902 (Montreal: ICAO, 1987).

15. U.S. Federal Interagency Committee on Urban Noise, *Guidelines for Considering Noise in Land-Use Planning and Control* (Washington, D.C.: U.S. Department of Transportation, June 1980).

16. R. Horonjeff and F. X. McKelvey, *Planning and Design of Airports,* 3d ed. (New York: McGraw-Hill, 1983), 593–601.

17. R. Doganis and A. Graham, *Airport Management: The Role of Performance Indicators* (London: Polytechnic of Central London, January 1987).

18. R. Schano, "Third-Party Development of Airport Facilities," *Airport Forum,* June 1987, 25–26.

19. "USA Needs Another 466," *Airports International,* December 1987–January 1988, 4.

20. Federal Aviation Administration, *NPIAS,* vi–ix.

21. Schano, "Third-Party Development of Airport Facilities," 25–26.

22. A.T. Wells, *Airport Planning and Management* (Blue Ridge Summit, Pa.: Tab Books, 1986).

23. "Why Eire Likes Liberalization," *Airports International,* February 1988, 15–16.

24. D. Woolley, "Regulation and Market Forces," *Airport Forum,* June 1987, 23.

25. S. Keeble, "USA: New Airports, Please," *Airline Business,* April 1988, 36–41.

26. R. Whitaker, "Europe: No Room for Competition," *Airline Business,* April 1988, 26–30.

27. J. Gallacher, "Asia/Pacific: The Curfew Conundrum," *Airline Business,* April 1988, 44–48.

28. R. Whitaker, "Europe: No Room for Competition," 27.

29. Federal Aviation Administration (FAA), *Airport Capacity Enhancement Plan* (Washington, D.C.: FAA, 1987), 2–5.

30. Ibid., 2–11.

31. "World Development Survey: Too Little, Too Late," *Airports International,* December 1987–January 1988, 29–54.

5
The U.S. Airline Industry
Past, Present, Future

I t was only about sixty years ago that airlines in the United States first
began to offer passengers transcontinental service, the flights taking more
than thirty hours, requiring more than a dozen refueling stops, and
costing about $400. Today, passengers can make the same journey in about
six hours, flying nonstop in a much more comfortable airplane and for a lot
less money. The improvements in services offered, combined with a reduction in passenger fares, have enabled the airlines to become the dominant
mode of common-carrier intercity travel. In 1987, U.S. airlines captured 92.2
percent of total common-carrier intercity passenger travel in the United States,
as measured in revenue passenger miles. Railroads—Amtrak—and motor
buses transported 1.4 percent and 6.4 percent, respectively.[1]

Since its inception, the airline industry, both in the United States and
worldwide, has been faced with continuous technical, economic, regulatory,
and political changes. Changes in the regulatory and technological climate
alone have been radical and overlapping, resulting in a major shift in the
industry's market structure, performance, and conduct. Moreover, the restructuring of the airline industry in the United States has had a significant
impact on the airline industry worldwide (see chapter 6). This chapter begins
with an overview of the structure of the U.S. airline industry, past and present. It next examines the economic, financial, and operating characteristics
of the industry and then analyzes major changes in the industry's market
structure, performance, and conduct since deregulation. The chapter con-
cludes with a discussion of future industry trends.

Industry Structure: Past and Present

Historical Review

Between 1938 and 1978, the commercial air transportation system in the
United States evolved according to the rules and policies of the Civil Aeronautics Authority and, subsequently, the Civil Aeronautics Board (CAB). The

technological development of the airplane also paced the industry's evolution. The CAB controlled all economic aspects of the industry—market entry and exit, passenger fares and cargo rates, and level and type of competition. During this period, the CAB established eleven different classes of air carriers operating in the United States: trunks, local service, international and territorial, all cargo, Alaskan, Hawaiian, helicopter, supplemental (charter), intrastate, commuter, and indirect air carrier.[2] Classification of air carriers, particularly the route networks they operated, largely reflected various stages in the development of the airplane. For example, as the trunk airlines— initially established by the CAB in the 1930s—began to acquire airplanes with longer range and larger capacity, they began to apply for routes that were more compatible with the new airplanes' operating characteristics. Consequently, the shorter-haul, thinner routes were turned over to a new class of airlines, the local-service carriers. Over time, the local-service airlines themselves began to acquire large and longer-range airplanes, leaving the bottom end of their routes to be taken over by air-taxi operators.

Air-taxi operators, recognized as commuters since 1969, were exempt from the CAB's economic (price and entry) regulations, with two exceptions. First, they could not offer scheduled service (a provision that was relaxed after 1960), and second, they were not allowed to operate airplanes with more than nine seats until 1969, at which time the limit was raised to nineteen seats. These restrictions were implemented by the CAB to control the level of competition among various groups of carriers. The seat limit was gradually raised to sixty after deregulation, when commuters were renamed regionals—carriers that provide regularly scheduled passenger service with airplanes having sixty or fewer seats. After deregulation, a few regionals/ commuters upgraded their operating certificates to enable them to operate even larger airplanes, for example, turbojets with more than sixty seats.

Until 1978, decisions about route entry and exit were also under CAB control. To approve a route application from an airline, the CAB had to establish first that the proposed service was required by the "public convenience and necessity" provisions of the Civil Aeronautics Act of 1938 (and subsequently by the Federal Aviation Act of 1958) and second that the airline applying for the route was "fit, willing, and able" to serve the route. Since most communities were interested in direct, point-to-point, nonstop service and many markets were too thin to justify such service, airlines built up traffic on main routes by tagging other routes to either or both ends. This process produced linear networks. Although hub-and-spoke systems (discussed later in this chapter), such as Delta's and Eastern's systems at Atlanta and United's and American's systems at Chicago, existed, they were limited. Because these airlines were prohibited from freely adding or deleting routes, they could not fully exploit their hub-and-spoke systems. The CAB also controlled an airline's decision to exit a market on the theory that in return for its privileged franchise, an airline had an obligation to provide the service for a relatively long time.[3]

Pricing policies were dictated by the CAB's regulatory policies and strongly influenced by airplane productivity. After World War II, for example, airlines introduced airplanes with higher speed and more capacity, such as the DC-6 and the Lockheed Constellation. Higher airplane productivity (the product of speed and capacity) resulted in lower unit operating costs (total operating costs divided by the number of seats or seat miles) and, in turn, lower fares. The introduction of jets in the late 1950s reduced unit operating costs even further because of their higher productivity. From the viewpoint of regulatory policy, the CAB adopted the rate-making philosophies used by the Interstate Commerce Commission and public utilities, with the goal of allowing the industry to earn sufficient revenues to cover its operating costs and provide an adequate return on investment. Approved fare levels were based on the average industry costs of providing the service, which meant that an individual airline could make better than the average return only by reducing its operating costs to a level below that of the average industry costs. Northwest is an example of an airline that followed this strategy.

Airline labor costs and labor-management relations were also influenced by the regulatory policies of the CAB. If, for example, the industry incurred cost increases because of higher wage settlements with the unions, the airlines could easily pass the higher costs on to consumers in the form of higher (CAB-approved) fares. The existence of this financial security tended to increase the bargaining power of the unions. Some observers of the airline industry argue that the airlines, for the most part, were more interested in protecting their market share than in resisting union demands, knowing that settlement costs could eventually be incorporated in the general fare level. While it was true that average fares had steadily declined, as a result of the gradual increase in the productivity of each new generation of airplanes, opponents of the CAB policy argued that the average fare would have declined even more had the unions not had the bargaining power that was indirectly provided by the CAB's regulatory policies.

The CAB's policies also had a substantial influence on airline labor relations because of (a) the imposition of labor-protective provisions in merger cases, such as the integration of seniority for certain classes of employees, and (b) the existence of the air carrier Mutual Aid Pact (MAP), a form of strike insurance. The MAP, approved by the CAB in 1959, provided financial assistance to an airline struck by a union. The arrangement called for paying to the struck carrier an amount equal to any resulting windfall profits that competing airlines received from handling the struck carrier's business. The MAP, designed to boost the bargaining power of airline management by increasing an airline's ability to withstand a strike, was opposed by the unions from the start, on the grounds that it discouraged management to bargain in "good faith." The unions further argued that the MAP brought into the bargaining process airlines not party to the basic labor dispute and interfered with the prompt settlement of disputes. Between 1964 and 1973, the CAB investigated the pact three times, each time reaffirming its merits and revising it to make it even more effective. The CAB effectively broadened the pact's scope, for example, by allowing local-service airlines to join the group.

By the mid-1970s, civil aviation policy began to shift in favor of less government involvement, on the premise that tight government control had led to inefficient operations by the airlines and to higher-than-necessary fares for the public. In October 1978, Congress enacted the Airline Deregulation Act of 1978, which placed maximum reliance on competitive market forces to determine the quality, quantity, and price of airline services to be provided. Phased out gradually was government control of entry, exit, fares, and service; eliminated was the MAP. The act even provided for termination of the industry's economic regulatory body, the CAB, by the end of 1984. Responsibility for international aviation was turned over to the Department of Transportation, which was also given the authority to approve airline mergers.

Present Industry Structure

In the history of the U.S. airline industry, the year 1978 was noteworthy. It marked the seventy-fifth anniversary of powered flight and the twentieth anniversary of both jet-powered flight and the Federal Aviation Act. It was a year in which the airlines set new records in passenger traffic and earnings and in which the Airline Deregulation Act became effective. During 1978, 30 airlines offered scheduled passenger service within the United States. Most of the passenger traffic was carried by the 11 trunks, which accounted for 92.2 percent of total domestic passenger traffic, as measured in terms of passenger miles. Among the trunks, a group called the Big Four, composed of American, Eastern, Trans World, and United, accounted for 53.1 percent of total passenger traffic.[4] Combined, the 8 local-service carriers accounted for only 41.8 percent of the traffic carried, as measured in passenger miles, and 65.8 percent of the revenue generated by the largest trunk carrier, United.[5] In addition to the trunk and local-service carriers offering scheduled service were 2 intra-Hawaiian airlines, 5 intra-Alaskan airlines, and 3 all-cargo airlines offering such service. International and territorial services were provided by 10 of the 11 trunk carriers; United, the largest trunk carrier, served the domestic markets. Commuter carriers, numbering 228, enplaned 11.3 million passengers,[6] slightly less than the number of passengers carried by the largest local-service carrier, Allegheny (now USAir), and only about a quarter of that carried by the largest trunk carrier, United.

In the years following deregulation, the list of airlines offering scheduled service increased by some 75 additional airlines, consisting of totally new carriers and of former supplemental (charter), intrastate, and commuter carriers. As a result of mergers and bankruptcies, however, most of those additional 75 airlines have ceased operations.[7] At the end of 1987, the number of commercial passenger and cargo carriers reporting traffic and financial data to the Department of Transportation was 69. (See table 5–1.) These carriers are now classified into four groups, based on annual revenue: (a) *major carriers,* which have annual operating revenues of more than $1 billion; (b) *national carriers,* which have annual operating revenues of $100 million to $1 billion; (c) *large regional carriers,* which have annual operating revenues of between $10 million and $100 million; and (d) *medium regional carriers,* which have annual revenues of less than $10 million. Of the 69 active commercial air carriers shown in table 5-1, 40 offered scheduled passenger service—10 more than existed at the time of deregulation in 1978. In fiscal 1987, the new Big Four—Texas Air Group, United, American, and Delta—accounted for 60.2 percent of the total scheduled passenger traffic.[8]

Air carriers are distinguished as well by the type of operating certificate

Table 5–1
Active U.S. Commercial Air Carriers

Majors	Nationals	Large Regionals	Medium Regionals
American	Air Wisconsin	Arrow	Aerial
Continental	Alaska	Aspen	Aeron
Delta	Aloha	Buffalo	Atlantic Gulf
Eastern	America West	Emerald	Challenge Air Cargo
Federal Express	America Trans Air	Evergreen	Challenge Air International
Flying Tiger	Braniff	Five Star	Connor
Northwest	Hawaiian	Florida Express	Florida West
Pan American	Midway	Horizon Air	Galaxy
Piedmont	MGM Grand	Key	Great American
Trans World	Pacific Southwest	Markair	Gulf Air Transport
United	Southwest	Mid Pacific	Independent Air
USAir		Midwest Express	Jet East
		Northern Air	Jet Fleet
		Cargo	Million
		Pacific Interstate	Orion
		Pilgrim	Rich
		Presidential Air	Rosenbalm
		Reeve	Skybus
		Royal West	Sun Coast
		Sky World	Sun Country
		Southern Air	Trans Air-Link
		South Pacific Island	Trans International
		Sunworld	
		Tower	
		Zantop	

Source: Federal Aviation Administration (FAA), *FAA Aviation Forecasts: Fiscal Years 1988–1999* (Washington, D.C.: FAA, February 1988), 175–77.

they hold. The major and national air carriers are regulated by the FAA's FAR part 121, which contains a broad spectrum of standards relating to

- certain categories of management personnel—for example, directors of operations and maintenance;
- requirements and qualifications for flight crews and ground crews— such as aircraft dispatchers—including the quality of training programs;
- aircraft and flight operations, including the development of a definitive operating manual;
- maintenance, including the development of a comprehensive manual and record-keeping system;
- passenger safety; and
- transportation of hazardous materials.

Carriers operating small airplanes—those with 30 seats or less and a maximum payload capacity of 7,500 pounds or less—comply with FAR part 135, which is less rigorous than part 121 requirements. H.P. Wolfe and D.A. NewMeyer provide an overview of FAR parts 121 and 135 in their book *Aviation Industry Regulation.*[9]

During 1987, common-carrier air transportation was provided by a fleet of 4,326 aircraft, belonging to the U.S. scheduled, supplemental, commuter, air-taxi, and cargo carriers. Most of the fleet—93 percent—was turbine powered, and more than half the fleet belonged to the majors. An examination of the fleet composition of the 21 U.S. and 2 Canadian airlines that are members of the Air Transport Association reveals that the Boeing 727, a three-engine, medium-range airplane, accounts for 33 percent of their fleets, or 1,148 out of 3,476 aircraft. The Douglas DC-9 and the Boeing 737, both of which are two-engine, short- to medium-range airplanes, make up another 39 percent of their fleets—21 percent and 18 percent, respectively. In other words, 72 percent of the total fleet consisted of these three types of airplanes belonging to the 23 member-carriers of the Air Transport Association of America.[10] The rest of the jet fleet spanned a broad spectrum in size and range characteristics, from the Fokker F-28, with about 85 seats and a range of approximately 1,000 miles, to the Boeing 747, with about 450 seats and a range exceeding 6,000 miles.

In 1987, the regional air carriers had a fleet of 1,841 airplanes, 1,514 in part 135 service and 327 in part 121 service. Turboprops and piston-engine airplanes made up 63 percent and 34 percent of the fleet, respectively, with the remaining 3 percent consisting of helicopters and jets.[11] A third of the airplanes had less than 10 seats, and 42 percent had between 10 and 19 seats; only 6 percent had more than 40 seats. The four most common types of airplanes were the Fairchild Metro (268 units), the Cessna 402 (135 units), the British Aerospace Jetstream 31 (120 units), and the Piper Navajo (114 units).[12] It should be kept in mind, however, that the U.S. air carrier fleet represents only a small fraction of the total civilian fleet: In 1987, active airplanes in the general aviation segment of the industry numbered close to 219,000.

Economic, Financial, and Operating Characteristics

Some characteristics of the airline industry are common to many other industries; others, at least in combination with one another, are unique to this industry. A basic understanding of these characteristics will be helpful in comprehending not only the industry's current market structure, performance, and conduct but also the probable future trends in the airline industry.

1. The airline industry has been influenced significantly by the forces of government regulation. Chapter 1 and the preceding section of this chapter discussed how the federal government regulated and promoted the development of this industry. Although the CAB no longer exists, the airline industry is still probably one of the most heavily regulated of all industries. The Department of Transportation has taken over some of the functions of the CAB, and the FAA regulates safety aspects of airline operations—for example, aircraft certification, flight operation, and maintenance procedures. In addition, many other federal and local government agencies influence the airline industry, including the National Transportation Safety Board, the Environmental Protection Agency, the Department of Justice, and local airport authorities. In the international arena, both economic and safety aspects continue to be regulated by the federal government.

2. Because airlines produce and sell a service—that is, scheduled air transportation of passengers and property from one place to another—they are subject to the usual constraints of a service industry. Examples of the basic differences between airline services and other products are that (a) an airline's output (a seat on a flight) cannot be inventoried to match fluctuations in demand, as can most physical products; (b) air services, unlike manufactured goods and products, are produced and consumed at the same time; and (c) the customer participates in the service delivery system.[13] Such differences have an enormous influence on the marketing management process—analysis, planning, implementation, and control.

3. The demand for airline services varies by season, month, week, day, and time of day. Whereas demand is heavy in the east-west direction during the summer, it is heavy in the north-south direction during the winter. There are demand variations around traditional holidays, such as Easter, Thanksgiving, and Christmas. During the day, demand is heavy in business markets between 7:00 and 9:00 A.M. and between 4:00 and 6:00 P.M. To accommodate peak demand, airlines must acquire additional assets, facilities, and personnel. These added investments lead in turn to higher average operating

costs, because the additional resources are underutilized during off-peak periods. Furthermore, because airlines provide a scheduled service, they cannot add or discontinue flights to match short-term variations in the level of demand.

4. The airline industry is labor-, fuel-, and capital-intensive. During 1987, the labor and fuel costs of airlines that were members of the Air Transport Association of America accounted for 35 and 16 percent, respectively, of total cash operating expenses.[14] In terms of the composition of assets, airplanes represent 55.8 percent of the industry's total asset acquisitions, a figure reflecting the price of aircraft purchased and the capitalized value of leased aircraft (excluding depreciation), as well as the value of total assets (excluding depreciation).[15]

5. For the airline industry, the acquisition of new assets involves long lead times. Orders for new airplanes are often placed years before the airplanes can be delivered, yet historical analysis has shown that the industry's traffic pattern is cyclical. Thus, on a number of occasions in the past, airplane orders were based on an optimistic forecast, because they were placed during an upturn in the economy, but deliveries came during an economic downturn, when the airlines needed them the least.

6. The airline industry is highly competitive. Prior to deregulation, the amount and type of competition in the industry were regulated by the CAB. On a typical route, two or three airlines competed with each other and competition was focused on service rather than price. Since deregulation in 1978, though, the degree of competition has increased substantially, as a result of (a) the increase in the number of airlines; (b) the existence of low-cost airlines; (c) airlines' freedom to enter and exit markets; and (d) airlines' ability to compete on price as well as service features.

7. The industry is highly leveraged in both a financial and an operating sense. In an operating sense, it is leveraged in that a small change in load factor—the percentage of seats filled—produces a large swing in profitability. In a financial sense, it is leveraged in that more than half the capital is debt. Once fixed interest charges on debt are covered, net income for stockholders increases rapidly and vice versa.

8. The net profit margin in the industry is extremely low relative to the industry's risk characteristics. Even during the most profitable year, 1978, the airline industry as a whole just matched the net profit margin generated, for example, by the Value Line's *industrial composite* (5.2 percent for airlines, versus 5.1 percent for the industrial composite). During their worst year, 1982, U.S. scheduled airlines posted a net loss of 2.5 percent, compared with a net profit of 3.7 percent by the industrial composite. For the ten-year period 1978–1987, the industrial composite averaged a net profit margin of 4.7 percent, compared with 0.7 percent for the U.S. scheduled airlines. The data from Value Line's *Industrial Composite* are based on more than nine hundred industrial, retail, and transportation companies (excluding rails),

which together account for about 80 percent of the income earned by all U.S. nonfinancial corporations.[16] (Net profit margin is defined as net profit after interest and taxes as a percentage of operating revenues. Operating profit margin is defined as operating profit—operating revenue minus operating expenses—as a percentage of operating revenues).

9. Technology turnover in the airline industry has been high. Although in the past, continuous improvements in technology benefited both the airlines and the public, they also shortened the reequipment cycle for the airlines, resulting in large capital investments every six to eight years; further, technologically advanced airplanes required that the industry infrastructure keep pace with the development of the vehicle. In recent years, however, technological advances have slowed, making it possible for airlines to keep existing airplanes longer. In addition, lower fuel prices have made it economically feasible to keep older airplanes in service.

10. The transportation services offered by airlines are highly dependent on the services provided by two other components of the air transportation industry: airports and the air traffic control system. In the United States, one component of the air transportation industry—namely, the airlines—has been deregulated and now conducts its business according to the rules of the free marketplace. In contrast, the other two components of the industry remain under the control of the government—the federal government, in the case of the air traffic control system, and local governments, in the case of the airports—and are managed with a focus on public policy and politics, rather than on profitability and efficiency. Consequently, the quality, quantity, and to some extent price of airline services are affected by external factors that are not only outside the airlines' control but, more important, not necessarily consistent with the airlines' competitive objectives.

At the end of 1987, there were twelve major carriers—ten providing a combination of air services, one providing traditional freight service (Flying Tiger), and one providing expedited package service (Federal Express).* Of the ten major carriers providing combination air transportation services, the annual total operating revenue ranged from $2.0 billion (Piedmont) to $7.9 billion (United), while the number of passengers carried ranged from 15 million (Pan American) to 56 million (American). (See table 5–2.) The number of airline employees ranged from 18,000 (Piedmont) to 60,000 (United). The average passenger trip length ranged from about 450 miles (Piedmont) to 1,750 miles (Pan American), and the average number of passengers carried per departure ranged from 56 (Piedmont) to 104 (Pan American).

In 1987, wide variation existed, too, in the financial performance of the major and national carriers. As a group, the nineteen U.S. airlines shown in table 5–2 reported a net profit of $591 million. Yet fourteen of those airlines

---

*In December 1988, Federal Express decided to acquire Tiger International Inc., parent of the Flying Tiger Line, the world's largest air-cargo carrier.

Table 5-2
ATA Airline Statistics, 1987

	Number of Aircraft	Employees	Aircraft Departures	Passengers (000)	Revenue Passenger Miles (000)	Passenger Revenues ($000)	Cargo Revenues ($000)	Total Operating Revenues ($000)	Operating Profit (Loss) ($000)	Net Profit (Loss) ($000)
Alaska	48	4,351	80,489	3,910	2,938,870	459,273	44,405	541,187	37,016	32,474
Aloha	10	1,117	56,025	3,056	404,108	90,832	11,870	118,153	12,276	6,251
American	410	57,275	663,561	55,584	56,748,531	6,147,715	260,912	7,124,481	473,184	213,828
Braniff	26	1,837	33,937	3,078	3,408,377	248,421	2,917	293,058	(17,778)	(10,364)
Continental	352	30,763	545,108	40,149	39,637,018	3,627,227	173,436	4,020,598	26,698	(258,085)
Delta	374	50,039	732,182	54,052	43,576,526	5,607,370	320,982	6,093,331	434,243	233,297
DHL	18	300	N/A	—	—	—	N/A	N/A	N/A	N/A
Eastern	284	43,776	528,471	44,674	36,704,358	4,051,641	193,672	4,529,208	58,898	(181,676)
Evergreen	38	588	—	—	—	—	—	126,213	17,708	8,016
Federal Express	80	45,151	148,705	—	—	—	3,494,931	3,572,699	381,278	166,226
Flying Tigers	38	6,072	18,838	158[a]	1,133,717[a]	84,935[a]	939,420	1,175,210	151,412	81,710
Hawaiian	29	2,344	79,375	4,773	2,910,354	232,309	9,561	298,777	(11,299)	(8,385)
Midway	38	2,304	65,636	3,619	2,568,074	329,675	2,715	340,689	25,014	19,759
Northwest	313	34,172	517,246	37,247	39,549,506	4,371,624	554,553	5,073,726	205,115	140,716
Pan American	125	21,883	143,451	14,888	26,093,636	2,613,015	216,556	3,121,574	(170,439)	(274,595)
Piedmont	181	17,818	452,553	25,359	11,465,932	1,867,304	62,744	1,963,706	154,905	98,550
Southwest	72	5,281	246,041	14,214	6,749,941	676,268	11,915	698,675	41,278	19,692
Trans World	213	30,089	309,649	24,623	32,860,518	3,414,808	226,414	4,056,435	240,438	106,200
United	378	59,669	669,743	55,184	66,292,264	6,774,078	488,826	7,862,795	151,217	33,338
United Parcel Service	100	N/A	N/A	—	—	—	N/A	N/A	N/A	N/A
USAir	162	15,768	391,427	24,773	13,071,613	1,948,858	55,484	2,070,311	263,456	164,113
Associate Members										
Air Canada	108	22,200	191,928	11,000	14,358,000	2,358,400	412,000	3,131,100	103,700	45,700
Canadian	79	13,454	155,402	9,539	11,060,513	1,084,450	118,992	1,417,509	96,347	13,802

Source: Air Transport Association of America (ATA), *Air Transport 1988* (Washington, D.C.: ATA, June 1988), 6–7.

N/A—Not Available.

[a]Includes nonscheduled service.

generated a total net profit of $1,324 million; American and Delta combined reported a net profit of $447 million. In contrast, five of the nineteen airlines reported a net loss, totaling $733 million, 37 percent of which resulted from the loss reported by just one airline, Pan American.

Average passenger yield—that is, revenue for carrying one passenger one mile—during 1987 ranged from 7.33 cents per passenger mile for Braniff to 45.73 cents for Air Wisconsin. Unit costs also showed a similar variation, ranging from 5.56 cents per available seat mile—that is, one seat flown one mile—for Braniff to 20.82 cents for Air Wisconsin. Unit yield or unit costs by themselves, however, are not necessarily accurate indicators of profitability. The relative spread between yield and cost, adjusted for load factor— that is, the ratio of seats occupied to seats available—is usually more informative. Since yield is based on passenger miles and cost is based on seat miles, it is necessary to consider load factor in the assessment of an airline's financial performance. For selected airlines, table 5–3 shows the data on unit costs, yield, passenger trip distance, and stage length. Unit costs decrease as stage length increases, and yield decreases as passenger trip length increases.

While all airlines have attempted to improve their operations in all three areas—yield, costs, and load factor—during the past ten years, the major emphasis has been on reducing costs. Since the beginning of the 1970s, the cost structure in the airline industry has changed dramatically because of the changes in the price of fuel and the impact of deregulation. (See table 5–4.)

Table 5–3
Unit Operating Costs and Revenues for Selected U.S. Airlines, 1987

Airline	Unit Costs	Yield	Passenger Trip Distance	Stage Length
American	7.50	10.83	1,021	775
Continental	6.20	9.15	987	750
Delta	7.25	12.80	810	631
Eastern	7.97	11.22	808	631
Northwest	7.89	11.05	1,062	690
Pan American	7.88	10.01	1,753	982
Piedmont	9.49	16.28	452	356
TWA	7.33	10.39	1,335	813
United	7.60	10.22	1,201	824
USAir	8.90	14.91	528	428
PSA	8.80	15.78	397	371
Air Wisconsin	20.82	45.73	157	127
Alaska	9.34	15.63	752	528
America West	5.93	9.66	515	442
Braniff	5.56	7.33	1,105	871
Hawaiian	6.06	7.98	610	287
Midway	7.03	12.84	710	619
Southwest	5.72	10.02	475	368

Source: Air Transport Association of America and author's calculations.

Table 5–4

Cost as a Percentage of Total Cash Operating Expenses

Category	1973	1981	1987
Labor	45.6	34.5	35.0
Fuel	12.1	29.3	16.0
Landing fees	2.6	1.7	2.0
Interest	3.3	3.3	3.4
Traffic commissions	3.2	5.4	8.6
Passenger meals	3.9	2.8	3.5
Advertising and promotion	2.4	1.9	2.2
All others	26.9	21.2	29.3

Source: D.A. Swierenga, *Airline Cost Index* (Washington, D.C.: Air Transport Association of America, May 5, 1988).

In 1973, when fuel cost 12.8 cents per gallon, fuel represented 12.1 percent of the total cash operating expenses; in 1981, when fuel prices rose to $1.04 per gallon, it represented 29.3 percent of total cash operating costs; and in 1987, when fuel prices, having bottomed out at 43.8 cents per gallon during the fourth quarter of 1986, rose to 55.7 cents per gallon, fuel represented 16 percent of total cash operating costs. While the airline industry has no control over the price of fuel, it does have some control over the efficiency with which fuel is consumed, as evidenced by the data presented in figure 5–1, which shows the increase in fuel-use efficiency based on passenger miles per gallon of fuel consumed.

After deregulation, airlines also began to be able to control their labor costs more effectively. Between 1970 and 1983, the average annual compensation for an airline employee increased from $12,915 to $41,847. Since 1983, the airlines have implemented a variety of methods to control their labor costs, with the result that the average annual compensation per employee increased only $1,197 between 1983 and 1987 (see figure 5–2 [a]). Moreover, airlines have also increased employee productivity, as measured in ton miles sold per employee, since 1981 (see figure 5–2 [b]). Consequently, airline employee compensation per ton mile produced has been declining since 1983 (see figure 5–2 [c]).

Since 1980, other categories of airline costs have also changed significantly. Advertising and promotion costs and travel agent commissions, for example, have increased as airlines have been forced to compete aggressively for market share. The increase in travel agents' commission rates, combined with an increase in the number of tickets written by travel agents, has increased total distribution costs.

The Impact of Deregulation

The deregulated marketplace is a remarkable contrast to the regulated environment. From the airlines' point of view, the freedom to exercise mana-

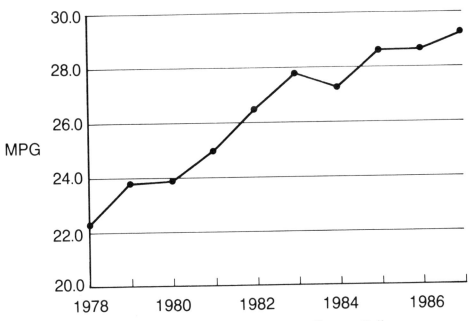

Figure 5–1. Fuel Efficiency: Revenue Passenger Miles per Gallon

Source: D.A. Swierenga *Airline Cost Index* (Washington, D.C.: Air Transport Association of America, May 5, 1988).

gerial initiative has been the greatest single benefit of deregulation. Deregulation has enabled airlines to become more cost efficient and innovative in marketing their perishable product. Whereas cost efficiency has been achieved by changing the labor wage level and structure, negotiating productivity improvements in labor contracts, and rationalizing the fleet mix, changes in marketing have involved all elements of the marketing mix: product, price, distribution, and promotion. The implementation of innovative marketing techniques, coupled with the changes in airline cost structures, has transformed the market structure, performance, and conduct of the airline industry in the United States. These developments have also affected the international airline industry (see chapter 6) and to some extent other modes of transportation, such as intercity bus transportation and the trucking industry (see chapter 7).

New Entrants

Deregulation allowed new airlines to begin offering service in the domestic interstate markets. Some of the new entrants, such as AirCal, PSA, and Southwest, were former intrastate carriers; others such as Arrow, World,

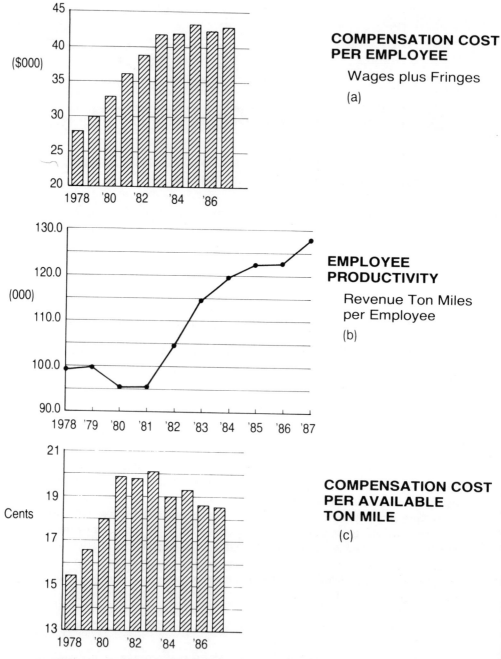

COMPENSATION COST PER EMPLOYEE

Wages plus Fringes

(a)

EMPLOYEE PRODUCTIVITY

Revenue Ton Miles per Employee

(b)

COMPENSATION COST PER AVAILABLE TON MILE

(c)

Figure 5–2. Employee Productivity and Compensation

Source: D.A. Swierenga *Airline Cost Index* (Washington, D.C.: Air Transport Association of America, May 5, 1988).

and Transamerica, were former charter carriers; and still others, such as Air Wisconsin and Horizon, were former commuter carriers. And some, such as Jet America, Midway, New York Air, People Express, and Regent Air, were completely new airlines. Although the following discussion focuses on the last group—those airlines which inaugurated jet service after 1978—the influence of the new entrants in other groups should not be overlooked. For example, Southwest, which started operations within the state of Texas in 1971, strongly influenced the decision of Congress to deregulate the airline industry and continues to serve today, moreover, as the model for other airlines whose goal is to become more efficient and innovative.

The changed environment in the airline industry encouraged new airlines to fill special niches in the marketplace. Each new entrant analyzed the marketplace to identify a particular price or service option that would satisfy the needs of a particular segment of the marketplace and produce a profit for the airline. Price and service options offered after deregulation ranged from the no-frills service offered by People Express to the all-frills service offered by Regent Air. Between those two extremes, other airlines experimented with various price/service options, such as first-class travel at standard coach fares and service from secondary airports. Some new airlines attempted to create new markets, while others attempted to divert traffic from existing airlines. A number of new entrants managed to develop a significant market identity (for example, People Express, New York Air, and Air Florida); however, as a group, they attained only a fairly small share of the total U.S. market. But despite the minute market share gained by the new entrants, they collectively made a substantial contribution in encouraging existing airlines to become more efficient and more responsive to the needs of the price-conscious segment of the marketplace. In addition, by meeting the needs of this segment of the marketplace with lower-fare services, the new entrants stimulated market growth.

In general, most new entrants followed the strategy of overall cost leadership. The new airlines were able to lower their unit operating costs as result of (a) lower labor costs, (b) higher labor productivity, (c) simplified operations, (d) high load factors, and (e) service designed to minimize costs. Low labor costs and high labor productivity were achieved typically by employing non-union labor. As a result, rigid job classifications were eliminated and each employee was required to perform several line and staff functions— flight attendants worked as secretaries, pilots as flight dispatchers, and so forth. In terms of service features, a number of new entrants offered a simplified reservation system, lower-quality in-airport and in-flight services, no interline capabilities, airplanes with higher seating density, lower schedule integrity in terms of on-time performance, and reduced reservation integrity in terms of the percentage of passengers whose reservations were honored. Consequently, different levels of resources were required to produce and market different types and levels of service. Most new entrants used their low-cost structure to offer low-fare service, People Express being the leader in this group. A few airlines, such as Regent Air, went to the other end of the spectrum and offered features such as exceptionally high levels of service on the ground and during flight. A few others, such as Air One and Midway Airlines, used their cost structure to offer the equivalent of first-class service at standard economy-class fares.

Overall, the financial performance of the start-up new entrants has been poor and in fact many new entrants have left the marketplace. Most of these carriers came into the marketplace with low operating costs and high productivity, hoping that their low-cost structure alone would give them the necessary staying power. Nevertheless, many new airlines discovered that they lacked (a) the ability to identify, develop, and maintain market niches; (b) sufficient financial resources; (c) marketing intelligence; and (d) credibility with travel agents. Consequently, those airlines which lacked these attributes and relied purely on their lower operating costs experienced losses or performed marginally at best. The mortality rate among the new entrants has thus been very high.

Assessing the impact of new entrants on the industry is a complex task because of their varied origins and diversity, the lack of appropriate resources available to the major carriers at the beginning of deregulation, and the influence of external factors, such as the state of the economy, fuel prices, and the air traffic controllers' strike. At the same time, it is possible to draw at least two general conclusions about the collective impact of new entrants: (a) They have increased the spectrum of price/service options available to the public, and (b) they have placed great pressure on incumbent carriers to reduce their operating costs and become more efficient.

Hub-and-Spoke Systems

As a result of the end of route regulation, airlines have altered their route structures to utilize their resources more efficiently. Specific steps taken have included opening up new cities, abandoning or downgrading service to other cities, and adding flights to strengthen their hub-and-spoke systems. A *hub-and-spoke* network allows an airline to schedule many of its flights from outlying cities to arrive at its hub airport at about the same time so as to maximize the number of online (same airline) connections; departures from the hub along the spokes are also scheduled as close together as possible. Such converging flights are often called connecting banks or connecting complexes, and their objective is to control traffic feed, improve load factors, broaden market coverage, diversify the network, and achieve a certain amount of insulation from competition. The airlines have achieved these ends by developing (a) strategically located hubs, (b) interline arrangements with feeder carriers, (c) a broad spectrum of nationwide routes (with different lengths of haul, traffic mix, and seasonality characteristics), and (d) international routes. And in addition to benefiting airlines, hub-and-spoke systems have also been advantageous for certain segments of passengers, such as those traveling in the lower-density, long-haul markets.

The development of these systems has not, however, been without disadvantages. Peaking of arrivals and departures, an inherent characteristic of hub-and-spoke systems, has contributed to the congestion of airports and airways and created a need for additional facilities to handle a large volume of traffic for short periods of time. From the passengers' standpoint, trip times in some markets have increased, because they have involved a stop or a change of plane at the hub. Moreover, competition on some spokes to and from major hubs has decreased, inasmuch as smaller carriers competing with the major airlines that dominate large hubs cannot easily offer cost-effective service on thinner spokes, which have local markets.[17]

The formulation of interline arrangements between larger and smaller carriers has been an integral part of hub-and-spoke development. To increase traffic feed, particularly from smaller communities, the major carriers initially allowed selected feeder carriers to use their two-letter designator codes, a process that allowed the schedules of lesser known (and in some cases virtually unknown) feeder carriers to show up with the identity of the well-known major carriers in the computer systems used to make reservations. Subsequently, many major carriers strengthened their relations with feeders by allowing the feeders to utilize the majors' livery on their aircraft. Some major carriers went even further and acquired the feeder carrier(s) that they felt fit best with their route system. Following are examples:

- October 1985   Piedmont acquired Empire Airlines
- January 1986   People Express acquired Provincetown-Boston Airways
- February 1986 People Express acquired Britt Airways
- April 1986   Pan American acquired Ransome Air
                        Texas Air acquired Rocky Mountain Airways
                        USAir acquired Suburban Airlines
- May 1986   Delta acquired Atlantic Southwest
                        Delta acquired Comair
- July 1986   Piedmont acquired Jet Stream International

Thus, interline arrangements have been used by major and national carriers to support their hub development strategies. Such arrangements have allowed the larger airlines to capture traffic from short-haul, low-density markets on a cost-competitive basis; they have also had an impact on the structure of the regional airline industry (discussed below) by decreasing the viability of those regional/commuter airlines which opted to remain totally independent.

Regional/Commuter Carriers

As noted earlier, the regionals/commuters have always operated in an un-regulated environment, subject only to the use of small airplanes. They could enter and exit markets and set fares in response to market conditions. Deregulation simply expanded the opportunities available to this segment of the airline industry. In addition to allowing regionals/commuters to operate larger airplanes, deregulation also made these carriers eligible for subsidies under the Essential Air Service program and qualified them for the FAA equipment loan guarantee program. These changes in the operating environment have resulted in a massive restructuring of this component of the air transportation industry.

One part of the restructuring process has pertained to airplane size, the restrictions on which had historically limited the growth potential of regionals/commuters; their image and quality of service, for example, were influenced by the size of the airplanes they could operate. But since deregulation, the average number of seats per airplane has been increasing steadily (see table 5–5), the greatest change occurring in the category of airplanes with more than forty seats (see table 5–6). With larger airplanes, the regionals/commuters have been encouraged to seek out higher-density and longer-haul markets, particularly those vacated by the former trunk and local-service carriers. Some of the larger commuters, such as Air Wisconsin, even upgraded their equipment to small jets, such as the BAe-146, to compete more aggressively on denser and longer-haul routes.

In markets abandoned by trunk and local-service carriers and picked up by the regionals, commmunities perceived a reduction in the quality of service offered. Although the regionals generally offered greater frequency of service, they did so with piston-engine airplanes and turboprops, some of which were unpressurized. Other complaints voiced by different communities pertained to the increase in average local fares and, in some cases, the instability of service caused by changes in carriers, schedules, and equipment. A number of communities were therefore concerned that a lack of reliable, consistent, and reasonably priced air service was undermining their ability to attract industry to enhance the strength of their local economy. On the issue of fares, while it is true that average local fares did increase and sometimes doubled in many markets, it should be recognized that before deregulation, the CAB had maintained fares in short-haul, low-density markets at an artificially low level, with hidden subsidies for more profitable routes.

Some of the concerns of small communities had been anticipated during the debate over deregulation. Consequently, to maintain a minimum level of air transportation service to and from the nation's smaller-size communities, the Essential Air Service program was made a part of the Airline Deregulation Act. This program provided for continuation of a minimum level of air service for ten years for all cities that had been certified to receive air service

Table 5–5
Regional Airline Industry Traffic Statistics, 1987 Calendar Year

Passenger Operations	1978	1979	1980	1981	1982	1983	1984	1985	1986	1987
Carriers operating	228	227	214	246	215	196	203	179	179	169
Passengers enplaned (millions)	11.3	14.0	14.8	15.4	18.6	21.8	26.1	26.0[a]	28.4	31.8
Average passengers enplaned per carrier	49,600	61,700	69,200	62,600	86,500	111,200	128,100	152,400	158,400	187,700
Revenue passenger miles (RPMs) (billions)	1.28	1.72	1.92	2.09	2.61	3.24	4.17	4.41[a]	4.47	5.00
Average RPMs per carrier (millions)	5.97	7.58	8.97	8.50	12.14	16.53	20.46	24.64[a]	24.98	29.60
Airports served	681	746	732	766	817	854	853	854	824	834
Average trip length (miles)	121	123	129	136	141	149	160	173	158	158
Aircraft operated	1,047	1,265	1,339	1,463	1,573	1,545	1,747	1,745	1,806	1,841
Average seating capacity (seats per aircraft)	11.9	12.5	13.9	15.1	15.6	18.1	18.4	19.2	18.4	19.7
Fleet flying hours (thousands)	1,131	1,390	1,740	1,994	2,160	2,415	2,764	2,854	2,929	2,942
Average annual utilization per aircraft (hours)	1,080	1,193	1,299	1,363	1,373	1,563	1,582	1,635	1,622	1,598

Source: Regional Airline Association (RAA), *1988 Annual Report of the Regional Airline Association* (Washington, D.C.: RAA, 1988), 8. Data inclusive of carriers that may have operated during only part of calendar year 1987.
[a]Adjusted to exclude Empire Airlines traffic, merged into Piedmont during 1986, to provide meaningful year-over-year comparison.

Table 5–6

Aircraft in Regional Airline Passenger Service: Comparison of Aircraft Seating Capacity by Fleet Size, 1978 versus 1987

	Passenger Seating Capacity					
	1–9	10–19	20–39	40 and Up	Other	Total
1978	667	270	72	22	16	1,047
1987	605	781	289	115	51	1,841
Percentage change	− 9%	+189%	+301%	+423%	+219%	+ 76%

Source: Regional Airline Association (RAA), *1988 Annual Report of the Regional Airline Association* (Washington, D.C.: RAA, 1988), 31.

Table 5–7

Essential Air Service Subsidy Payments

Year	Section 406 Subsidy (Millions)	Section 419 Subsidy (Millions)
1950	35.0	—
1976	72.5	—
1977	82.2	—
1978	73.9	—
1979	72.1	0.5
1980	80.1	9.0
1981	106.7	15.0
1982	55.1	26.0
1983	13.5	39.8
1984	-0-	36.0
1985	-0-	33.7
1986	-0-	33.4
1987	-0-	24.0
1988	-0-	24.4

Source: Regional Airline Association (RAA), *1988 Annual Report of the Regional Airline Association* (Washington, D.C.: RAA, 1988), 25.

prior to the day the act became law—October 24, 1978. Historically, the federal government had, under section 406, paid subsidies to trunk and local-service carriers to maintain a minimum level of service to small communities; the level of subsidy paid under section 406 varied from $35 million in 1950 to a high of $107 million in 1981, but such subsidies were phased out at the end of 1983. As part of the Essential Air Service program, however, the federal government agreed (under section 419) to pay subsidies, if necessary, to regional carriers to compensate them for losses incurred in providing service to eligible communities. The subsidy level was set at $500,000 in 1979; it increased to a high of $40 million in 1983 and declined to $24 million in 1987 (see table 5–7).

Another part of the restructuring process has pertained to the compo-

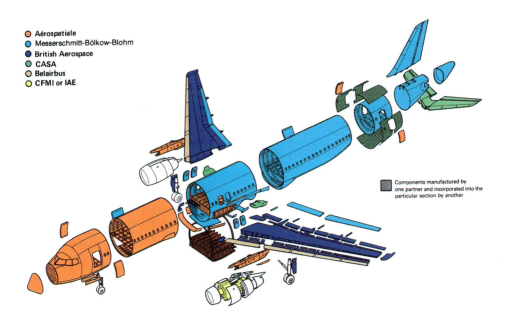

Figure 1–7. A-320 Production Sharing. Courtesy of Airbus Industrie of North America.

LIFE VEST

DANGER

Figure 2–10. Airbus Industrie A-320 Flight Deck. Courtesy of Airbus Industrie of North America.

Figure 3–4. Engineering Model of Advanced Automation System Controller Display. Courtesy of the Federal Aviation Administration.

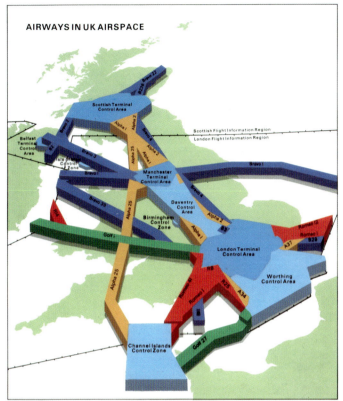

AIRWAYS IN UK AIRSPACE

Figure 3–5. United Kingdom Airways System. Courtesy of U.K. Civil Aviation Authority.

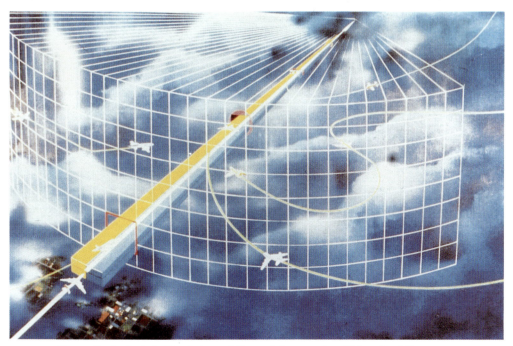

Figure 3–6. Artist's Depiction of Curved Approaches Using the Microwave Landing System. Courtesy of the Federal Aviation Administration.

Figure 8–5. Modern Corporate Aircraft Cabin Configuration. Courtesy of KC Aviation.

sition of the regional/commuter segment of the industry. Even before dereg-ulation, this segment was able to enter and exit from the marketplace relatively easily; indeed, more than 600 different carriers have operated as commuters since 1969.[18] But because the number of commuter carriers operating in any given year has not exceeded 250, it is clear that turnover in this segment of the industry has been high. Among the many reasons for the high turnover rate are lack of knowledge and experience in management, particularly mar-keting; undercapitalization; and intense competition. With the exception of the larger companies, most regionals/commuters do not have the necessary skills or data to conduct basic market analysis; consequently, route, fleet, and pricing decisions are made with virtually no quantitative analysis. The majority of the commuters are also undercapitalized, some with a deficit equity (liabilities exceeding assets) and many with an unacceptable debt-equity ratio. Moreover, competition has compounded the problems of com-muter carriers, in that many commuter markets cannot support more than one carrier.[19]

Table 5–5 shows that the number of regional carriers has generally been declining since 1981. Moreover, the operations within the regional industry are highly concentrated. In 1987, 169 regional air carriers offered passenger services, the top 50 of them accounting for 92 percent of the passengers carried. The level of concentration is expected to increase as a result of code-sharing agreements, which represent yet another part of the restructuring process. Code-sharing, as noted earlier, is a form of cooperative marketing between a regional carrier and a major or national carrier. Under code shar-ing, the regional uses the officially recognized two-letter code of the major or national carrier; these two-letter codes are used to identify various air-lines' flights in the computer reservation systems and the *Official Airline Guide,* a publication showing the entire airline industry's scheduled flights and services. Commuters, particularly smaller ones that did not establish alignments with larger carriers, faced severe economic and operational prob-lems, some of which threatened their very survival. Recognizing this threat, the independent commuters began to pursue aggressively code-sharing and other cooperative arrangements. In 1980, for example, only 10 Allegheny commuters shared the code (AL) of USAir. In 1987, 43 of the top 50 regional carriers had code-sharing agreements with major and national carriers.

Fares, Computers, and Brand Loyalty

In the regulated environment, the CAB attempted, to the extent possible, to base fares on the cost of the service provided. Since many categories of airline costs are related to distance flown, for example, the CAB implemented a fare formula that was based on distance. But today, in the deregulated en-vironment, little or no relationship exists between costs and fares on a mar-ket-by-market basis. Fares are now much more a function of competition (and their "fit" in the overall marketing mix) than a function of the costs of the service provided. In some markets, fares are considerably higher than average costs; in other markets, they are fairly close to marginal costs. The emphasis is now focused on market-oriented pricing policies that capitalize on the strengths of a carrier while compensating for its weaknesses.

From the perspectives of airlines and passengers, the free and open marketplace has both advantages and disadvantages. For the airlines' part, carriers can now offer a wide variety of price/service options, such as peak/off-peak prices and lower-priced nonrefundable tickets, to take advantage of the laws of supply and demand and maximize their return on investment. They can, for example, offer extremely low fares to fill seats that would otherwise go empty, and they can also charge higher fares in markets in which competition is limited. Still, carriers have also had to offer lower competitive fares, even if such fares were unwarranted in terms of their cost structures. And for the consumer's part, while low fares introduced to fill excess capacity have been highly beneficial, passengers have also had to pay higher prices when demand has exceeded supply, such as during certain holiday periods or in markets with little or no competition.

To a large extent, airlines' pricing policies have become dependent on the availability and use of sophisticated management information systems (computer reservation systems, or CRSs) that can monitor changes in travel demand patterns and the actions of competitors in thousands of markets. Consequently, those airlines which invested large sums of money in developing sophisticated CRSs—American and United, for example—have been in the best position to capitalize on these investments. Initially, the owners of CRSs placed their systems at the offices of travel agents. Any airline that did not have its own CRS and by default had to use another airline's CRS was required to pay a fee. Moreover, airlines that did not have their own CRSs claimed that the CRS-vendor carriers had incorporated a competitive bias into their systems—an accusation related to the manner in which competitors' schedules and fares were displayed on the terminals in travel agents' offices. Although the bias issue continues to be debated, no one doubts that CRSs have provided their owners with both enormous marketing power and handsome profits.

The availability of sophisticated CRSs proved very timely in the development of *seat-inventory management systems,* which enable airlines to deal with the proliferation of discount fares. These systems aid airlines in deciding how many seats to offer in each fare class on each flight, based on historical booking patterns. As discussed earlier in this chapter, the financial performance of an airline is a function of three variables: yield, costs, and load factor. The judicious use of seat-inventory management systems allows an airline to balance these factors to maximize net revenue; consequently, the systems are sometimes also referred to as yield management systems or revenue enhancement systems. These systems have also provided an indirect way for airlines with higher cost structures to compete with low-cost airlines and for all airlines to implement peak-period pricing policies. For example, by carefully managing its seat inventory, a high-cost airline is able to match—and sometimes even beat—a low-cost competitor's fares on a selected number of seats that would otherwise go empty. Airlines have used these systems, too, to restrict the number of discount seats available on flights with high demand.

Automation has also enabled the airlines to implement a powerful marketing tool for developing passenger loyalty: the frequent-flyer program. Because an airline can offer its passengers flights to more markets on which to accumulate mileage "credits" and a wider choice of flight award destinations, these programs are most successful among those airlines which have comprehensive route networks. Consequently, the more popular frequent-flyer programs belong to the larger carriers, such as American, TWA, and United. Even these carriers have attempted to broaden their award offerings by forming frequent-flyer-program partnerships with foreign-flag carriers, examples being American and Singapore Airlines, United and British Airways, and TWA and Qantas.

The rise of the frequent-flyer program has been an integral component in the development of the hub-and-spoke system, for the program created brand loyalty at a time when the airlines were designing their hub-and-spoke systems. The role played by the frequent-flyer program in developing brand loyalty and in supporting individual carriers' route development strategies is exemplified by the following data: Whereas in 1977, 13 percent of all passengers interlined, that is, used the services of more than one airline to complete a trip, in 1986, only 3 percent of all passengers interlined.[20] Thus, frequent-flyer programs, coupled with hub-and-spoke systems, have enabled airlines to keep an increasing proportion of connecting passengers on their own airplanes. Moreover, frequent-flyer programs have given airlines added marketing advantages, such as ready-made mailing lists that can be used to promote "specials" to selected segments of the marketplace or even to bypass the normal distribution channel—the travel agent.

While frequent-flyer programs are considered a success story thus far, some concerns exist about the liability they have produced for the airlines. If large numbers of passengers decide to redeem their "free flights" quickly—a situation that could be triggered, for example, if the Internal Revenue Service decided to tax passengers on the mileage they earned—the results could be detrimental, particularly for financially weaker airlines. A related concern is that the airlines might be required to show the value of the unredeemed mileage on their balance sheets as a liability, a decision that could force the airlines to set aside as much as 10 percent of their revenues to cover future frequent-flyer liabilities.[21]

Labor Practices

Deregulation of the airline industry and the resultant changes in the industry's structure have led to marked changes in airline industrial relations, particularly in the collective bargaining process. By removing barriers to entry, allowing airlines to compete on price, and eliminating the airline Mutual Aid Pact, deregulation has forced older airlines to reduce their labor costs both directly and through improvements in productivity. In exchange for improvements in employee productivity and lower wages and benefits, managements at certain airlines have offered a variety of incentive programs, including profit sharing plans, employee stock-ownership plans, and employee/union representation on the board of directors. ·

Airlines have implemented a number of different measures to reduce labor costs. As noted earlier, new entrant carriers tended to enter the marketplace with non-union labor that was paid considerably lower wages and benefits. To compete more effectively with the new entrants, the incumbent carriers used a variety of techniques to reduce their labor costs. Some carriers turned to their employees with demands for concessions, pointing out that without financial sacrifices by employees, their companies would not be able to survive. In some cases, management went further, proclaiming that without concessions, there was a likelihood of bankruptcy that would eliminate jobs and might even jeopardize employees' back pay and pension funds. Although such managements conceded that in the event of bankruptcy, some of the displaced employees could obtain jobs with the new entrants, they also pointed out that the displaced employees would have to accept much lower wages and generally work longer hours.

Another approach to reducing labor costs involved the outright revocation of labor contracts via a declaration of bankruptcy. Here, the established airline would first declare bankruptcy to abrogate its existing labor agreements and would temporarily cease operations; it would then recommence operations with non-union labor. This approach results in an immediate reduction in labor costs, and examples of companies that employed it include Continental and Braniff. Consider the case of Continental: In 1982, Continental's labor costs were 35 percent of its total costs, in comparison with an industry average of 37 percent. Declaring bankruptcy in 1983, Continental immediately began operations with lower-paid employees and as a result, reduced labor costs to 22 percent of total costs in 1984. Such an approach to reducing labor costs, while dramatic and having immediate impact, can also produce great bitterness among employees. And since air transportation is a service industry, the ramifications of an unhappy work force can prove highly detrimental to an airline's long-term viability.

Still another approach to reducing labor costs, one pioneered by American Airlines, has involved the two-tier structuring of wages as a way of reducing average costs without having to resort to cutting the wages of incumbent employees. Under this scheme, new employees are paid a level of wages lower than that of existing employees. The two-tier pay system, however, provides meaningful immediate benefits only for those carriers in a position to aggressively expand their systems or implement early retirement programs. Significant expansion, particularly if it is to be achieved quickly, requires the availability of resources to acquire additional fleet, personnel, and facilities. Consequently, the real beneficiaries of the two-tier approach have been those carriers in a strong financial position.

In addition to forcing the incumbent carriers to reduce direct labor costs, new entrants also caused established carriers to improve productivity—for example, by increasing the "hard time" for flight-deck crews, making greater cross-utilization of all employees, and using part-time employees. *Hard time* refers to the number of hours the flight crew actually flies an airplane. Cross-utilization involves the use of employees across different craft classifications to reduce the impact of restrictive work rules. And the use of part-time employees is cost-effective in an industry whose production process varies widely by time (of day and season) and geographic location; overnight package-delivery airlines, for example, need vast numbers of employees for a short time during each night. An example of a carrier that achieved employee productivity in all three areas well in excess of the industry average was People Express, though unfortunately, such productivity advantages were not sufficient to sustain that airline's success.

Consolidation

During the debate preceding the Airline Deregulation Act, serious concerns were raised about potential consolidation in the airline industry—a process that could diminish competition. Since 1985, the consolidation process has gained momentum, as exemplified by the following partial listing of mergers and acquisitions (this list is not all-inclusive, nor does it cite mergers or acquisitions involving commuters or all-cargo operators):

- October 1985   Piedmont acquires Empire
                  People Express acquires Frontier
- January 1986   Northwest proposes to purchase Republic
- February 1986   Texas Air agrees to purchase Eastern
                  Trans World agrees to purchase Ozark
- September 1986 Delta agrees to purchase Western
                  Texas Air agrees to purchase People Express
                  Alaska Airlines agrees to purchase Jet America
- October 1986   American announces its intent to purchase AirCal
- December 1986   USAir announces it intent to purchase Pacific Southwest
- March 1987   USAir announces its intent to purchase Piedmont
- November 1987   Braniff announces its intent to purchase Florida Express

The list of reasons, stated or otherwise, for mergers and acquisitions is a long one: economies of scale, acquisition of a more appropriate fleet, traffic feed, reduction in competition, acquisition of infrastructure facilities (such as CRSs and airport slots, gates, and ticket counters), more desirable balance sheets, and/or an attempt to take advantage of an opportunity created by the Reagan Administration's lenient interpretation of antitrust laws.

Interpreting the impact of consolidation is a difficult task. Although the number of scheduled airlines operating in 1987 far exceeded the number operating in 1978—forty versus sixteen—the airline industry has become more concentrated. For example, in 1987 the market share of the four largest airlines was 60.2 percent (counting Texas Air as one airline), compared with 53.1 percent in 1978. Moreover, the market share captured by the majors in 1987, 93.0 percent, was 2.4 percentage points higher than the combined market share of the same airlines in 1978.[22] The FAA has also analyzed the change in operations at selected airports where competing airlines combined their operations. This analysis shows that whereas air carrier operations increased by 6.3 percent in fiscal year 1987 at all FAA-towered airports, the operations at St. Louis and Minneapolis/St. Paul International declined by 6.3 percent and 5.1 percent, respectively.[23] At those two airports operations were affected by acquisitions: Trans World's acquisition of Ozark at St. Louis and Northwest's acquisition of Republic at Minneapolis/St. Paul.

The FAA's findings about the impact of concentration at individual airports are confirmed in a recent research report produced by Solomon Brothers Incorporated and reported in *Air Transport World*.[24] Solomon Brothers' research is based on use of the Herfindahl-Hirschman Index (HHI) to measure the degree of horizontal market concentration. This index is computed by first squaring the market share of each airline and then summing the results for all airlines. Economists suggest that an HHI score below 1,000 is indicative of little concentration; between 1,000 and 1,800, indicative of moderate concentration; and above 1,800, indicative of high concentration. In the past, such guidelines have been used by the U.S. Department of Justice to measure market concentration before and after a proposed merger.

The Solomon brothers' report first computed this index for the entire U.S. airline industry between 1977 and the first quarter of 1987, based on each airline's share of total systemwide passenger enplanements. Making up the industry were a total of twenty-seven airlines, not all of which existed in both 1977 and 1987. The HHI score was 842 and 1,303 for 1977 and 1987, respectively. While this analysis indicated an increase in concentration in the overall industry between 1977 and 1987, the level of concentration was still in the moderate range, according to the statistical guidelines. But Solomon Brothers then computed the HHI based on market share of competing airlines at the top fifty airports, and this time the HHI varied from 1,208 at Las Vegas to 10,000 at Dallas Love Field (where 100 percent of the market share is held by Southwest Airlines). At the ten largest airports, the index varied from 1,283 (Los Angeles) to 4,606 (Dallas/Ft. Worth). For nine of those ten airports, the index was above 1,800.[25] Thus, while concentration in the airline industry may not be high when measured at the national level, it is very high when measured at the individual airport level.

The ramification of this conclusion has been illustrated by the following example: Whereas a passenger traveling between Boston and Phoenix has a wide choice of routings and airlines and therefore a wide choice of service/price options, a passenger traveling to or from St. Louis, where one airline controls 82 percent of the market, has very little choice.[26] Some analysts hypothesize that as an airline becomes more dominant at a hub—that is, as one airline accounts for a very high percentage of operations—it is in a position to increase its average fares for travel to and from that airport. It should be noted, however, that in addition to the level of concentration, average yield realized by an airline in a given market is a function of a number of other variables, including length of haul, market density, mix of passenger traffic (business versus leisure), and whether or not there is a low-cost/low-fare competitor.

Future Trends

Deregulation provided an opportunity for the airline industry to radically alter its market structure, performance, and conduct—in other words, to shed management practices built up over forty years. Although the industry is still in transition, the extent and speed of change under deregulation have been remarkable, given the events the industry has had to cope with that have been essentially outside management control. Examples of such events, which have tended to stretch out the transition process, include an increase in the price of fuel from an average of 39.3 cents per gallon in 1978 to $1.04 per gallon in 1981, the air traffic controllers' strike in 1981, and the "double dip" recession between 1980 and 1982. During the early period of deregulation, the incumbent airlines were as concerned about developing strategies to address these external factors as they were about dealing with the emergence of new competitors. Since 1983, however, the incumbents have begun to take greater advantage of their newfound freedom and have become more innovative, competitive businesses, as exemplified by

- the radically different approaches implemented to reduce labor costs;
- the proliferation of second-tier hubs;
- the introduction of deep-discount fares supported by the development of sophisticated seat-inventory management systems;
- the increase in merger and acquisition activity; and
- the establishment of domestic and international marketing alliances.

Without any consideration of the influence of external factors, the two key trends in the airline industry can be stated as follows: (a) The market structure of the U.S. airline industry is clearly headed toward oligopoly, a situation in which the control of the passenger airline industry may eventually be in the hands of about a half-dozen airlines, and (b) With the help of automation and experiences gained from other industries, airlines are beginning to develop a much greater appreciation of the role of marketing. With the respect to concentration, it is relatively clear that the process will continue into the near future, as the remaining weaker major and national airlines and the remaining independent regionals are forced to leave the marketplace because they lack certain requisite strengths. Those strengths include but are not limited to a large size, encompassing a national and/or international network; a number of strategically located hubs with a large number of feeder airlines; a sophisticated CRS; an efficient cost structure; a productive labor force; a low debt-equity ratio; an attractive frequent-flyer program; and a marketing orientation. The lack of a number of these attributes not only will force some existing airlines to leave the marketplace but will also preclude new airlines of any significant size from entering the marketplace. This process has increased the degree of concentration by a moderate percentage at the national level and by a much higher percentage at the local airport level for most large airports.

The airlines are also becoming much more market oriented and innovative in developing, pricing, distributing, and promoting their product. The direction being followed to develop and implement innovative marketing concepts has been influenced partly by the use of automation (for example, the use of computers to manage seat inventory) and partly by the lessons learned from other industries (for example, the use of frequent-flyer programs to build brand loyalty). Further exploitation of automation and experience gained from other industries will continue to shape future marketing programs in the airline industry. Some airlines, for example, have thought about a la carte pricing as used in the restaurant industry and have considered pricing policies based on the methods used in the stock market industry, wherein the price of a stock is a function of not only the change in demand but also the rate at which demand is changing. In the distribution system, an example of a potential change is the use of personal computers to make reservations and obtain tickets. And in promotion, strategies are being examined, for example, for an airline to promote those travel agents who use its CRS.

A greater focus on marketing is, however, only one variable in the equation related to the future market structure, performance, and conduct of the airline industry. Two other key variables that are outside the industry's control are (a) the approach adopted by the government and individual airports to attack the airport/airway congestion problem and (b) the approach adopted by the government in promulgating Stage 2 and Stage 3 aircraft-noise regulations. If, for example, the development of new airports and the expansion of existing airports do not keep pace with the growth in traffic and, furthermore, if proposed technological solutions (for example, to reduce aircraft separation standards) do not provide the needed increase in capacity, the airline industry may be forced into a different mode of operation, including, perhaps, a proliferation of smaller, less congested hubs; the acquisition of larger airplanes; a reduction in the services provided by smaller carriers feeding the larger carriers at major congested airports; and an increase in passenger fares. Similarly, a decision by the government to compress the Stage 3 compliance deadline (as a result of political pressure) would have a serious economic impact on the entire U.S. airline industry and a potentially devastating impact on selected airlines. Moreover, the impact of the airport/ airway congestion problem and of noise legislation will not be limited to the U.S. airline industry; it will also affect the international aviation industry, the topic of chapter 6.

Notes

1. Air Transportation Association (ATA), *Air Transport 1988* (Washington, D.C.: ATA, June 1988), 12.
2. N.K. Taneja, *The Commercial Airline Industry: Managerial Practices and Regulatory Policies* (Lexington, Mass.: Lexington Books, 1976), 21–27.
3. W.E. O'Connor, *An Introduction to Airline Economics*, 3d. ed. (New York: Praeger, 1985), 36.
4. U.S. Department of Transportation, *FAA Aviation Forecasts: Fiscal Years 1987–1988* (Washington, D.C.: Federal Aviation Administration, February 1987), 27.
5. Air Transport Association of America (ATA), *Air Transport 1979* (Washington, D.C.: ATA, June 1979), 20–23.
6. Regional Airline Association (RAA), *1988 Annual Report* (Washington, D.C.: RAA, 1988), 8.
7. U.S. Department of Transportation, *FAA Aviation Forecasts: Fiscal Years 1987–1998*, 27.
8. U.S. Department of Transportation, *FAA Aviation Forecasts: Fiscal Years 1988–1999* (Washington, D.C.: Federal Aviation Administration, February 1988), 34.
9. H.P. Wolfe and D.A. NewMeyer, *Aviation Industry Regulation* (Carbondale: Southern Illinois University Press, 1985), chap. 6.
10. Air Transport Association of America (ATA), *Air Transport 1988*, 8–9.
11. Regional Airline Association, *1988 Annual Report*, 33.
12. Ibid., 30–31.
13. D.A. Collier, *Service Management: Operating Decisions* (Englewoods Cliffs, N.J.: Prentice Hall, 1987).
14. D.A. Swierenga, *Airline Cost Index* (Washington, D.C.: Air Transport Association of America, May 4, 1988).

15. Air Transport Association of America, *Air Transport 1988,* 14.

16. Data supplied by the Airline Industry Data Division of the Air Transportation Association of America, Washington, D.C.

17. M.A. Brenner, J.O. Leet, and E. Schott, *Airline Deregulation* (Westport, Conn.: ENO Foundation for Transportation, 1985), chap. 7.

18. U.S. Department of Transportation, *FAA Aviation Forecast: Fiscal Years 1988–1999,* 57.

19. J.F. Molloy, Jr., *The U.S. Commuter Airline Industry: Policy Alternatives* (Lexington, Mass.: Lexington Books, 1985), 144–49.

20. S. Keeble, "The Cost of Flying Free," *Airline Business,* May 1988, 44–46.

21. Ibid.

22. U.S. Department of Transportation, *FAA Aviation Forecasts: Fiscal Years 1988–1999,* 34–35.

23. Ibid.

24. P. Flint, "Too Many Mergers, Too Little Competion?" *Air Transport World,* January 1988, 81–84, 131.

25. Ibid.

26. Ibid.

6
International Air Transport

Unlike the U.S. domestic airline industry described in the preceding chapter, the international air transport industry functions in a far more complex environment, one characterized by multilateralism, bilateralism, interline agreements, and government ownership. The regulatory framework of bilateral and multilateral agreements controls market entry, capacity, and pricing—factors that determine the competitive environment for international air transport operations. In addition, the operating objectives of most international airlines that are partially or totally owned by their governments reflect a wide spectrum of national interests, ranging from tourism to business development to foreign policy to defense. The airlines' pursuit of national objectives, some of which extend far beyond the pure economics of airline operations, necessitates the establishment of commercial managerial policies and practices that are in harmony with national policies.

During the past ten years, both the structure and the mode of operation of the international airline industry have been affected by such trends as the liberalization of regulatory policies, the exploitation of automation as a competitive tool, the privatization of government-controlled airlines, and the redeployment of assets in order to offer alternative price/service options. This chapter traces the development of the framework in which the international air transport industry functions. It also provides an overview of the current industry structure and briefly comments on the trends that are reshaping this component of civil aviation.

Evolution of International Commercial Aviation

Paris and Havana Conventions

Louis Bleriot's flight across the English Channel in 1909 did more than just demonstrate the technical viability of the airplane; his flight crossed sovereign aerial boundaries, an event that had ramifications for both national defense and international commercial relations. This aspect of Bleriot's flight, coupled with previous border crossings by balloons, prompted France in 1910 to hold a multilateral conference on the regulation of air navigation. Although the conference reviewed a number of technical issues relating to air navigation, such as crew competence and rules for departures and landings, its fundamental issues pertained to the "rights and privileges" of aircraft operations in sovereign territories. A comprehensive international convention, containing more than forty articles, was drafted; however, because of differences in opinion among the countries, agreement could not be reached on those articles relating to the issue of rights and privileges.

After World War I ended, the French government proposed the establishment of an aeronautical commission as part of the 1919 Paris Peace Conference. Once formed, this commission was given the responsibility of drafting the principles to be contained in a single international convention for civil aviation. From the start it was agreed that the proposed convention should recognize the basic principle of each nation's complete sovereignty over the airspace above its territories and territorial waters—a principle that continues to be the foundation for economic regulation of the international air transport industry. The draft convention, containing forty-three articles and eight annexes, was ultimately signed by thirty-eight nations and became known as the International Convention for Air Navigation, later called the *Paris Convention*.

In addition to establishing the sovereignty principle, the convention dealt with navigation and other related issues, such as the airworthiness of aircraft and the competency of pilots. It also called for establishment of the International Commission for Air Navigation, an organization that was formed and held its first meeting in Paris in 1922.[1] The commission's purpose was twofold: (a) to monitor developments in aviation and, if warranted, propose to contracting states amendments to the convention and revisions and updates of annexes and (b) to collect and disseminate aeronautical information related to international air navigation.

The year 1919 brought two other significant events. First, Aircraft Transport and Travel established the first daily scheduled international passenger air service between London and Paris. Second, a number of European airlines founded the International Air Traffic Association (IATA), whose purpose was to make international air transportation convenient and more acceptable to passengers.[2]

Although the Paris Convention was a comprehensive document, it had three significant shortcomings. First, it contained language that precluded flights by airlines from those nations which were not parties to the convention over the territories of those nations which were parties to the convention. This provision was presumably intended to (a) encourage all allied and neutral nations to adhere to the convention and (b) place wartime enemy nations at a disadvantage. Second, the convention provided for a weighted voting power in favor of the principal Allied Powers—France, Italy, Japan, the United Kingdom, and the United States—and thereby created a basic inequality among convention signatories. Third, some of the world's largest nations—for example, China, the United States, and the USSR—were not party to the convention. Although the United States had participated in the formulation of the convention, as part of President Woodrow Wilson's League of Nations, it could not become an actual signatory, since the Senate did not endorse U.S. participation in the League of Nations.[3] China and the USSR, too, were not members of the League of Nations and therefore were not parties to the convention.

As a result of these shortcomings, a number of nations decided not to participate in the Paris Convention but instead to draft another convention. In 1926, Spain led the way, inviting all Latin American and Caribbean nations and Portugal to form the Ibero-American Congress, which drafted the Ibero-American Air Convention, an agreement based almost entirely on the Paris Convention. Although the proposed Ibero-American Air Convention did remove the unacceptable language contained in the Paris Convention, it was not ratified by a sufficient number of nations and thus never became effective. In 1928, yet another alternative to the Paris Convention, known as the Pan American Convention of Commercial Aviation, emerged at the Pan American Conference held in Havana. This convention was ratified and adopted by the signatory nations.[4]

Chicago Conference

As World War II came to an end, the world's nations once again began to focus on a framework in which to establish global civil aviation. Two key factors that led to renewed interest in worldwide aviation policy were (a) a serious concern on the part of some nations about the effects that two different conventions, Paris and Havana, would have on the future development of the international civil aviation industry and (b) the desire of three countries, Canada, the United Kingdom, and the United States, to play a prominent role in the postwar development of international civil aviation.[5] The U.S. government took a leadership role and in 1944 invited more than fifty nations to attend an international conference in Chicago; the USSR chose not to participate. The Chicago Conference had two ambitious goals: to unify the framework for international aviation at the multilateral level and to effect agreement on various economic issues.

Whereas the previous two conventions had addressed primarily technical issues and left economic issues to be resolved either by airlines or through bilateral channels,[6] the Chicago Conference, by contrast, included on its agenda a discussion of economic issues at the multilateral level. The economic issues proved far more contentious than the technical issues. Five countries presented very different and very controversial proposals, one each by Canada, the United Kingdom, and the United States and a joint proposal by Australia and New Zealand. The British advocated strict regulation of international services by an international aeronautics authority (similar to the U.S. CAB), with control over routes, rates, flight frequency, and market shares. The United States stressed the policy of "open skies," with no control on tariffs or capacity. The United States did not object to the formation of an international authority so long as its responsibilities were limited to the promulgation of technical standards; in terms of economics, the United States saw the role of the international authority as strictly advisory.

Although the deadlock over economic regulation was not resolved, the Chicago Conference did produce the Convention on International Civil Aviation, a document augmented by twelve technical annexes. This unifying convention made the Paris and Havana conventions obsolete and established general rules under which international air transport could be operated. It also called for establishment of the Provisional International Civil Aviation Organization (PICAO), which was to be governed by a council composed of regularly elected representatives from signatory nations. This intergovernmental agency immediately began to establish a network of air routes and a global air navigation infrastructure. Immediately after World War II, for example, there was an urgent need for a navigational infrastructure across the North Atlantic, the world's most heavily traveled transoceanic air corridor, and PICAO, convening special conferences, obtained an agreement from nine member nations—Belgium, Canada, France, Ireland, the Netherlands, Norway, Sweden, the United Kingdom, and the United States—to participate in the support and operation of a number of Atlantic Ocean weather ship stations.[7] In 1947, PICAO was made a permanent organization, as a specialized agency of the United Nations.

During the Chicago Conference, an attempt was also made to establish a multilateral agreement on the *five freedoms of the air,* defined as follows:

- The right of one country's airline to fly through the sovereign airspace of another country without landing

- The right of one country's airline to make a landing in a foreign country for technical or emergency reasons without picking up or deplaning revenue traffic (passengers or cargo)

- The right to carry international revenue traffic from an airline's home state to a treaty partner's state

- The right to carry international revenue traffic from a treaty partner's state to the carrier's home state (the converse of the third right)

- The right of one country's airline to carry international revenue traffic between two foreign states (for example, a U.S. airline carrying passengers between London and Rome)

It was the fifth freedom that caused the most controversy at the Chicago Conference. Although the majority of delegates supported the first two freedoms because those principles did not involve commercial traffic rights, they rejected the fifth freedom. The Europeans, having little domestic traffic, feared that the fifth freedom would provide U.S. carriers with access to their valuable international traffic. As a result of the controversy surrounding fifth freedom, the conference produced the International Air Services Transit Agreement, containing only the first two freedoms; this agreement was accepted and subsequently ratified.

Bilateral Agreements

Since the delegates at the Chicago Conference could not reach a longer-term multilateral agreement concerning how international tariffs—passenger fares and cargo rates—should be established, they decided that the airlines themselves should coordinate and agree to tariffs on a routine basis and then submit them to governments for approval. The delegates also agreed that the airlines should hold their own meetings to discuss the possibility of establishing a worldwide association. Subsequently, at a 1945 meeting in Havana the airlines decided to reestablish IATA.

Because the different perspectives of the British and the Americans had not been reconciled during the Chicago Conference, the development of international air transport services between the two nations stalled after World War II. Eventually though, in February 1946, the United Kingdom invited the United States to Bermuda for the purpose of negotiating a bilateral air transport agreement. At the Bermuda meeting, the two countries reached a compromise and an agreement was signed.

The United Kingdom delegation agreed to the reciprocal grant of the third, fourth, and fifth freedoms, without formal restrictions on capacity or frequency. On the issue of rate control, the United States agreed to let IATA's traffic conference machinery establish fares, subject to government approval. It was agreed that (a) from the viewpoint of governments, fares negotiated multilaterally through IATA would meet the divergent requirements of sovereign governments, avoid direct government conflict, and reduce the possiblity of subsidy wars with government-owned or-controlled carriers and (b) from the viewpoint of carriers, multilaterally negotiated fares would coordinate. tariffs on a worldwide basis; facilitate long-haul, multi-stop operations; and meet the needs of passengers, shippers, and airlines.

This agreement between the United Kingdom and the United States, commonly known as the Bermuda Agreement, became, for the next thirty years, the global prototype for establishing bilateral agreements between countries, an arrangement deemed necessary for airlines to offer service in international markets. The Bermuda bilateral agreement, together with those signed and modeled after it, made a significant contribution to the postwar expansion of international air transportation.

A typical bilateral agreement has three parts. The first part involves general provisions, including the regulation of tariffs and capacity. Usually, it is agreed that tariffs are to be coordinated by the designated airlines, with their respective governments having final approval. The regulation of capacity varies from country to country—from minimal control to extremely tight control—yet even with a relatively liberal capacity clause, the matter of capacity still tends to be subject to governmental review. In addition, this part of the bilateral agreement may also contain provisions relating to such issues as airport charges, airport handling policies, and customs duties. The second part of the bilateral agreement is an explicit statement of the destinations to be served, including the behind-and-beyond traffic rights (feeder routes) that can be used by the designated airlines. The third part of the document lists any special notes, agreements, or memorandums exchanged between the two parties.

In general, most bilateral agreements allow the designated airlines to offer services on routes between their home countries. In some cases, fifth-freedom carriers are allowed to offer additional services as long as the additional capacity offered pursuant to the fifth freedom is relatively small compared with that offered under the third and fourth freedoms. *Sixth-freedom rights,* which allow an airline to combine third- and fourth-freedom rights to attain fifth-freedom rights, generally are not negotiated explicitly in bilateral agreements, although references to them have been made in confidential memorandums of understanding.[8] For example, Lufthansa could combine its New York–Frankfurt service (fourth-freedom right) with its Frankfurt–New Delhi service (third-freedom right) to carry traffic between New York and New Delhi (fifth-freedom traffic). Finally, *cabotage rights,* whereby an airline from one country is allowed to carry revenue traffic between two points within another country, are granted only rarely.

Although the Bermuda Agreement established a general framework for the negotiation of bilateral agreements, the actual process is extremely complex. While the overall philosophy governing bilateral agreements is to provide a fair and equal opportunity for the contracting parties' carriers, other considerations must be taken into account. With the exception of the U.S. airlines, most of the airlines in the world are at least partially owned by and to varying degrees subsidized by governments. Moreover, the government subsidies are based on a variety of motives—for example, to compensate an airline for providing mandated service on routes considered important from the standpoint of public need, commercial trade, national defense, or simply politics. The ability to compete in the free marketplace also varies from national airline to national airline. Consequently, governments use the bilateral process to control and protect their airlines by controlling the degree of competition through regulating market entry, price, and capacity. Governments also use the bilateral process to negotiate nonaviation issues related to defense, politics, and other sectors of commercial trade. Access to strategically located military bases and export-import quotas, for example, have been used as bargaining chips in the negotiation of bilateral agreements.

The preceding factors have led to the development of bilateral airline agreements that are similar in principle but different in details. One difference, once prevalent in Europe and still so in Asia, is the existence of *pooling agreements*—interline agreements to share capacity and revenue according to a prearranged formula. (It is also possible to have revenue-cost pools, in which services are offered by only one carrier but revenues and costs are shared by all partners in the pool.)[9] In addition to sharing capacity and revenue, pooling agreements can also include such activities as joint advertising and promotion, ground services, and reservations. Further, on some routes one airline may be required to pay royalties to another airline for the right to carry traffic that could have been transported by the airline receiving royalties, had the carrier actually offered the service. Royalty payments can take different forms, such as a fixed charge per passenger or a percentage of the total revenue generated in the market.

Since their inception, pooling agreements have been highly controversial and indeed are illegal for U.S. airlines to enter into. Proponents argue that these agreements reduce operating costs and thus provide passengers with lower fares and better schedules. With respect to quality of service, proponents contend that without such agreements, there would be a concentration of departures at peak periods and fewer, if any, departures during off-peak periods. In contrast, opponents argue that pooling agreements reduce the incentive to compete, leading to inefficient operations, poorer service, and higher prices.

For about thirty years after World War II, the international scheduled air transportation system continued to work on the basis of cooperation among nations and airlines. Cooperation between countries in technical, operational, and legal areas was achieved largely through the efforts of the International Civil Aviation Organization, (ICAO), which obtained its authority and guidance from the convention signed in Chicago in 1944. ICAO, for example, played an instrumental role in the decision to place a cable system on the floor of the Atlantic Ocean to connect the Newfoundland, Greenland, Iceland, and Scotland area control centers, which greatly improved the safety and efficiency of transatlantic operations. Cooperation between international airlines was achieved through the efforts of IATA, which was established in 1945, and through bilateral and interline agreements. An example of the valuable work of IATA, the interline system enabled a passenger to travel from one part of the world to another using a standard airline ticket purchased in one currency from any participating airline or one of thousands of accredited travel agents. This cooperation at the multilateral level, coupled with the regulatory framework of bilateral agreements, effectively controlled entry, capacity, and pricing—the key factors that determine the level of competition in international air transport operations.

Procompetitive Developments

After working reasonably well for about thirty years, the international air transportation system, built on the principles of bilateralism and multilateralism, began to fall apart in the mid-1970s. At least five factors were responsible for straining the system. First, the number of scheduled international airlines increased dramatically after World War II, and most of the new airlines had different and often conflicting objectives. Second, the number of airlines offering lower-priced charter service proliferated. Third, the introduction of wide-body airplanes increased capacity, and the economic viability of these airplanes required changes in route systems and scheduling policies. Fourth, excess capacity existed during the mid-1970s and became a contributing factor to financial losses incurred by airlines around the world. And fifth, U.S. international aviation policy began to change drastically during the mid-1970s, placing greater reliance on competitive market forces to determine the quantity, quality, and price of air services.

The dynamic changes cited above and other important developments, such as the capacity imbalance in U.S.–United Kingdom markets, led to the announcement in 1976 by the British government of its intention to renegotiate the Bermuda Agreement.[10] A new agreement, signed in 1977 and known as Bermuda II, was once again a compromise between the two different positions taken by the United Kingdom and the United States. Although neither party got all it wanted, the final agreement did provide a foundation of mutual benefits. For example, Bermuda II imposed a restriction on the number of U.S.-flag carriers (U.S. airlines operating in international markets) in the U.S.–United Kingdom markets. In addition, it established a mechanism for the British to control capacity, and it limited the beyond points to which the U.S. carriers could carry United Kingdom fill-up traffic, that is, traffic originating in the United Kingdom. Bermuda II also introduced additional U.S. and United Kingdom carriers; opened up more gateways, or commercial airports of entry for foreign carriers; and brought about lower fares.

After Bermuda II, U.S. international aviation policy became aggressively more liberal. According to Rigas Doganis in *Flying Off Course,* three factors explain this shift in policy. First, high-ranking U.S. government officials truly believed in the economic benefits of airline competition. Second, whereas the early stages of deregulation in the U.S. domestic markets had produced some desirable results, particularly lower fares, it was reasoned that if deregulation could produce favorable results in domestic markets, it could also produce similar results in international markets. And third, the Carter administration felt that a more liberal environment could stabilize the declining market share of U.S. carriers operating on the North Atlantic.[11]

In 1978, the Carter administration stated that its policy would be to extend fair competition between airlines to provide the greatest possible benefit to passengers and shippers. This policy was to be implemented in as many future bilateral negotiations as possible, through such provisions as multiple designation (more than one airline from a country), change-of-gauge rights (the right to change the size of an airplane), country-of-origin rules (operations conducted according to the rules of the country in which the flight originated) for charter operations, and double-disapproval clauses for tariffs, whereby both governments must disapprove fares proposed by airlines in order to block a tariff. During these negotiations, the United States allowed foreign carriers access to additional gateways in the United States in return for their implementing the liberal policies it advocated, such as lower fares.

In stark contrast to the U.S. government's open-skies policy, several U.S. international airlines, such as Braniff, Flying Tiger, Northwest, Pan American, and TWA, questioned their government's economic rationale for the free-for-all competition in international aviation. These airlines cited the following counterpoints: (a) Most foreign-flag airlines are not privately owned; (b) the air transportation policies of most governments include non-economical objectives; (c) different nations have different antitrust philosophies; and (d) the existence of government subsidies, coupled with the absence of a common regulatory framework and the operations of fifth-freedom airlines, increases the probability of predatory pricing. (Predatory pricing policies are generally based neither on cost nor on market; rather, they are set at a level to drive a competitor out of the marketplace.) The U.S. international airlines also argued that air transportation is both a public service and an integral part of many nations' economies, hence some foreign governments might be compelled to protect their national airlines from uncontrolled competition, employing such tactics as excessive user charges, forced use of ground-handling monopolies, restricted access to the market, and controls on the exchange of foreign currency.

The foreign aviation community, too, questioned the wisdom of the U.S. procompetitive policy, although for different reasons. Foreign governments and airlines did not argue with the need to stimulate productivity, efficiency, and innovation; the issue was the method of achieving such goals. Australia, for example, demonstrated that lower fares could be achieved through strict regulation. Nations in Africa and South America voiced the most severe criticism of the U.S. policy, pointing out that the nature of their operations did not warrant implementation of procompetitive policies. In Africa, the majority of markets have extremely small volumes of traffic, there are many airlines, and with few exceptions most of the traffic is long-haul. Moreover, operating costs are high relative to other domestic and international carriers, because of the seasonal nature of the traffic, low utilization of airplanes, and high costs of fuel and maintenance. As a result, most airlines in Africa operate at best very close to the break-even point. These characteristics, combined with the desire of governments to fulfill higher-priority national interests, have led most African nations to adopt restrictive aviation policies. Similar points were raised by the nations in South America.

Despite the marked differences in policy that existed among international carriers, the Carter administration continued to pursue its hands-off, procompetitive policies. During bilateral negotiations, the U.S. government aggressively sought to trade hard rights for foreign-flag carriers (for example, more gateways in the United States) for some hard rights for U.S. carriers (for example, multiple designations, more than one U.S. airline with access to a foreign gateway, and the removal of charter restrictions) and some soft rights (for example, the promise of low fares and the relaxation of the requirement to use monopoly ground-handling agencies). These developments were followed by passage of the International Air Transportation Competition Act of 1979, which amended the Federal Aviation Act for the purpose of providing competition in the international marketplace.

Essentially, the 1979 act adopted the general theme of the domestic Airline Deregulation Act of 1978, its overriding objective being to introduce more competition into international markets as a way of promoting a wider spectrum of price/service options.

The changes in U.S. international aviation policy during the late 1970s also influenced the U.S. government's view of the future role of IATA in establishing international tariffs, particularly for travel to and from the United States. Until the mid-1970s, all international markets were divided into three traffic conferences and four joint traffic conferences. For example, traffic conference 1 represented the Western Hemisphere; traffic conference 2 included Europe, the Middle East, and Africa; and traffic conference 3 represented the Far East and Southwest Pacific. Transatlantic operations were covered by joint conference 1-2. Joint traffic conference 1-2-3 represented around-the-world services. Tariff officials from airlines that offered scheduled service in particular markets participated in the appropriate traffic conference meetings; these meetings were closed to outsiders, and proposed tariffs had to be agreed upon unanimously by all airlines and approved by the governments of the countries and carriers in attendance before they could be implemented.

Since the Chicago Conference in 1944, the U.S. government had been opposed to the idea of an international body having the authority to regulate international tariffs. The United States did agree to this provision, however, in the Bermuda Agreement, and the CAB did endorse, although reluctantly, IATA's rate-coordinating functions. Then, in June 1978, as an outgrowth of its free-market international aviation policy, the CAB issued a show-cause order proposing to (a) disapprove the IATA traffic conference provisions and related resolutions and (b) subject IATA's multilateral activities to U.S. antitrust laws. The CAB's basic premise was that the IATA rate-making system was adverse to the public interest, on the grounds that the system was anticompetitive, inefficient, and unnecessary.

Many airlines and states opposed the CAB proposal, claiming that IATA's multilateral activities were in the public interest and had been providing substantial benefits to international commerce and tourism. More specifically, they argued that the association had developed a workable, integrated international network, one that had been consistent with the bilateral system and the sovereignty concept and that had provided an effective mechanism for the coexistence and harmonization of regional differences and disparate government pricing philosophies. These groups not only questioned the wisdom of the CAB order; they also saw no viable alternative to the existing system.

In 1979, IATA streamlined its procedures and regulations to keep abreast of the changing environment and to address some of the criticisms raised in the CAB show-cause order. The conference system was restructured by introducing the following changes:

- Participation in tariff coordination, which had been mandatory, was now made optional.
- Major geographical conference areas were subdivided into smaller units to expedite agreements.
- Mechanisms were established to allow the introduction of innovative fares without disturbing the basic agreement.
- Certain previously regulated items, such as in-flight services, were no longer considered part of the conference agreements.
- Third parties (non-airlines) were allowed to have limited participation in the conference.[12]

These changes were designed to eliminate many of the criticisms of the IATA tariff-coordination process and to encourage the development of tariffs that (a) were more responsive to consumers, (b) preserved the essential elements of the integrated worldwide system, and (c) harmonized the different pricing philosophies of the airlines and their governments. Despite these major changes, however, the CAB proceeded with its show-cause order and also began to introduce new, more liberal tariff provisions in the bilateral agreements that came up for renegotiation. Examples of these new provisions included double-disapproval clauses and country-of-origin clauses that permitted an individual government to regulate the tariffs for its outbound traffic. To get foreign governments to accept these liberal tariff provisions, the U.S. government, of course, paid a price: in most cases, by agreeing to give foreign airlines additional gateways in the United States.

Worldwide opposition to the CAB show-cause order, the lack of viable alternatives to the IATA tariff-coordination system, and the attempt by IATA to restructure its procedures forced the CAB, in 1980, to approve the IATA tariff-coordination process for a two-year period. The CAB hoped that its interim decision would encourage the development of innovative pricing policies. Indeed, in 1982 the United States and ten members of the European Civil Aviation Conference agreed to establish a *zone of reasonableness* for setting North Atlantic fares. This system, whereby governments automatically approved airline fare requests that fell within specified upper and lower boundaries, achieved three objectives: (a) It introduced a new concept in pricing, (b) it worked within the framework of a multilateral government agreement, and (c) it operated outside the IATA machinery. The CAB show-cause order was abandoned when the U.S. Department of Transportation took over the remaining functions of the CAB. Consequently, despite the restructuring of IATA, its influence on transatlantic tariffs was reduced, first by the actions of the U.S. government and second by the new zone-of-reasonableness fare scheme. Moreover, a number of subsequent bilateral agreements have been less forceful in clauses requiring the use of IATA tariff procedures, and a few other governments have discussed the possibility of withdrawing antitrust immunity for a number of IATA cooperative activities.

IATA was not the only organization that had to restructure itself to respond to the changes in the marketplace. ICAO also had to make adjustments to address issues that were not foreseen at the Chicago Conference in 1944. For example, although initially twelve annexes to the convention were drafted in 1944, subsequent developments in the international airline industry required ICAO to modify the original twelve annexes and establish additional annexes to address new issues. Annex 16 ("Environmental Protection") was added to deal with protecting the environment from the effect of aircraft-noise and -engine emissions; annex 17 ("Aviation Security") was added to address the increase in crimes of violence that adversely affected the safety of civil aviation; and annex 18 ("Dangerous Goods") was added to codify international regulations and procedures for transporting dangerous goods—explosive, corrosive, flammable, toxic, and/or radioactive goods. To keep abreast of changes in the industry, ICAO also established, in 1983, a special committee on Future Air Navigation Systems (FANS) to study and make recommendations related to a global civil aviation air navigation system.

From its inception, ICAO had addressed mainly technical problems, challenges, and issues. By the mid-1970s, however, numerous governments around the world were calling for ICAO to deal as well with commercial issues, including the establishment of methods to control capacity in scheduled operations, bring harmony between scheduled and charter operations, intercede when airlines or governments could not agree on tariffs through the IATA process, and handle the proliferation of tariff violations. These developments led to ICAO's First Special Air Transport Conference in 1977, which (a) reaffirmed the merits of bilateral agreements as an appropriate mechanism for dealing with international scheduled operations, (b) called upon ICAO to develop criteria and methods for regulating capacity in scheduled and charter operations, and (c) adopted recommendations for improving procedures for developing and monitoring international tariffs. The complexity of these issues led to a second and third air transport conference in 1980 and 1985, respectively. Whereas the second conference recommended a multilateral but more liberal system in response to the U.S. open-sky policy, the third conference dealt with the policy concerning commercial rights for international scheduled and nonscheduled air transport; the unilateral measures affecting international air transport; and the role of governments, the rules and conditions, and the enforcement associated with the international air carrier tariffs.[13]

The three ICAO conferences were convened to address the radical changes in the international air transportation industry, most notably the U.S. pro-competitive international aviation policies. Despite the initial general rejection of U.S. aviation policies, a number of countries around the world— among them Great Britain, Canada, Australia, and more recently even Japan—have been investigating the merits of a more liberal regulatory environment. Moreover, other emerging trends are expected to have a profound impact on the future of international aviation; these trends and their ramifications are discussed in the last section of this chapter.

Industry Structure

Whereas most of the 158 member-nations of ICAO have a single international airline that provides scheduled services, only about a half-dozen countries—including Canada, France, Japan, Mexico, the United Kingdom, and the United States—have more than one such airline. Some groups of countries own multinational airlines—for example, the Scandinavian Airlines System (SAS), owned by Denmark, Norway, and Sweden; Gulf Air, owned by Bahrain, Oman, Qatar, and the United Arab Emirates; and Air Afrique, owned by the 10 nations that are signatories to the Yaounde Treaty: Benin, Burkina Faso, the Central African Republic, Chad, the Congo, Côte d'Ivoire, Mauritania, Niger, Senegal, and Togo. International scheduled air services provided by the airlines of just 6 countries—the United States, the United Kingdom, Japan, France, the Federal Republic of Germany, and the Netherlands—account for about 50 percent of total international operations, as measured in ton-kilometers performed, of the 158 ICAO member-nations. (A ton-kilometer is one ton flown one kilometer.) U.S. airlines alone account for about 17 percent of total international scheduled services.[14]

Table 6–1 lists the top 50 IATA member-airlines offering international

Table 6–1
IATA Members' Rankings, 1987: Top Fifty Airlines

	Scheduled Passengers Carried International			Scheduled Passenger-Kilometers Flown International			Scheduled Freight Tonnes Carried International	
Rank	Airline	Thousands	Rank	Airline	Millions	Rank	Airline	Thousands
1	British Airways	14,482	1	British Airways	44,085	1	Flying Tiger	564
2	Air France	10,518	2	Japan Air Lines	34,821	2	Lufthansa	523
3	Lufthansa	9,888	3	Pan American	33,519	3	Air France	434
4	Pan American	9,376	4	Lufthansa	29,048	4	Japan Air Lines	401
5	Japan Air Lines	6,639	5	Air France	24,481	5	KLM	285
6	Iberia	6,426	6	Qantas Airways	22,709	6	British Airways	220
7	SAS	6,384	7	KLM	21,797	7	Swissair	177
8	Swissair	6,119	8	TWA	19,759	8	Alitalia	157
9	KLM	5,875	9	United Airlines	17,609	9	El Al	146
10	Alitalia	5,330	10	Iberia	14,909	10	Pan American	140
11	American Airlines	5,021	11	Alitalia	13,532	11	Qantas Airways	119
12	Eastern Air Lines	4,214	12	Swissair	13,519	12	Saudi Arabian Airlines	118
13	Air Canada	3,790	13	American Airlines	12,902	13	Iberia	114
14	United Airlines	3,475	14	Air Canada	10,614	14	Air Canada	110
15	Saudi Arabian Airlines	3,366	15	Saudi Arabian Airlines	10,342	15	SABENA	102
16	Qantas Airways	3,314	16	SAS	10,155	16	Air-India	81
17	TWA	3,234	17	Continental Airlines	10,002	17	VARIG	80
18	Mexicana	2,906	18	British Caledonian	8,559	18	Nippon Cargo	74
19	Continental Airlines	2,776	19	Air-India	8,335	19	SAS	74
20	Gulf Air	2,486	20	Air New Zealand	8,036	20	Kuwait Airways	71
21	SABENA	2,362	21	Canadian Airlines International	7,919	21	British Caledonian	70
22	Aer Lingus	2,233	22	VARIG	7,874	22	UTA	69
23	British Caledonian	2,114	23	P.T. Garuda Indonesia	7,510	23	United Airlines	67
24	Olympic Airways	2,093	24	Philippine Airlines	7,486	24	TMA	E
25	Egyptair	1,811	25	El Al	7,284	25	Pakistan International	61
26	Pakistan International	1,769	26	Mexicana	6,494	26	TWA	56

Rank	Airline	Value	Airline	Value	Airline	Value
27	Air-India	1,740	SABENA	5,973	Air New Zealand	54
28	Austrian Airlines	1,730	Eastern Air Lines	5,968	P.T. Garuda Indonesia	53
29	Air Algérie	1,720	Pakistan International	5,774	Continental Airlines	53
30	El Al	1,608	Olympic Airways	5,764	ZAS Airline of Egypt	E
31	P.T. Garuda Indonesia	1,604	Gulf Air	4,639	American Airlines	51
32	Finnair	1,543	Egyptair	4,467	Gulf Air	48
33	JAT	1,517	Aerolineas Argentinas	4,422	Royal Jordanian	46
34	Kuwait Airways	1,511	UTA	4,293	Avianca	45
35	Air New Zealand	1,507	TAP–Air Portugal	4,090	Air Afrique	43
36	Philippine Airlines	1,457	JAT	4,078	Iran Air	40
37	TAP–Air Portugal	1,444	South African Airways	E	Federal Express	39
38	Canadian Airlines International	1,403	Kuwait Airways	3,771	Egyptair	38
39	Aeroméxico	1,389	Royal Jordanian	3,485	Eastern Air Lines	37
40	MALEV	1,231	Aeroméxico	3,131	Philippine Airlines	34
41	THY	1,199	Finnair	2,815	Aer Lingus	33
42	VARIG	1,180	Aer Lingus	2,727	Canadian Airlines International	31
43	Royal Jordanian	1,120	Icelandair	2,467	TAP–Air Portugal	30
44	Royal Air Maroc	1,111	THY	2,351	Olympic Airways	30
45	Aerolineas Argentinas	1,059	BWIA International	2,314	VIASA	E
46	LOT	1,057	Air Algérie	2,248	South African Airways	E
47	Tunis Air	996	Royal Air Maroc	2,194	Finnair	25
48	Iran Air	955	Air Afrique	2,135	Mexicana	24
49	BWIA International	836	LOT	2,098	Aerolineas Argentinas	20
50	CSA	785	CSA	1,935	Royal Air Maroc	20

Source: International Air Transport Association (IATA), *World Air Transport Statistics* (Geneva: IATA, June 1988).

Note: Ranking are based on total IATA membership with estimates (E) being used for those airlines that did not report in time for inclusion in this analysis.

services, the rank order depending on the unit of measurement. In this table the ranking is shown with respect to three measurements: the number of scheduled passengers carried; the number of scheduled passenger-kilometers flown, which takes into account the distance flown by passengers; and the amount of freight carried in scheduled service. Note that this list represents only the operations of airlines that are members of IATA. Because many airlines belonging to the ICAO contracting states are not members of IATA, the list excludes certain large, non-IATA international scheduled airlines, such as Singapore, Thai (Thailand), and Aeroflot (USSR); moreover, charter airlines are not included in the list. In 1987, IATA member-airlines accounted for 62.2 percent of the total worldwide traffic, measured in tonne-kilometers performed, or 72.0 percent of the international traffic and 50.3 percent of the domestic traffic.[15]

International air transportation services, in addition to being provided by scheduled airlines, are also provided by charter airlines, largely in the passenger area. During 1987, charter traffic accounted for 18.7 percent of total passenger traffic, as measured in passenger-kilometers. About half the total international charter traffic was carried by charter airlines; the other half, by scheduled airlines in their charter operations. Charter activity, however, varies tremendously by region. Most of the international charter activity is concentrated within the 22-country European Civil Aviation Conference (ECAC), a region in which the volume of charter traffic is comparable to that of scheduled traffic. On the North Atlantic, charter traffic in 1987 represented 5.9 percent of total traffic. In recent years, the liberalization movement, particularly in Europe, has been changing the structure of the international charter industry.[16] On the North Atlantic, for example, scheduled carriers historically were able to attract a significant percentage of charter traffic to their scheduled operations by introducing lower fares, but subsequently a more liberal regulatory environment enabled some charter airlines to offer scheduled services. Yet although the basic structure of the nonscheduled airline industry has changed, the percentage of traffic carried by nonscheduled airlines remained relatively constant between 1982 and 1987 (see table 6–2).

For the purpose of monitoring growth patterns in air traffic, ICAO has divided the world into six regions. The largest region in terms of international scheduled traffic, as measured in ton-kilometers, is Europe, the other two major areas being North America and the Asia-Pacific regions. Table 6–3 shows the regional distribution of scheduled air traffic, both domestic and international, and the shift in regional shares between 1978 and 1987. During this ten-year period, there was a remarkable increase in the share of scheduled international air traffic accounted for by the Asia-Pacific region: from 20.6 percent in 1978 to 28.2 percent in 1987. This shift in regional shares is explained in part by the rate of development of a number of Far East airlines and in part by the economic growth of this region relative to

Table 6–2
Development of Nonscheduled Traffic, 1978–87

| Year | Nonscheduled Traffic (Millions of Passenger-kilometers) | | | Scheduled Traffic | Nonscheduled Traffic as Percentage of Total |
	Nonscheduled Carriers	Scheduled Carriers	Total		
1978	70,600	41,100	111,700	384,800	22.5
1979	72,300	36,700	109,000	440,200	19.8
1980	59,600	43,100	102,700	466,500	18.0
1981	57,600	41,100	98,700	494,400	16.6
1982	64,900	40,600	105,500	496,500	17.5
1983	69,500	38,800	108,300	510,800	17.5
1984	75,200	40,600	115,800	555,300	17.3
1985	72,700	49,000	121,700	589,300	17.1
1986	63,900	69,900	133,800	602,400	18.2
1987[a]	75,900	81,300	157,200	685,400[a]	18.7

Source: International Civil Aviation Organization (ICAO), *Bulletin,* July 1982, p. 31; July 1987, p. 35; and the *Annual Report of the Council,* June 1988, p. 11.
[a]Preliminary.

Table 6–3
Regional Distribution of Scheduled Traffic, 1978–87

| Percentage of Total Tonne-kilometers Performed by Airlines Registered in Each Region | All Services | | International | | Domestic | |
	1987	1978	1987	1978	1987	1978
North America[a]	39.7	41.0	20.5	20.5	60.3	59.2
Europe	31.3	35.0	36.7	42.4	25.5	28.4
Asia and Pacific	18.8	13.5	28.2	20.6	8.7	7.2
Latin America and Caribbean	4.7	5.0	5.7	6.6	3.7	3.5
Middle East	3.2	3.0	5.3	5.6	0.9	0.8
Africa	2.3	2.5	3.6	4.3	0.9	0.9
ICAO World	100	100	100	100	100	100

Source: International Civil Aviation Organization (ICAO), *Annual Report of the Council: 1987* (Montreal: ICAO, June 1988), 8.
[a]Canada and United States only.

other regions because of the move to the Far East by major components of world industry.

Some airlines from the Asia-Pacific region have developed into large entities, their growth particularly impressive given their late start. Korean Air, for example, which began operations in late 1962, now ranks with such major airlines as Swissair and SAS. And even more dramatic is the growth of Singapore Airlines, which started in 1972 and now ranks among the world's leading airlines, comparable in size to KLM (The Netherlands), Qantas (Australia), and Air Canada.

The single largest international market in terms of passenger-kilometers flown is the North Atlantic, which in 1987 accounted for 27.4 percent of total international traffic. In terms of passengers carried, however, the largest international market consists of international routes within Europe. During 1987, 74 million passengers traveled within Europe, compared with 20 million passengers who traveled to and from North America and Europe. Table 6–4 shows a breakdown of the total world international passenger market by various IATA regions. Annual traffic volumes range from 74 million international passengers within Europe to virtually no international traffic between the Middle East and Mid America, that is, Central America and the Caribbean.

At the end of 1987, IATA member-airlines which, again, represent about three-fourths of all international airline operations—operated a fleet of some 5,600 aircraft. Jet wide-body equipment and jet standard-body equipment represented 24 percent and 60 percent of the aggregate fleet, respectively. (See table 6–5.) The average age of aircraft in the fleet is twelve years, and almost 1,300 jet airplanes and more than 300 nonjet airplanes are eighteen or more years old. The aged status of the international fleet and pending noise regulations affecting major airports may require airlines to make a substantial investment over the next several years to purchase new airplanes. Financing these new fleet requirements will be a principal challenge for carriers based in certain regions of the world. In contrast, a number of carriers in the Far East, such as Singapore Airlines, enjoy an advantageous position because of the young age of their fleets.

The majority of international airlines outside the United States are either completely or partially owned by their governments. Private ownership in non-U.S. international airlines is increasing, however, with respect to both the number of airlines and the percentage of private ownership in each airline; Swissair and Japan Air Lines are examples. The operations of state-owned airlines, domestic or international, reflect a wide spectrum of national interests, some of which extend far beyond the pure economics of airline operations: employment; balance of payments; tourism; the development of political, commercial, and social links with other regions; and so on. As a result, a number of airlines operate services that are not economically viable and therefore require state support. Since making a profit, though desirable, is not always the ultimate or even an essential goal for some international airlines, it is difficult to evaluate and compare airlines from the perspective of financial performance.

Although not all international airlines view profitability as their primary goal, the relative financial condition of the world's scheduled airlines is an important consideration. During the past ten years, the industry's net profit margin has varied from a high of 4.1 percent in 1978 to a low of −1.4 percent in 1982. (see table 6–6). There is, of course, wide variation in the financial performance of airlines based in different parts of the world. Table

Table 6–4
IATA International On-flight–Origin–Destination Traffic Statistics, 1987

Passengers (thousands) by Major Region Pairs (both directions combined)	Year 1987 Preliminary		Average Annual Changes 5-year
All Services	Number	± Change	1987/1982
North America–Middle America	13,132	22.3%	9.4%
North America–South America	3,179	6.2%	0.9%
North America–Middle East	849	16.5%	6.7%
North America–Europe	20,424	23.1%	7.4%
North America–Africa	175	− 34.6%	− 10.1%
North America–Far East	4,667	23.2%	10.0%
North America–Southwest Pacific	1,721	18.6%	8.4%
Within North America	7,801	23.1%	6.9%
Middle America–South America	644	3.1%	− 1.8%
Middle America–Middle East	—	—	
Middle America–Europe	1,363	24.7%	10.6%
Middle America–Africa	1	− 68.1%	− 50.0%
Middle America–Far East	14	− 8.1%	− 8.9%
Middle America–Southwest Pacific	—	—	
Within Middle America	1,404	63.6%	9.4%
South America–Middle East	17	20.0%	15.1%
South America–Europe	2,107	− 0.9%	2.8%
South America–Africa	66	− 17.6%	0.4%
South America–Far East	68	1.7%	17.5%
South America–Southwest Pacific	40	33.4%	17.9%
Within South America	2,369	− 0.5%	1.1%
Middle East–Europe	6,952	4.0%	3.7%
Middle East–Africa	3,965	6.0%	− 1.5%
Middle East–Far East	5,723	4.7%	5.9%
Middle East–Southwest Pacific	22	3.6%	9.8%
Within Middle East	4,784	− 0.1%	1.3%
Europe–Africa	13,109	5.6%	0.2%
Europe–Far East	4,997	16.4%	8.3%
Europe–Southwest Pacific	849	8.1%	4.4%
Within Europe	74,058	10.4%	5.4%
Africa–Far East	353	16.0%	1.4%
Africa–Southwest Pacific	44	− 12.1%	− 4.8%
Within Africa	2,958	1.0%	2.2%
Far East–Southwest Pacific	2,803	19.2%	8.5%
Within Far East	7,035	12.2%	5.5%
Within Southwest Pacific	2,616	12.6%	6.2%
Total OFOD—all services	190,311	12.2%	5.1%

Source: International Air Transport Association (IATA), *World Air Transport Statistics* (Geneva: IATA, June 1988), 30.

Table 6–5
IATA Members' Aircraft Fleet, 1987

Aircraft Type	1977 or Before	1978	1979	1980	1981	1982	1983	1984	1985	1986	1987	Total
A-300	23	7	14	28	35	40	18	23	2	3	4	197
A-310	—	—	—	—	—	5	23	20	17	9	10	84
B-747	240	27	45	46	37	16	10	7	16	25	11	480
B-767	—	—	—	—	3	19	32	16	10	19	23	122
DC-10	191	14	32	32	14	7	—	1	—	5	1	297
L-1011	86	2	5	11	21	10	6	1	—	—	—	142
B-707	136	—	—	—	—	—	—	—	—	—	—	136
B-727	772	71	90	93	65	16	7	8	—	—	—	1,122
B-737	320	21	39	52	52	48	25	16	50	91	74	788
B-757	—	—	—	—	—	8	16	8	10	9	5	56
DC-8	87	—	—	—	—	—	—	—	—	—	—	87
DC-9	454	10	29	11	4	—	—	—	—	—	—	508
MD-80	—	—	—	6	36	14	34	46	53	77	65	331
F-28	24	4	—	5	4	4	13	6	2	—	—	62
Other jets	135	13	22	6	13	18	17	12	6	6	5	253
Total jets	2,468	169	276	290	284	205	201	164	166	244	198	4,665
Propellers/ helicopters	497	23	38	42	41	34	24	34	68	59	74	934
All types	2,965	192	314	332	325	239	225	198	234	303	272	5,599

Source: International Air Transport Association (IATA), *World Air Transport Statistics* (Geneva: IATA, June 1988), 27.

Table 6–6
Operating and Net Results for Scheduled Airlines of ICAO Contracting States, 1977–87

Year	Operating Revenues U.S.$ (Millions)	Operating Expenses U.S.$ (Millions)	Operating Result Amount U.S.$ (Millions)	Operating Result Percentage of Operating Revenues	Net Result Amount U.S.$ (Millions)	Net Result Percentage of Operating Revenues	Direct Subsidies U.S.$ (Millions)	Income Taxes U.S.$ (Millions)
1977	50,344	47,715	2,628	5.2	1,656	3.3	127	−631
1978	58,769	55,669	3,100	5.3	2,412	4.1	116	−540
1979	70,755	70,019	736	1.0	588	0.8	69	−145
1980	87,676	88,310	−635	−0.7	−919	−1.0	166	−123
1981	92,992	93,684	−692	−0.7	−1,150	−1.2	76	9
1982	93,240	93,400	−160	−0.2	−1,300	−1.4	210	100
1983	98,300	96,200	2,100	2.1	−700	−0.7	380	−340
1984	105,400	100,300	5,100	4.8	2,000	1.9	235	−1,100
1985	112,200	108,100	4,100	3.7	2,100	1.9	220	−660
1986	124,600	120,000	4,600	3.7	1,500	1.2	280	−1,100
1987[a]	144,500	138,000	6,500	4.5	NA	NA	NA	NA

Source: Various annual reports of the International Civil Aviation Organization.
[a]1987 data preliminary.

Table 6–7
Variation in Revenue-Cost Ratios among Airlines, 1986

Route Groups (Short Title)	Average Revenue-Cost Ratio	Number of Airlines in this Analysis	Revenue-Cost Ratio Range				
			Less Than 0.7	0.7–0.9	0.9–1.1	1.1–1.3	Greater Than 1.3
			Number of Airlines				
I. All World International Routes	0.99	73	3	14	44	9	3
II. *International Route Groups*							
1. North–Central America	0.90	6		1	2	3	
2. Central America	—	2			2		
3. North America	0.90	12	1	5	5	1	
4. North–South America	1.10	13		2	6	3	2
5. South America	1.05	8		1	3	2	2
6. Europe	1.05	19	1	1	10	6	1
7. Middle East	1.15	5		1	2	1	1
8. Africa	0.90	7		3	2	2	
9. Europe–Middle East	0.90	20	2	10	6	1	1
10. Europe–Africa	0.95	24	2	7	8	4	3
11. North Atlantic	0.90	33	3	14	13	2	1
12. Mid Atlantic	0.95	13	2	3	6	1	
13. South Atlantic	1.05	12		3	7	2	
14. Asia/Pacific	1.05	18	1	1	10	4	2
15. Europe–Asia/Pacific	1.00	32	3	7	14	6	2
16. North/Mid Pacific	1.00	10		3	3	2	2
17. South Pacific	0.90	8		5	2	1	

Source: International Civil Aviation Organization (ICAO), *Regional Differences in Fares, Rates, and Costs for International Air Transport, 1986* (Montreal: ICAO, October 1988), 15.

6–7 shows, for example, the variation in the average revenue-to-cost ratio during 1986 for airlines operating in seventeen different parts of the world, the ratio varying from 0.85 to 1.10, with a ratio of less than 1 indicating that operating costs exceed revenues. This table also shows the variation in the financial performance of airlines within each of the seventeen route groups. Consider, for example, the airlines operating between Europe and the Asia-Pacific region. In 1986, thirty-two airlines, as a group, reported break-even operations—that is, revenues equaling costs. Included in this group, however, were three airlines whose revenues were less than 70 percent of costs and two airlines whose revenues exceeded costs by more than 30 percent.

Numerous factors account for the differences in financial performance among airlines based in different parts of the world. Affecting financial performance are factors like fare levels, competitive pressures, average length of haul, average size of airplane, average load factor, price of fuel, enroute facility charges, and travel agent commission rates. Tables 6–8 and 6–9 show the influence of these factors among the airlines operating in seventeen different route groups. For example, length of haul, which affects direct operating costs, varies from 652 kilometers for travel between and within Central America and the Caribbean to 5,119 kilometers for travel on the North and Mid Pacific (see table 6–8). Similarly, fuel costs range from 1.0 cents per passenger-kilometer for the North Atlantic to 2.7 cents per passenger-kilometer for Africa (see table 6–9). Some of these factors, such as the price of fuel, are outside the control of individual airlines. Then, too, movements in foreign exchange rates—beneficial to some airlines and detrimental to others—also affect the revenues and costs of international airlines. Figure 6–1 shows the foreign exchange rate development, relative to the U.S. dollar, between 1977 and 1987. Moreover, fluctuations in exchange rates have also altered travel patterns around the world, because of the changes in the purchasing power of different currencies.

The government ownership that characterizes the majority of non-U.S. airlines has both advantages and disadvantages for an airline so owned. In light of the industry's generally dismal net profit margin, the most obvious advantage is financial. In addition to providing direct subsidies, governments can furnish indirect subsidies, including exemption from various taxes, interest-free or guaranteed loans, generous mail revenues, exemption from customs duty on equipment and parts, and free or low-cost use of infrastructure facilities. Governments can also help in the acquisition of desirable fleets, traffic rights, and training facilities. On the negative side is state interference with commercial managerial decisions concerning employment, investment, routes, and tariffs. Ultimately, the degree of government involvement and the net benefit (or cost) of that involvement will vary from country to country.

Government ownership is a critical factor underlying the ability of many international carriers to withstand financial losses year after year. Although no government wants its airline to experience losses, some combination of

Table 6–8
Basic Operational Data and Financial Results for Scheduled Passenger Services by International Route Group, 1986

Route Group	Number of Airlines (1) No.	Percentage of World's International Traffic (Available Seat-kilometers) (2) %	Average Length of Flight Stages (3) Km	Average Number of Seats per Aircraft (4) No.	Average Passenger Load Factor (5) %	Average Revenue per Passenger-kilometer (6) US cents	Average Passenger Costs per Passenger-kilometer (7) US cents	Ratio Revenue/Costs (8) —
I. All World International Routes	208	100.0	1,680	241	63	7.42	7.49	0.99
II. International Route Groups								
1. Between North America and Central America/Caribbean	33	3.2	1,184	187	63	7.2	7.8	0.90
2. Between and within Central America and the Caribbean	19	0.2	652	136	—	—	—	—
3. Between Canada, Mexico, and the United States	29	5.5	1,021	159	60	6.3	7.1	0.90
4. Between North America/Central America/Caribbean and South America	31	3.2	2,038	245	57	7.8	7.2	1.10
5. Local South America	15	0.6	913	152	57	9.4	9.0	1.05
6. Local Europe	48	9.4	816	133	61	15.6	14.5	1.05
7. Local Middle East	16	1.2	873	180	57	14.9	12.7	1.15
8. Local Africa	30	0.4	855	135	55	10.8	12.0	0.90
9. Between Europe and Middle East	42	4.4	2,086	215	54	9.3	10.2	0.90
10. Between Europe/Middle East and Africa	64	5.0	2,703	233	62	8.2	8.5	0.95
11. North Atlantic	47	24.6	3,658	308	61	5.8	6.3	0.90
12. Mid Atlantic	20	2.0	3,638	260	64	5.5	5.9	0.95
13. South Atlantic	19	1.8	3,488	254	70	7.0	6.6	1.05
14. Local Asia/Pacific	38	8.0	1,608	271	70	7.5	7.2	1.05
15. Between Europe/Middle East/Africa and Asia/Pacific	57	17.5	3,457	304	67	6.1	6.1	1.00
16. North and Mid Pacific	18	10.5	5,119	325	67	5.9	5.8	1.00
17. South Pacific	13	2.5	4,392	317	67	5.0	5.5	0.90

Source: International Civil Aviation Organization (ICAO), *Regional Differences in Fares, Rates, and Costs for International Air Transport,* 1986

Table 6–9
Estimated Passenger Costs per Passenger-kilometer, by Cost Item, 1986

Route Groups (Short Title)	Total Operating Costs (Sum of Columns 1–9)	Aircraft Operating Costs		Landing and Associated		Other Operating Costs				
		Aircraft Operating Costs Excluding Fuel and Oil 1	Aircraft Fuel and Oil 2	Landing and Associated Airport Charges 3	En Route Facility Charges 4	Station Expenses 5	Passenger Services 6	Commission 7	Ticketing, Sales, and Promotion 8	General, Administrative, and Miscellaneous 9
I. All										
US cents	7.49	2.07	1.15	0.27	0.14	0.81	1.01	0.75	0.78	0.51
Percentage of total costs	100.0	27.6	15.3	3.7	1.9	10.8	13.5	10.0	10.4	6.8
II. International Route Groups (U.S. cents)										
1. North–Central America	7.8	2.2	1.2	0.2	0.0	1.2	0.8	0.7	0.7	0.8
2. Central America	—	—	—	—	—	—	—	—	—	—
3. North America	7.1	2.0	1.1	0.1	0.0	1.4	0.9	0.6	0.5	0.5
4. North–South America	7.2	1.9	1.4	0.2	0.1	0.7	0.8	0.9	0.8	0.4
5. South America	9.0	1.9	1.9	0.5	0.3	0.8	0.9	1.2	1.2	0.3
6. Europe	14.5	3.7	1.4	1.1	0.6	2.2	1.7	1.4	1.9	0.5
7. Middle East	12.7	3.9	1.7	0.4	0.1	1.4	1.3	1.4	1.1	1.4
8. Africa	12.0	3.4	2.7	0.6	0.2	1.6	0.9	0.9	0.8	0.9
9. Europe–Middle East	10.2	3.2	1.4	0.4	0.3	1.0	1.3	0.8	0.9	0.9
10. Europe–Africa	8.5	2.3	1.6	0.3	0.2	0.8	1.1	0.7	0.8	0.7
11. North Atlantic	6.3	1.8	1.0	0.1	0.1	0.7	0.9	0.5	0.6	0.6
12. Mid Atlantic	5.9	1.6	1.2	0.2	0.2	0.5	0.8	0.4	0.6	0.5
13. South Atlantic	6.6	1.7	1.3	0.2	0.2	0.5	0.9	0.7	0.9	0.2
14. Asia/Pacific	7.2	2.2	1.0	0.3	0.1	0.7	1.0	0.8	0.8	0.3
15. Europe–Asia/Pacific	6.1	1.7	1.0	0.2	0.1	0.4	1.0	0.5	0.7	0.5
16. North/Mid Pacific	5.8	1.6	1.0	0.1	0.1	0.3	0.9	1.0	0.5	0.3
17. South Pacific	5.5	1.5	0.9	0.1	0.0	0.5	0.8	0.7	0.6	0.4

Source: International Civil Aviation Organization (ICAO), Regional Differences in Fares, Rates, and Costs for International Air Transport, 1986 (Montreal: ICAO, October 1988), 12.

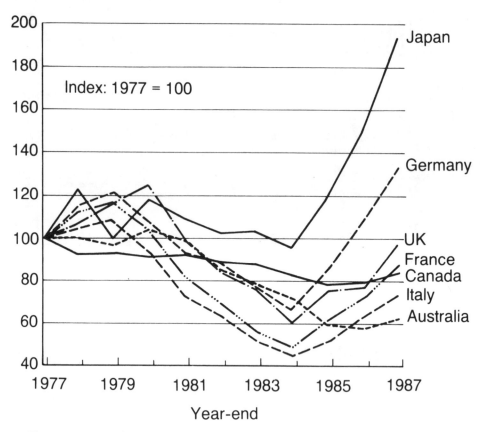

Figure 6–1. Exchange Rate Development

Source: International Air Transport Association (IATA), *World Air Transport Statistics* (Geneva: IATA, June 1988), 15.

nonfinancial national objectives may simply be given higher priority. As a consequence, historically the industry has rarely achieved a level of profitability that could be considered adequate in terms of the industry's risk characteristics or its need to replace equipment. It is possible, however, that the industry's financial performance could be improved by the trends discussed in the following section.

Trends and Implications

In recent years, several factors have caused the international air transportation industry to undergo significant structural and operational changes. Some of these factors are external to the industry, among them (a) a rising global interest in the free enterprise system as a means of obtaining faster economic and social development, (b) the Pacific gaining on the Atlantic as a center of economic might, (c) discussions relating to the desirability of including services in the General Agreement on Tariffs and Trade (GATT), and (d) consumer demands, at least in more mature markets, for lower fares and broader price/service options. Other factors are internal to the industry, among them (a) the liberalization movement, (b) the increasing use of automation in the marketing process, (c) the trend toward privatization, and (d) the implementation of operating restrictions on aircraft that do not meet Stage 2 (chapter 2) requirements. This section addresses the potential impact of three internal factors: liberalization, automation, and privatization.

Liberalization

The most dramatic changes in commercial air transportation during the past ten years have resulted from airline deregulation in the United States. Despite the initial general rejection of U.S. aviation policies by the world aviation community, a number of countries have begun to investigate the merits of a more liberal regulatory environment. In Europe, for example, despite the disparity of opinion among governments regarding the benefits and feasibility of airline deregulation, the tide is turning toward a more liberally regulated environment as a result of pressure from four main sources: consumer groups; charter and regional airlines; individual nations, such as Great Britain and the Netherlands; and multilateral entities, such as the ECAC, the twelve-member European Community (EC), and the European Court of Justice.[17] The pressures exerted by these parties, combined with the threat of significant competitive incursions by U.S. mega-carriers, have already started the movement toward a more procompetitive air transportation system in Europe.

Characterizing the liberalization movement are the development of regional services, growing implementation of the zone concept for tariffs, and more freedom in bilateral agreements for capacity deviations and pooling arrangements, especially with respect to the division of revenue. Further changes are likely to take place as a result of external developments, such as (a) the decision by the European Court of Justice that competition rules of the Treaty of Rome apply to air transport; (b) the Single European Act, signed by the twelve nations in the EC, which will facilitate passage of proposals promoting competition within the EC; and (c) the decision by the twelve EC states to establish, by 1992, a borderless intra-European market— an area without internal frontiers, in which members' goods, citizens, services, and capital can move freely. The industry is now beginning to regroup, as evidenced by the acquisition of British Caledonian by British Airways; the decision by SAS to form a partnership, including financial equity, with another international airline; and the "marketing merger" between British Airways and United Airlines, by which the two airlines will share flight-destination codes and facilities at selected airports.

Individual countries are also beginning to respond to these changes. In the United Kingdom, the aviation regulatory authority has, since the 1970s, been using different methods to decrease the burden of regulation. As a result of the desire to relax regulatory control, for example, inclusive tour charters in Europe were allowed to operate without specific route and price control, cargo charter services were liberalized, and regulations relating to domestic scheduled services were progressively relaxed. While licensing of competitors on existing routes has a long history in the United Kingdom, the process has accelerated in recent years. According to a recent study by the United Kingdom Civil Aviation Authority, an increase in competition on main domestic routes produced positive benefits for passengers in terms of quality of service and lower fares.[18] Based on the experience of the British, it can be argued that the gradual approach to liberalization has merit in that it does not suddenly disrupt the existing structure and it allows the appropriate government agencies to monitor public reaction to regulatory change.

To date—and with the exception of the United States—Canada has moved furthest toward a more liberalized environment. The Canadian government studied the pros and cons of U.S. deregulation for several years and in 1984 decided to initiate its first phase of regulatory reform by introducing the "freedom to move" policy. This policy led to (a) the cancellation of the rule that had previously limited intra-Canada competitors to 25 percent of Air Canada's route mileage and (b) the opening to competition of the most heavily traveled routes in southern Canada. The immediate reaction of the airlines to this new policy was similar to that of domestic carriers in the United States to U.S. deregulation—mergers and acquisitions. Ten years ago, there were three groups of airlines in Canada: Air Canada and Canadian Pacific Airlines; five smaller airlines, each confined to a regional territory; and "third-level" airlines, connecting small communities to one another and to larger airports. Today there are essentially only two large airlines: Air Canada and Canadian Airlines International. The latter was formed through the merger of Canadian Pacific Airlines and Pacific Western Airlines; these two airlines had previously acquired the other four regional airlines.

The government of Australia has also examined alternative, more liberal regulatory frameworks. In 1985, it commissioned an independent review of the economic regulation of domestic aviation (the "May Review"). This review, which lasted almost two years, was critical of the existing regulatory regime, particularly of the Airlines Agreement Act of 1981, which ensured that government-owned Australian Airlines and privately owned Ansett be the only two airlines to provide scheduled passenger service on trunk routes. Under this regulatory policy, the two airlines were required to charge only those fares approved by the government and to comply with the Airlines Equipment Act of 1958, under which (a) the government determined the capacity to be provided by the two airlines and (b) the two airlines were required to share capacity. The May Review issued its report in 1987, identifying five options for future government policy on aviation, ranging from status quo to deregulation. The government selected the option of more or less full deregulation and has given the three-year required notice for terminating the Airlines Agreement Act of 1981. Although deregulation will allow additional competition in domestic operations, no change is expected in the role of Qantas—Australia's flag carrier. The decision not to allow additional competition with Qantas from another Australian carrier is the result of the relatively small passenger traffic base in Australia and the existing competition provided by a large number of foreign carriers serving Australia.

Even Japan, a strong opponent of deregulation, is being nudged a little further toward some form of deregulation. Until recently, Japan Air Lines (JAL) was the only national carrier authorized by the Japanese government to operate overseas services. In 1982, All Nippon, the second-largest carrier in Japan, was authorized to offer limited charter services to some Southeast Asian countries, China, Guam, and Saipan. Nippon Cargo Airlines, owned by a consortium of shipping entities and All Nippon Airways, also received authority to operate cargo flights to the United States. In 1985, All Nippon's authority was expanded to include scheduled service to the United States, and services began on the Tokyo–Los Angeles route in July 1986. Progress in relaxing the domestic regulatory environment has been slow, however, even though organizations like Japan's Fair Trade Commission advocate the introduction of competition in the air transportation industry. Given that JAL now faces competition on international routes from other Japanese carriers, it appears likely that JAL will obtain additional lucrative domestic routes. Such a move would lead the Japanese government further toward deregulation.

Developing countries, such as those in Africa and South America, continue to oppose the deregulation movement. The perspective of many of these nations is that they do not have the luxury of multiple airlines offering competitive service that would be ready to take over abandoned markets were a competing airline to go bankrupt. Further, in many of these countries investment in an airline tends to be at the expense of other desirable public expenditures, rather than to provide a return on investment commensurate with the risks. In this context, it is generally the case that developing nations are extremely concerned when developed nations promote open-skies policies and deregulation. Nevertheless, at least some developing nations and their airlines are beginning to realize—and with encouragement from the financial lending institutions—that it is no longer a question of *whether* government and airline policies should change but of when and to what extent they will change.[19]

Automation

The role of automation as a competitive marketing tool is the second most significant trend in the international airline industry. Once simply a tool to improve operational efficiency and telecommunications (which meant either telephone lines or links to reservation systems), automation has begun to be used as a managerial tool to help solve the airline industry's most critical problem: its inability to match supply with demand. Computer reservation systems (CRSs), coupled with data networks providing critical information in a timely manner, are proving extremely valuable in solving this problem through cost-effective market segmentation and pricing/revenue management systems. Additionally, U.S. airlines that own their own CRSs—for example, American and United—have been using automation and information technology to gain a competitive edge in the distribution system. Because a large percentage of international travel arrangements are made through travel agents —as much as 90 percent for some international airlines—the airline that owns the CRS system being used by a group of travel agencies is able to capture a disproportionate share of business from the agencies and additional revenue in the form of user fees.

Once the major U.S. airlines began to market their CRSs outside the United States, large foreign airlines, particularly those based in Europe, became concerned that they might lose control of the international distribution system, the activities of which include dispensing flight information, booking reservations, collecting fares, and issuing tickets. As a result, two groups of European airlines initiated the development of their own CRS consortium. One system, known as Amadeus, is being developed in cooperation with Texas Air, which now owns the CRS System One developed initially by Eastern Airlines. Amadeus is not planning to acquire an equity interest in System One; rather, System One will simply be a vendor of technology. The other system, known as Galileo, is being developed in cooperation with Covia, a subsidiary of United Airlines. Unlike the members of Amadeus, Galileo's members do have an equity interest in Covia, which operates Apollo, the CRS developed by United. The airlines based in the Asia-Pacific region are also in the process of forming consortia to develop competitive CRSs. At present, one system in the planning stage, called Abacus, involves an agreement for technical support with PARS, a CRS owned jointly by TWA and Northwest.

The growing interest in the development of CRSs is based on the premise that such a system is vital for controlling travel agency business, which in turn is important to an airline's success. Marketing power, however, is only one ramification of the trend to develop CRSs. A related development is the establishment of four or five highly competitive global alliances: Whereas Amadeus and Galileo have already divided the airlines in Europe into two groups, airlines in the Asia-Pacific region are similarly beginning to segregate into different alliance groups. Moreover, consumer groups, particularly in North America and Europe, are raising concerns about the role of the CRS in such areas as the relationship between travel agent and airline, CRS bias, and restricted access. Consumer groups question, for example, the loyalty of a travel agent who is receiving a higher commission from an airline for using a particular system. CRS bias refers to the manner in which an airline's schedule, relative to competitors' schedules, is displayed on the computer system used by a travel agent. And restricted access refers to the situation in which a travel agent using a particular CRS cannot sell seats on certain airlines that have refused—usually for competitive reasons—to distribute their seats through the system. Thus, it appears that a fierce competitive battle within the more liberalized international environment is being fought over the issue of CRSs, an issue that now includes the interests of consumers as well as airlines.[20]

Privatization

The trends toward liberalization and automation are forcing international airlines to become more efficient and more innovative competitors. Some governments that own their national airlines believe that one way to make their airlines even more efficient is to reduce the government's share of equity in the airline; it is assumed that greater efficiency and improved profitability will result from reducing a national airline's financial dependence on its government. In recent years, then, countries in Europe, Asia, and other parts of the world have taken steps to privatize a larger share of the ownership in their airlines, examples being British Airways, Singapore Airlines, and Japan Air Lines. Privatization, however, is no simple process. Indeed, it is an exceedingly complex one, raising some very thorny issues and questions. For example: Since many international airlines are instruments of national policy, would the governments of inefficient airlines allow the national airlines to fail? If privatization efforts require displacing large numbers of employees in order to gain efficiency, are these governments willing to accept the political ramifications of reductions in the labor force? And even in the case of national airlines that become efficient as a result of the privatization movement, to what extent will governments force their airlines to serve routes that are in the national interest but unprofitable?

Such issues and questions, many of which have not yet been resolved, suggest that in general, governments will always retain some percentage of equity in their national airlines to ensure that national interests are not overlooked. Government's share of equity will vary widely from one national airline to another. At one extreme, in those cases in which the national airline is clearly a survivor whatever the environment—for example, in the case of Air France, British Airways, Lufthansa, and Japan Air Lines—the number of politically motivated routes are minimal, and the nation has a large origin-destination traffic base, the government is likely to privatize its national airline, completely in some cases and partially in other cases. At the other extreme, in those cases in which the national airline is operated more for political reasons than for commercial purposes, the government is likely to retain a majority share of equity in the airline.

The trends discussed in this chapter, coupled with the ongoing development of a global economy, have already begun to influence the market structure, performance, and conduct of the international air transport industry. Evidence in this regard can be seen in increased merger activity, the decision by various carriers to form multilateral alliances, and the decision on the part of many governments to increase private ownership so that their airlines can become more efficient and better able to enter into cooperative arrangements. Unlike changes in the U.S. domestic airline industry, however, changes in the international arena will take place more slowly and will not be so extensive, because of the interrelationship that exists in many countries between airline operations and national interests. For example, since it is more difficult and in some cases almost impossible to merge international airlines, they are more likely to form cooperative arrangements to achieve some of the benefits of size, such as economies of scale and marketing power. These kinds of cooperative arrangements, sometimes called marketing mergers, as opposed to true ownership participation, will enable the resulting "multinational airlines" to undertake joint marketing programs, share flight codes, and develop CRSs in partnership while maintaining national identities.

Notes

1. D.W. Freer, "A Convention Is Signed and ICAN Is Born: 1919 to 1926," (part 3 of a twelve-part series on international civil aviation), *International Civil Aviation Organization Bulletin*, May 1986, 44–46.

2. International Air Transport Association (IATA), *Membership Services Directory* (Geneva, Switzerland: IATA, May 1986), sec. 1, p. 3.

3. D.W. Freer, "Regionalism Is Asserted: ICAN's Global Prospects Fade— 1926 to 1943" (part 4 of a twelve-part series on international civil aviation), *International Civil Aviation Organization Bulletin*, June 1986, 66–68.

4. Ibid.

5. D.W. Freer, "Enroute to Chicago: 1943 to 1944" (part 5 of a twelve-part series on international civil aviation), *International Civil Aviation Organization Bulletin*, July 1986, 39–41.

6. D.W. Freer, "Chicago Conference (1944): U.K.-U.S. Policy Split Revealed" (part 6 of a twelve-part series on international civil aviation), *International Civil Aviation Organization Bulletin*, August 1986, 22–24.

7. D.W. Freer, "PICAO Years: 1945 to 1947" (part 8 of a twelve-part series on international civil aviation), *International Civil Aviation Organization Bulletin*, October 1986, 36–39.

8. R. Doganis, *Flying Off Course: The Economics of International Airlines* (London: George Allen and Unwin, 1985), 257.

9. Ibid., 30.

10. N.K. Taneja, *U.S. International Aviation Policy* (Lexington, Mass.: Lexington Books, 1980), 21.

11. Doganis, *Flying Off Course*, 52.

12. International Air Transport Association (IATA), *Membership Services*, sec. 2, pp. 9–10.

13. International Civil Aviation Organization (ICAO), *Third Air Transport Conference* (Montreal: ICAO, January 1986), 1.

14. International Civil Aviation Organization (ICAO), *ICAO Bulletin*, July 1987, 28.

15. International Air Transport Association (IATA), *World Air Transport Statistics* (Geneva, Switzerland: IATA, June 1988), 20.

16. International Civil Aviation Organization (ICAO), *ICAO Bulletin*, July 1987, 35–36.

17. S. Wheatcroft and G. Lipman, *The Air Transport in a Competitive European Market* (London: The Economist, 1986).

18. The U.K. Civil Aviation Authority (CAA), *Competition on the Main Domestic Trunk Routes* (London: CAA, March 1987).

19. N.K. Taneja, *The International Airline Industry: Trends, Issues, and Challenges* (Lexington, Mass.: Lexington Books, 1988), chap. 5.

20. R. Katz, "Passenger Power,"*Airline Business*, May 1988, 36–41.

7
The Air-Cargo Industry

A s was shown in chapter 1, the early operators of civil aviation enterprises relied heavily on subsidized airmail contracts to fund the development of passenger services. Over the past fifty years, however, passenger service has grown so rapidly that it now overshadows air-cargo operations. Moreover, the air-cargo business—freight, various kinds of express delivery services, and airmail—is minute in relation to the volumes of cargo transported by other modes, particularly by rail and shipping. Yet, air cargo is poised to become a much more significant portion of the aviation industry. This conclusion is based on recent regulatory changes internationally—for example, deregulation of the airline industry in the United States and passage of the Single European Act, which will significantly liberalize commercial air service in Europe by 1992—that will enable the air-cargo industry to be more responsive to the needs of the marketplace. Too, the needs of the marketplace itself have been changing: Just-in-time inventory policies require timely deliveries of critical supplies; miniaturization and automation have increased the need to transport fragile and expensive, high-technology components; the transfer of domestic manufacturing capacity to foreign sites has increased the demand for air-cargo services; and shifts in the patterns of employment across industries are also expected to contribute to the growth of air cargo. Another trend that will bolster air cargo is an increase in the number of firms that now view the attributes of shipping by air as a competitive edge in producing and marketing their products and services. This chapter provides an introduction to the air-cargo component of the aviation industry. Specifically, this chapter discusses the characteristics of the airfreight market and its services, the structure of the industry, and the importance of the air-cargo infrastructure.

Market and Services

Market Characteristics

In 1987, the world air-cargo market, excluding the air-cargo movements in the USSR, amounted to some 60 billion ton-kilometers. U.S. airlines transported about a third of world air-cargo shipments; non-U.S. airlines transported the balance. By contrast, total world air-cargo in 1960 was only 3.2 billion ton-kilometers, of which almost 60 percent was carried by U.S. airlines.[1] The increase in market share by non-U.S. airlines reflects the growing importance of third-country carriage—for example, the participation of a German airline in the United States–France market or the participation of a Japanese airline in markets between the United States and countries in the Far East other than Japan.

Within the U.S. air-cargo industry, the express package business has been growing at a phenomenal rate compared with that of heavy airfreight and airmail. Whereas in 1983, for example, domestic small/express package air traffic revenues were $2.8 billion on 118 million shipments, in 1987 revenues were $5.2 billion on 292 million shipments. These figures, provided by the Air Transport Association of America (ATA), are based on domestic operations of airlines reporting to the ATA, freight forwarders that operate their own aircraft, and the U.S. Postal Service.

Not only is the airfreight market smaller than that for passenger transportation, but other characteristics of the two markets are also quite different. It is the existence of such differences, as highlighted below, that explains the unique nature of airfreight marketing and operations.

1. Each individual air-cargo shipment generally makes a one-way journey, whereas most passengers travel on a round-trip basis. This difference leads to the "backhaul" problem—that is, finding suitable cargo to fill the airplane for the return flight. To prevent the inefficient use of resources that would result from underutilization of capacity on return flights, carriers often resort to creative pricing policies to attract backhaul business.

2. Unlike the passenger market, the freight market is heterogeneous. Shipments vary in size, shape, weight, fragility, and value. Consequently, the rate structure for airfreight is even more complicated than that for passenger fares.

3. Compared with passenger service, airfreight is "nonambulatory," that is, passive. Assembling, loading, unloading, and dispensing airfreight requires a wide range of ground-handling services, whereas passenger transportation is self-handling.

4. In contrast to passenger activity, a significant percentage of freight movement takes place during the late evening hours to allow close coordination with the normal daytime business activities of the shipper and the receiver. Unfortunately, the need for late-night aircraft departures creates noise problems and some airports have implemented curfews that restrict the in- and outbound flow of airfreight.

5. In the freight transportation industry, there is some intermodal competition among airplanes, trucks, trains, and ships at all haul lengths. In passenger transportation, intermodal competition decreases as length of haul increases and is virtually nonexistent across the oceans.

6. In airfreight transportation, routing is not as important as it is in passenger transportation, so long as the freight arrives according to the promised delivery schedule. Therefore, it is not uncommon for freight shipments to be sent hundreds of miles in the wrong direction—for example, to a carrier's hub—before being sent on to its ultimate destination. Although such routing flexibility benefits the air carriers, it also increases competition among carriers because of the existence of multiple routings between various origins and destinations.

7. Whereas passenger transportation is characterized by a two-party transaction involving the passenger and the airline, freight shipments are multiparty transactions involving packers, ground-transportation companies, insurance brokers, warehousers, and customs agencies.

While reading the following discussion on the airfreight market, it is important to keep in mind the preceding seven characteristics. The airfreight business is much more complex and the opportunities more challenging than merely finding available space on scheduled passenger flights.

Today, all kinds of commodities move by air—electronic equipment, chemicals, auto parts, fruits, vegetables, medical supplies, live animals, artwork, and clothing. Historically, the total market for airfreight, including express delivery service, involved three broad categories: (a) emergency traffic, (b) perishable traffic, and (c) traffic that could be diverted from some other mode of transportation. *Emergency freight* is highly sensitive to time, which implies for the receiver a significant opportunity cost if the freight is not available or delivered on time. Typical emergency freight shipments arise from such common occurrences as a shutdown of manufacturing operations because a critical part is broken and the threat of lost sales from a large order that exceeds on-site inventory. The important characteristics of emergency freight are that (a) it is not planned and (b) from the viewpoint of the receiver, the cost of transportation is small in relation to the opportunity cost of not receiving the goods as quickly as possible. Over the years, air carriers have developed an image as transporters of emergency goods. Since an emergency can occur at any time and in any place, airfreight operators hoping to attract emergency freight business must offer services to and from a multitude of cities, at a high level of frequency, and with sufficient space available to accommodate last-minute requests. It is generally assumed that the future growth potential of this segment of the airfreight market is limited, since nearly all emergency shipments are already moving by air.[2]

Perishable freight traffic is also sensitive to time, but unlike emergency freight traffic, it is planned. The perishability of the goods may be physical, as in cut flowers, fruit, or fresh fish, or related to the product's demand, as in magazines and fashionable clothes. Although the cost of transportation is more significant to the receiver of perishable versus emergency freight, price is still not the prime consideration in deciding whether or not to ship by air. The extent to which a shipper or a consignee (that is, the receiver of the shipped goods, such as a wholesaler) is willing to pay a premium price for air transportation of perishable freight depends largely on the extent to which the ultimate customer is willing to absorb the added cost of shipment by air in the form of higher prices.

Freight that can be diverted to the air mode, principally from trucks and ships, is planned, but it is more sensitive to pricing than emergency or perishable freight is. However, for freight that is diverted to air, either the *total* cost for using the air system must be less than the total distribution cost for other modes or the shipper/consignee must perceive some other significant competitive advantage in air shipment that can be converted into increased profits. When analyzing the potential of diverted traffic, airfreight operators examine total distribution costs, including inventory carrying costs and transportation costs.[3] On the revenue side, the analysis takes into account such factors as the ability to broaden the market base and the ability to sell the product at a premium price. This particular category of airfreight represents significant growth potential for air-cargo carriers and suppliers.

Although the express category of air cargo, consisting of small packages, letters, and envelopes, has been around for decades, it was not exploited by the industry until about the mid-1970s. Since then, this category has grown rapidly. Express delivery is a premium-priced business that requires swift, reliable, door-to-door service. The threat of product substitution from electronic mail and electronic transmission of documents is likely to slow the growth of express delivery to some degree. Nevertheless, because of the potential size of this business and its comparatively high yield, express delivery is expected to become an even more significant source of revenue and profits relative to the traditional airfreight segment and the passenger market.

Air-Cargo Services

Airlines offer a variety of air-cargo services. Some are dependent on time—same day, overnight, second day, and so forth—while others include services provided on the ground, such as door-to-door service. Goods to be shipped—consignments—can be tendered in either shippers' containers or carriers' containers. Shipments can be given directly to the airlines or to freight forwarders that provide additional services, such as consolidation, pickup and delivery, documentation, and customs clearance. Many combination carriers, or those transporting both passengers and cargo, are expanding their services in an effort to attract additional air-cargo business. The implementation of door-to-door services; the development of alternative price/service options, such as lower price for second-day delivery; the simplification of tariffs; and the pursuit of retail customers on a direct-sale basis, bypassing intermediaries such as freight forwarders, are examples of these expanded services.[4]

Over the years, the industry has attempted to identify the common attributes of products that can be cost-effectively shipped by air. Although there is no single, unique set of such attributes, the industry does consider the value of a commodity, per unit weight, to be one important criterion for determining air eligibility: The higher the value per unit weight, the greater the merits of shipping by air. In general terms, some air carriers suggest that goods must be worth $10 per pound to justify space on an airplane,[5] a line of reasoning that is justified on at least two counts. First, because air transportation costs are higher than those of surface modes, it is easier to pass those higher costs through to customers if the value of the commodity is high. Second, the higher the value of a commodity, the greater the total benefit derived from transporting it by air, including lower inventory costs, less capital tied up in on-site storage, and minimized losses from damage and pilferage.

Although the value of a commodity continues to be key in determining air eligibility, the industry has also identified other important product characteristics, such as density, fragility, time sensitivity, market growth rate, perishability, shipment size, and shipment weight. Using data pertaining to a full range of characteristics, cargo operators attempt to identify air-eligible commodities and alternative ways to market their services to meet shipper needs and requirements.[6] Cargo operators demonstrate to specific businesses, for example, how their financial performance can be improved by using air transportation based on the concept of total distribution cost (TDC), which takes into account all costs related to the distribution system, including inventory and transportation costs. Inventory costs include the cost of holding inventory in storage and the cost of in-transit goods; whereas storage costs include the actual value of inventories and the associated costs of warehousing, in-transit goods tie up capital, preventing a firm from realizing its goal of obtaining early cash recovery. For some commodities, the use of air transportation can reduce some of these inventory costs sufficiently to offset the somewhat higher cost of air transportation. By integrating air cargo into a TDC analysis, airlines have shown that total distribution costs for selected businesses can be reduced significantly, from about one-third of a finished product's total cost to less than one-quarter.[7]

Use of the TDC concept has convinced some shippers to broaden their focus from the objective of simply minimizing transportation costs to that of improving the company's bottom line. By using the more expensive air mode, many shippers are able to increase profits either by expanding into new markets or by charging a premium price that certain segments of the marketplace are willing to pay. These shippers rely on the theory of cost-effectiveness as a basis for marketing. In a market where competition is intense and time is short, it is important to balance supply and demand quickly to take advantage of short-lived market opportunities. The rapid shipment of supply is best accomplished by airfreight, even if surface modes offer lower costs. Consider, for example, the retail clothing business. Some ready-to-wear clothes have a very short life, and unless the store is able to obtain the garments while they are in style and demand, it is generally forced to liquidate them at a reduced selling price. Consequently, there is pressure to place these garments on the selling floor as quickly as possible. In such a case, airfreight—with its garments-on-hangers service—can help a clothier increase its profit even though the cost of air transportation is higher than that of slower modes. In this context, airfreight has been viewed as a cost-effective merchandising strategy.

Drawing upon its successful use of the TDC approach, the air-cargo industry has begun to investigate whether air cargo can be integrated beyond the distribution process, into the actual manufacturing process. This broader approach to marketing air-cargo services is consistent with the expanded role of logistics management. Historically, the management in charge of logistics in a manufacturing enterprise dealt with two basic aspects of distribution: movement (transportation) and storage (warehousing and inventory). Today, the responsibilities of logistics management have expanded considerably and include a more formal and complex liaison with other corporate functions, such as marketing, finance, and production, as well as interface with customers and vendors. Consequently, logistics management is now a more integral part of the total planning process.[8]

Capitalizing on the broader role of the logistics function, air-cargo operators have begun to investigate the potential role air cargo can play in the "just-in-time" concept of inventory management. When capital was inexpensive and transportation services were limited in scope (in terms of speed, reliability, network size, and so forth), manufacturers accumulated large warehouse inventories of raw materials, parts, and supplies to keep their production lines going. In recent years, capital has become significantly more expensive and certain manufacturers have begun to appreciate the flexibility, speed, and reliability with which air cargo can deliver the raw materials, components, and so forth, that feed the production process. Consequently, manufacturers are coordinating the complementary functions of production and inventory control, which enhances overall company efficiency. These manufacturers work with air-cargo operators to ensure that parts and materials are delivered at the right place immediately before they are needed in the production process (just-in-time). Thus, for some manufacturers, air-cargo transportation has become an integral component of the production line.

In recent years, a substantial increase in multinational manufacturing and distribution has made the role of air cargo more vital.[9] Increasingly, companies are searching the worldwide marketplace for lower-cost raw materials, components, and production facilities in order to gain competitive advantage and/or to meet the needs of particular market segments, and air cargo is proving to be a key element of this global strategy. Among the many familiar examples of this globalization strategy are the jazzy fashion house

Esprit and the U.S. automobile manufacturer General Motors. In an effort to make its products stand out among many competing brands, Esprit buys uniquely designed plastic shoe boxes in Brazil. But because Esprit's high-fashion shoes have a short shelf life, the boxes are transported by air to Taiwan, where Esprit shoes are made. In Taiwan, the shoes are then loaded into the Brazilian-made boxes and shipped by air to San Francisco for distribution.[10] At General Motors, the company has integrated air cargo into the production and distribution of its top-of-the-line automobile, the $55,000 Allante. Car bodies produced by a firm in Italy are transported by a Luft Hansa Boeing 747 from Turin to Detroit, where the chassis and drivetrain assembly are completed. On the return trip, the Boeing 747 freighters carry Allante subassemblies and other auto parts for GM customers in Europe. Air cargo thus makes it possible for GM to (a) effectively extend its production line more than 3,000 miles; (b) reduce in-transit time to less than a day, versus three weeks by ship; (c) substantially reduce in-transit damage; and (d) keep its delivery schedule short, thereby increasing its responsiveness to market demand.[11] Lower in-transit inventory carrying costs and fewer losses from goods damaged in transit more than offset the higher cost of air transportation and result in a net saving to the company.

Prospects

During the next ten years, the growth in air cargo is expected to remain strong as a result of four trends. First, manufacturers increasingly are moving away from large-scale, single-site, heavy manufacturing facilities and toward smaller, specialized facilities. Moreover, manufacturers in the industrialized world are turning away from heavy products, such as sheet metal, and toward lighter, more compact products, such as computers and telecommunications equipment. Because of their size, density, and value, the miniaturized components for these products are more likely to move by air. Semiconductor chips made by Texas Instruments in Lubbock, Texas, for example, are flown to Singapore for processing, and the finished products are then flown back to Texas to be put into telecommunications equipment.[12] Second, as noted earlier, companies around the world are integrating air cargo into their manufacturing and distribution systems to take advantage of the speed, predictability, and dependability of air transportation. Third, the trend toward a global economy is expected to lead to an increasing need for the speed of express services. And fourth, increased competition in the air-cargo industry, arising from the partial deregulation of other modes, a proliferation of air-cargo carriers, and an increase in air-cargo services provided by passenger carriers, has resulted in average load factors for freight in the lower hold of combination carriers—that is, the empty space beneath the passenger compartment—that are well below passenger load factors. Consequently, there have been a widespread reduction in air-cargo prices and intensive efforts to develop new markets for air-cargo services. The exploitation of the demand for fresh fish offers an example of how air-cargo services can be marketed to capitalize on a new trend: Fresh fish is now transported regularly within a short period of time—for example, from Alaska to the lower states and from as far away as Scotland and New Zealand to the United States—to meet the demands of wholesalers catering to the needs of higher-class restaurants.

Equipment

Air-cargo services are offered by a broad spectrum of airlines that have an equally diverse mix of aircraft. There are full-service, all-cargo airlines, such as Cargolux and Flying Tiger*, that have worldwide route networks. There are integrated, expedited small-package carriers, such as Federal Express and United Parcel Service (UPS)—termed *integrated* because they operate their own trucks as well as their own airplanes. Whereas most passenger airlines carry air cargo only in the lower holds of passenger airplanes, some, such as Northwest, Japan Air Lines, and Luft Hansa, also operate freighters. Additionally, passenger airlines like KLM and Qantas operate combination, or "combi," airplanes, in which the main deck is shared by both passengers and air cargo. Finally, certain freight forwarders, such as Emery, now operate their own airplanes. Although historically, freight forwarders only collected smaller shipments from a variety of different shippers, consolidated them into larger shipments, and then negotiated with airlines for a volume discount, ownership of lift capacity by freight forwarders today has added another competitive dimension to the air-cargo industry.

Of the 7,000 or so jet aircraft in airline fleets worldwide, about six hundred are jet airplanes used exclusively for all-cargo operations, ranging in size from the Boeing 747 to the BAe-146, and even smaller, as in the case of Dassault Falcons. The Boeing 747 freighter has a capacity of some 100 tons; the BAe-146, of about 12 tons. The total capacity available for air cargo in the lower holds of passenger airplanes far exceeds the combined capacity offered in the world's fleet of all-cargo airplanes. Carrying a full load of passengers and their baggage, a Boeing 747 still has a payload capacity of about 75,000 pounds of cargo; a DC-10, about 50,000 pounds; and a Boeing 767-200, about 40,000 pounds. In practice, full-volume payloads are reached at about half these weights. Figure 7–1 shows the inside of a Boeing 747 being used to transport freight. Figure 7–2 shows, in a sketch form, the inside of a loaded Boeing 747.

The majority of existing all-cargo airplanes are not dedicated freighters (sometimes called uncompromised freighters). Instead, most of these aircraft

---

*In December 1988, Federal Express decided to acquire Tiger International Inc., parent of the Flying Tiger Line, the world's largest air-cargo carrier.

Figure 7–1. Inside of a Boeing 747

Photo Courtesy of Boeing Commercial Airplanes

Figure 7–2. Artist's Depiction of a Boeing 747 Carrying Freight on the Main Deck and in the Lower Hold

Photo Courtesy of Boeing Commercial Airplanes

are converted passenger airplanes. Airplanes expressly designed to carry freight—for example, the Armstrong Whitworth Argosy, the Lockheed Hercules L-100, the Canadair CL-44, and the Boeing 747F—have such features as a payload capacity that reflects the density characteristics of goods moving by air; a floor close to the ground, at truck-bed height; doors of a more suitable size and location; and perhaps even a more suitable cross-section of the fuselage. The flight deck of a Boeing 747 freighter, for example, is located high to enable the installation of a nose door for loading large containers (see figure 7–2). In general, however, based on the excess capacity in the lower holds, the demand for uncompromised freighters is insufficient for them to be produced at a competitive price, given the high costs of research and development, testing, and certification of new airplane designs.

In the lower holds of narrow-body passenger airplanes, such as the DC-9, air cargo is generally carried as loose—for example, noncontainerized—bulk freight. The lower holds of wide-body airplanes, by contrast, carry freight in specially built containers or on pallets. The lower-deck, LD-3 container, for example, is flat across the top, with one side contoured to correspond to the interior of the lower hold, and is designed to carry cargos weighing typically 20 pounds per square foot. The LD-7 is flat across the top and has straight sides and rounded corners at the top. Pallets are designed to carry typically 10,000 pounds. In practice, pallets are generally loaded in a rectangular shape; sometimes they are arranged with a contour to gain more useable volume, and some are contoured on their top ends to permit transfer to standard-body freighters. Main-deck containers for combi and all-cargo Boeing 747s are rectangular boxes (an 8-by-8-foot cross-section) that come in two lengths, 10 feet (M1) and 20 feet (M2); see figure 7–3. In addition, there is an array of containers to accommodate special consignments, such as garments-on-hangers containers and temperature-controlled containers. In some cases, the use of these containers lowers distribution costs by reducing handling and storage requirements, and in other cases, such containers are needed because of the unique attributes of the commodity being shipped. For instance, whereas transporting clothes in garments-on-hangers containers avoids the need to pack the clothes in boxes, unpack them at the destination, and then iron them before putting them out on display, a temperature-controlled container is required to transport frozen fish and other types of food.

A number of international carriers that do not operate freighter service have elected to offer substantial cargo capacity in combi airplanes. These airplanes can play an important role in those international markets in which freight demand is insufficient for freighter service and belly-hold capacity is either insufficient or unable to accommodate bulky shipments. Combi airplanes can also be ideal for sharing main-deck capacity between freight and passengers according to demand variations.[13] (Figure 7–4 shows the loading process for containers on the main deck of a Boeing 747 combi.) Such an

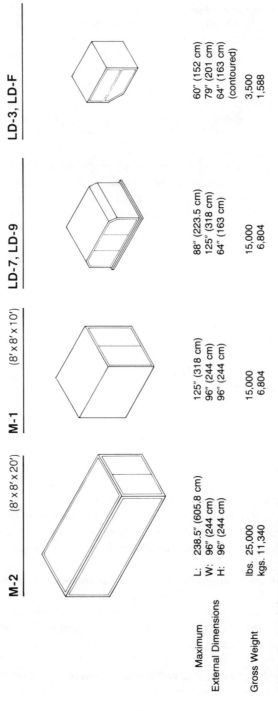

	M-2 (8'×8'×20')	M-1 (8'×8'×10')	LD-7, LD-9	LD-3, LD-F
Maximum External Dimensions	L: 238.5" (605.8 cm) W: 96" (244 cm) H: 96" (244 cm)	125" (318 cm) 96" (244 cm) 96" (244 cm)	88" (223.5 cm) 125" (318 cm) 64" (163 cm)	60" (152 cm) 79" (201 cm) 64" (163 cm) (contoured)
Gross Weight	lbs. 25,000 kgs. 11,340	15,000 6,804	15,000 6,804	3,500 1,588

Figure 7–3. Selected Airfreight Containers

Figure 7–4. Boeing 747 Combi Being Loaded

Photo Courtesy of Boeing Commercial Airplanes

arrangement is particularly advantageous in situations in which one set of market characteristics dictates a unique aircraft capability, say, a long-range airplane, but other market characteristics dictate a contrasting choice, say, small load capacity. There may not be enough separate passenger or freight demand on a transpacific flight, for instance, to commit a single-purpose airplane, but a combi may be able to operate profitably. Transporting freight in combi airplanes, however, may pose disadvantages, such as scheduling conflicts between freight and passenger priorities, fluctuations in capacity, problems in weight and balance, and limitations on the transportation of hazardous material and livestock.

Rates

The air-cargo rate structure is not only more complex than the passenger tariff structure but also much more controversial. The complexity arises because airfreight rates, unlike many passenger air fares, are a function of more than just length of haul. Several factors, including type of commodity, weight and size, degree of consolidation, density of shipment, and direction of movement, all play a part in determining the rate for a particular shipment.

In most parts of the world, transportation rates, including airfreight tariffs, are still regulated. In the United States, although the airfreight business was deregulated in 1977, the domestic industry continues to utilize some of the nomenclature as well as the rate structure that evolved during the regulatory era. Whereas prior to deregulation the CAB set air-cargo rates, now the airlines are free to set their own rates for domestic services. The air-cargo industry has traditionally offered general commodity rates and specific commodity rates. *General commodity rates,* applicable to all commodities, are based on shipment weight and distance for each pair of cities in the shipping itinerary. A weight-break incentive, sometimes called volume spread, exists for heavier shipments, and rates also vary by direction to compensate for spatial imbalance in traffic flows. *Specific commodity rates,* applicable to specific classes of commodities, are usually lower than general commodity rates and were developed to attract both commodities moving by a surface mode and those not being transported at all, such as fresh flowers and fruit from the West Coast. Specific commodity rates were also developed to attract certain types of freight particularly suited for air transportation, such as high-density freight, freight with a high value per pound, and freight requiring special handling. These rates, too, depend on weight and feature weight-break incentives for heavier shipments. Consequently, specific commodity rates tend to be based on market rather than cost, and there have been allegations that such rates are discriminatory. Moreover, because a specific rate must be published for each commodity, by weight and city pair, this type of rate structure tends to become unwieldy.

Besides general and specific commodity rates, there are numerous other kinds of rates, among them *exception rates,* for commodities requiring higher handling costs, such as valuable artwork and live animals; *container rates,* which provide consolidation and density incentives; *priority rates,* which offer shippers fast and reliable service at premium rates; *small-package rates,* for shippers that may tender their packages at an airline's baggage counter and have them picked up by the consignee at the destination airport's baggage counter; and *contract rates,* for shippers and forwarders that agree to tender a minimum amount of freight over a given period of time. These and many other categories of rates have been established to target a certain segment of the market or to meet certain airline requirements, such as the need to reduce ground-handling costs, and conditions in the marketplace, such as overcapacity. Consolidation incentives, for example, reflect the reduction in terminal handling costs, while density incentives represent an inducement to pack more freight in a container, beyond the minimum weight, to reduce the severity of the "cube out" problem, which commonly occurs when an airplane's storage space is filled before the airplane reaches its maximum weight limit. Additionally, certain container rates have enabled the air mode to become more competitive with surface modes.

The controversy in pricing airfreight services reflects the disparate rate-setting philosophies of the various industry participants. Disagreements over air-cargo pricing center on the contrasting approaches of by-product versus joint-product costing and of cost-based versus market-based rates. The *by-product* approach to determining costs holds that airfreight is a by-product of passenger service and should be offered and priced on an as-available basis. Proponents of the *joint-product* approach argue that passenger and freight services are both profit centers and that each should be priced according to the cost of providing the service. In addition, differences between airfreight and passenger movements, such as the fact that freight is a one-way movement, exacerbate the complexity and controversy surrounding the setting of airfreight rates.

Airline analysts remain divided over the appropriateness of by-product costing in which rates are based on the incremental costs of providing cargo service on passenger airplanes. These rates are established on the assumption that because the airplane will be flying to transport passengers regardless of whether any cargo is carried, the airline should fill all available cargo space as long as the price charged is high enough to cover the incremental cost of handling the additional cargo. Implementation of this philosophy can produce rates that may be competitive with those of surface modes; however, they do not cover fully allocated costs. Rates developed from by-product costing can, though, make a contribution to fixed costs.

Another point of controversy in airfreight pricing is whether rates should be based on cost or market. Whereas cost-based rates are set to recover the costs of providing service, market-based rates are set at levels the market will bear. While resolving this issue is difficult, the consensus appears to be that pricing policies should reflect the cost of production without overlooking the total sales potential of market-based rates. It is similarly difficult, if not impossible, to determine all the true costs uniquely associated with air-cargo service, given the imprecise and arbitrary nature of cost-allocation techniques. And even if the true costs could be established, one might question the desirability of having a purely cost-based rate if it cannot be marketed. Consequently, it can be argued that a more appropriate way to view this issue is not whether rates should be based on cost or market but, rather, how much weight should be given to each factor.[14]

Compared with the prices charged for other modes of transportation— trucks, railroads, and ocean ships—airfreight rates are generally higher.[15]

This premium price proved to be a handicap during the early development of the air-cargo industry, when price was the primary criterion for carrier selection. The air-cargo industry did not begin to grow until shippers broadened their criteria for carrier selection by including such factors as total transit time, reliability, carrier capability and accessibility, and security against loss and damage. For example, while airfreight rates are much higher than the rates charged by shipping companies, the use of the air mode reduces transit time and provides greater security against loss and damage. Consideration of such trade-offs is clearly evident in the case of General Motors' decision to ship its expensive cars by air.

Air cargo does compete with trucking, particularly in markets of less than 500 miles, for which the air mode offers no significant time advantage. For longer hauls, however, the air mode does offer a time advantage in return for its higher rates. In short-haul markets, the truck is becoming even more competitive, partly because of an increase in the quality of service offered: Trucking companies now offer much more reliable schedules, the ability to handle palletized freight, and tracking capability.[16] Tracking capability, enhanced by the emergence of bar-code labels, is particularly important to the users of express services. At the same time, airlines that already own and operate trucks for their feeder services could offer all-truck service in short-haul markets, provided the shipper did not perceive that it was paying airfreight prices while receiving surface transportation service.

Over the years, selected modes of transportation have attempted to offer intermodal joint services and joint rates, moving goods via two or more modes of transportation. The intermodality concept does open up new opportunities for the marketing and distribution of certain commodities, and it does have the potential to be more cost-effective for shippers. In the past, however, intermodality in its purest form achieved only limited success— particularly with respect to combining the air mode with any other mode— because of institutional problems and lack of coordination and integration.[17] More recently, though, the environment for intermodal transportation has become more conducive, as a result of the relaxation of regulatory control. Deregulation of the U.S. airfreight industry in 1977 opened up entry to the industry and provided pricing freedom in both the air carrier and the airfreight forwarding industries. The Interstate Commerce Commission deregulated rail rates for certain commodities in 1979, and the Motor Carrier Act of 1980 lowered barriers to entry and relaxed rate regulation in the truckline business. The Staggers Rail Act of 1980 deregulated piggyback carriage, allowed railroads to abandon unprofitable lines, and eased intermodal ownership restrictions. Finally, the Shipping Act of 1984 called for a review of the role of ocean freight forwarders. All these relaxations of regulatory control have facilitated the development of intermodal freight movements. And from an operational standpoint, the increasing application of computers has improved control of traffic movements, helped shippers identify and plan for changing requirements, and enhanced tracing, billing, and document-transmission capabilities.

These changes in the environment, coupled with the globalization of the air-cargo marketplace, have led to the development of limited movements of "sea-air" shipments between the Far East and Europe. Some products now move by ship between Japan and the U.S. West Coast, where they are transferred (in-bond) to airplanes destined for Europe and South America. This type of intermodal movement provides the shipper with an attractive price/service option: the combination of the low cost of ships and the speed of airlines.

Industry Restructuring in the Liberalized Operating Environment

During its early years, the air-cargo industry promoted the benefits of air-speed in order to penetrate the marketplace. Following the emergence of regulatory policies that limited the degree to which it could develop and market new services, the industry became preoccupied with rates and pricing policies. During the past decade, however, the air-cargo industry worldwide has been undergoing a restructuring process, largely because of changes in the regulatory climate and in the marketplace.

Deregulation of the airline industry in the United States allowed new carriers to enter the marketplace and incumbent carriers to introduce new price/service options. In Europe, the liberalization movement has had a similar effect, though not to the same degree as full deregulation in the United States. Yet ultimately, passage of the Single European Act will move Europe closer to a deregulated environment. This act, which could take effect in 1992, will remove all internal trade barriers within the European Community, thereby creating a single market encompassing a population of about 350 million.

Changes in the marketplace include the proliferation of multinational manufacturing, the success of expedited delivery services, and the evolution of "just-in-time" inventory management procedures. The market restructuring process will allow the industry not only to restore an emphasis on the quality of air transportation services provided but also to offer new service/price options. New services and new service/price options will in turn allow the industry to capitalize on other trends as they emerge in the marketplace.

The most significant marketplace change already under way is the substantial increase in expedited delivery services for small parcels and documents. These services, developed first within the United States and more recently within Europe, emphasize expedited handling, such as next-day delivery. Initially, passenger airlines began to accept small packages at their airport passenger counters for specific flights, the packages then being picked up at the destination airports by the shipper's representative. Subsequently, Federal Express pioneered an overnight small-package service that included pickup and delivery in trucks operated by the carrier. Following "Fed Ex," a number of other firms, such as United Parcel Service (UPS), began offering similar services. The market for these services, despite their relatively high price, has grown at a tremendous rate, and some carriers have begun to offer expedited services in international markets. Similarly, the air express industry is mushrooming within Europe, where the European Community is making significant progress in broadening the internal market by eliminating barriers to free trade. Like the U.S. market, the European express market is huge—estimated by TNT, a large Australian-based transportation conglomerate, to be $6 billion per year.[18]

Three reasons can be cited for the success of air express. First, the advent of computer-processing technology has greatly increased the requirement for information exchange among the developed economies of the world. Second, integrated carriers—those flying their own airplanes and operating their own trucks—have exploited technology to provide a high level of service, including computerized documentation and up-to-the-minute parcel tracking. Third, successful express service operators have not only bypassed the intermediary (the agent) and gone directly to the shipper but have also bypassed traditional scheduled airlines and in some cases traditional airports.

Changes in the freight-forwarding submarket represent another aspect of industry restructuring. Airfreight forwarders were once called indirect air carriers because they did not operate any airplanes of their own but instead consolidated smaller shipments into larger shipments and then used the lift provided by airlines. Thus, to the shipper, a freight forwarder was the carrier; to the carrier, the freight forwarder was the shipper. Freight forwarders also supplemented the ground and marketing services offered by airlines, by providing such services as pickup and delivery, documentation, and a sales force to promote and develop the market for airfreight. Forwarders made their money from the rate breaks incorporated in the rate structure—the larger the shipment, the lower the unit rate offered by airlines. Thus, by consolidating small shipments from many shippers into larger units, forwarders received lower rates from airlines, passing some of these savings along to customers. Another reason for the airlines' dependence on freight forwarders was the geographic limitation of an individual airline's network. As a result of these characteristics of airfreight forwarders, the airline industry has traditionally had a love-hate relationship with forwarders: On the one hand, forwarders have been one of the largest customers of airlines; on the other hand, they have also been competitors.

In the past few years, a significant change in the operating and competitive environment for airfreight forwarders has occurred as a result of (a) the emergence of integrated carriers, (b) more exacting requirements demanded by shippers, and (c) the decision by some forwarders to operate their own airplanes. The integrated express carriers, which started by transporting time-sensitive documents and high-value small packages, are penetrating the heavier freight (lower-yield) market by promoting their concept of one-stop shopping for door-to-door service. Shippers' demands for new services reflect the realities of doing business in a dynamic marketplace in which a proliferation of multinational manufacturers has turned to air cargo as a means of reducing manufacturing and distribution costs. Consequently, many shippers are demanding that forwarders have, among other things, computer capabilities, which currently can be provided cost-effectively by only the largest forwarders. Further, to maintain their revenues most cargo operators are scrambling to build volume as a result of the competitive pressure on yields—a situation that presents a strong incentive for forwarders to become large and computerized. Alternatively, some freight forwarders may have to scale back the scope of their operations in hope of prospering in a special niche. Moreover, a number of freight forwarders have begun operating their own airplanes, claiming a lack of sufficient prime-time lift after most scheduled airlines eliminated their freighter operations. This action has increased competition between airlines and forwarders. At the same time, those freight forwarders which have their own fleets appear to be vulnerable to attack from the mega–combination carriers, for two reasons: (a) Mega–combination airlines can approach large shippers directly, and (b) combination carriers can capitalize on their inherent strengths relative to the newly established flight operations of forwarders, such strengths including broader geographic networks and lower rates resulting from by-product pricing policies, which some would argue is a form of subsidy.

Another aspect of industry restructuring involves the decision by most major U.S. combination carriers to discontinue all-cargo freighter service. For several years, service in all-cargo freighters had been unprofitable for various reasons, including the quantity of space available for cargo in the wide-body fleet; the marketing leverage of freight forwarders, in terms of their access to large quantities of freight; and the increase in the price of fuel. In April 1985, Eastern Air Lines attempted to revive its freighter service with two new twists. First, Eastern found a freight forwarder, CF Airfreight, that contracted for all of Eastern's nighttime cargo capacity. Second, Eastern supplemented its cargo revenue with extremely low passenger fares on the main deck for late-night flights operating through its freight hub in Houston. Thus, for the first time in the history of the airline industry, passengers instead of cargo became the incremental factor, though this service was dropped after two years, when Eastern was acquired by Texas Air Corporation.

Regulatory reform in the United States has also led to changes in mail transport practices. Prior to deregulation, mail rates in the United States were set by the CAB, and airlines were obligated to carry mail on all flights and to give priority to mail above all other freight. Now, however, an individual airline is not required to carry mail under contract, though if an airline chooses to sign a contract for the carriage of mail, then mail is given priority above other kinds of freight. Transportation of mail to foreign destinations continues to be regulated by the Department of Transportation. The U.S. Postal Service, the largest single customer of the airline industry, now contracts for air transportation on the basis of bids that include price and service features. In addition, the U.S. Postal Service no longer has a monopoly on U.S. airmail going to foreign destinations; new regulations now allow private carriers to compete against the U.S. Postal Service with alternative price/service options.[19] Accordingly, there has been a corresponding and simultaneous effort by postal authorities in Europe, the Far East, and the United States to charter their own airplanes to fly mail in competition with private companies.

The scope of the operation of Air Cargo, Inc., the airlines' jointly owned pickup and delivery company, has also changed as a result of airline and trucking deregulation in the United States. Prior to 1980, Air Cargo trucks operated on behalf of the airlines and were generally limited in their airfreight pickup and delivery services to a 125-mile radius of city centers. Deregulation of the trucking industry has allowed the airlines to provide door-to-door truck service between any two points.

The foregoing offers a few examples of the regulatory and marketplace changes that have been principal contributors to the recent restructuring of the air-cargo industry. In general, the old demarcations among shippers, forwarders, and airlines have eroded. In addition, the industry has recently witnessed the successful development of integrated carriers. Further alterations, both in the structure of the industry and in the services offered, are expected as a result of (a) a continued evolution in the nature of competition and cooperation with other modes of transportation and (b) changes in the infrastructure.

Infrastructure Considerations

Because of the basic differences between the two industries, the infrastructure plays a more important role in air cargo than in passenger transportation. Consider, for example, terminal operations for routine freight and sort facilities for express packages. Not only are terminal operating costs high because these operations tend to be labor-intensive, but the amount of time required to process a shipment on the ground, relative to the actual flight time, undermines the chief advantage of air transportation—the speed of the airplane. Cargo that moves from across the Atlantic in hours and then sits at the destination airport for days before it can be processed and delivered to the customer negates the benefit of airspeed. In the case of sort facilities at hub airports for overnight service, ground time is even more critical in light of the need for late departures from inbound cities to the hub sort facility and for early departures from the hub facility to outbound cities. That these requirements are affected by airport restrictions is another example of the infrastructure constraints faced by the air-cargo industry: Airport curfews affect air-cargo movements more than passenger movements, since a large percentage of air cargo moves at night.

The processing of traditional airfreight at airport terminals is a labor-intensive function. Freight delivered by truck to a terminal needs first to be sorted, consolidated, and stored in a safe place and then loaded on an airplane. At the destination airport, the process is reversed. In addition, a large amount of paperwork usually needs to be completed at the terminal: maintaining accounting records, compiling statistics for management and government agencies, and tracking the status of a particular shipment. International airfreight necessitates even more paperwork because of restrictions imposed by customs. Given the labor-intensive nature of terminal operations, terminal costs tend be high relative to other categories of airfreight operating and nonoperating costs. And terminal costs are especially high for freight moving in short-haul markets, where competition from trucks is more intense and terminal costs have to be spread over shorter line-haul distances, resulting in higher airfreight rates. Several carriers have attempted to reduce their terminal costs by automating their freight terminal operations. Labor productivity can in fact be improved significantly by computerizing certain portions of the required paperwork and sorting/collecting processes and by increasing the degree of containerization, to avoid handling several smaller pieces.

Containerization provides many other benefits besides reducing terminal operating costs. For example, the development of lower-deck (LD) containers reduced turnaround time, ramp congestion, and ground-handling costs and improved security. Introduction of the Boeing 747F—F designates freighter—made possible the transportation of intermodal containers, at least between air and motor carriers. In addition, the development of special containers, such as garments-on-hangers containers and refrigerated containers, has been instrumental in attracting completely new air-cargo customers. Unfortunately, the program of developing containers has not been without its problems, such as the substantial investment required initially, the backhaul problem, the weight penalty of the container itself, the lack of standardization, and the cost of repairing containers. On balance, however, the container program has been successful in increasing the productivity of ground operations and its net benefit will increase even further as technological advances are incorporated, producing, for example, lighter, see-through plastic containers.

Two elements of the infrastructure that influence the development of the air-cargo industry are customs facilities and access to airports. Although in recent years customs agencies have introduced some improvements in facilitating the clearance of international air cargo, the rate of progress has not kept pace with the expansion of services offered by international air couriers. The international flow of air cargo is particularly affected by habitually slow processing at border crossings, most of the problems arising from language differences and sometimes conflicting documentation. Recent efforts directed at having the European Community, the United States, Canada, and the Pacific Rim nations adopt the *Harmonized Commodity Description and Coding System,* to provide a uniform international classification system for imports and exports, should save time and money. A uniform and simplified classification system should, among other things, allow importers and exporters to determine more accurately the category and customs duty on products, facilitate the preparation and processing of documents, and increase awareness of and compliance with foreign customs regulations. Leading the effort to develop this system has been the Brussels-based Customs Cooperative Council, whose mission is to harmonize customs procedures on a worldwide basis.

In conjunction with the movement toward a uniform, global air-cargo system, leading airports around the world are developing computerized cargo systems to alleviate delays in customs clearance. These systems allow pertinent air-cargo documents, such as air waybills and commercial invoices, to be transmitted to customs before cargo arrives at an airport, thereby facilitating the release of a large percentage of routine shipments. Three examples of such automated systems are the Air Cargo Fast Flow system at New York, the Miami International Cargo system, and London's ACP-90—Air-Cargo Processing in the 90s.

In recent years, a highly charged political groundswell has prompted the enactment of stifling curfews on nighttime operations at several airports, causing airlines and shippers to be concerned about the continuing efforts of environmentalists and noise activists to find new and creative ways to enact noise restrictions. At the federal level, the workhorses of the air-cargo industry—the originally equipped Boeing 707s and DC-8s—have already been phased out of domestic operations as a result of Stage 1 noise regulations; in the United States, such airplanes could not be operated after January 1, 1985, unless they had been exempted or retrofitted with costly engine modifications. Stage 2 noise regulations, effective January 1, 1988, are undoubtedly affecting carriers that operate the unmodified Boeing 727, DC-9, and BAC-111 jet airplanes. In addition, at the local level a number of airports have imposed onerous restrictions, including curfews, on the use of their airports by certain types of airplanes. Although the airlines have suggested that to preserve a "national" transportation network, the FAA should intervene and replace existing local airport restrictions with more reasonable restrictions, the FAA has been reluctant to take such action for fear of being liable for all noise-damage litigation. Consequently, action by Congress may be necessary to resolve this issue.

Air cargo is already handicapped with total operating costs that are much higher than those for other modes, and infrastructure constraints further reduce the competitiveness of the air mode. Consequently, improvements in the infrastructure can significantly increase the air mode's competitiveness by reducing indirect operating costs, bettering the quality of door-to-door service, and facilitating innovative ways to respond to the demands of an increasingly global marketplace.

Notes

1. Boeing Commercial Airplane Company, *World Air Cargo Forecast* (Seattle: Boeing Commercial Airplane Company, May 1987).
2. S. Shaw, *Airline Marketing and Management*, 2d ed. (London: Pitman Publishing, 1985), 39.
3. J.J. Coyle, E.J. Bardi, and C.J. Langley, Jr., *The Management of Business Logistics*, 4th ed. (St. Paul, Minn.: West Publishing, 1988).
4. M.W. Lyon, "Cash In on New Markets," *Air Cargo World*, December 1987, 18–22.
5. E.A. Finn, Jr., "Twenty-first-Century Truckers," *Forbes*, April 4, 1988, 80–86.
6. N.K. Taneja, *The U.S. Airfreight Industry* (Lexington, Mass.: Lexington Books, 1978), 92–96.
7. J.A. Cronin, "Global Trends Seen Promising for Pure Air-Cargo Operations," *Traffic World*, November 16, 1987, 9–14.
8. Coyle, Bardi, and Langley, *The Management of Business Logistics*, 14.
9. R.I. Kirkland, "Entering a New Age of Boundless Competition," *Fortune*, March 14, 1988, 40–48.
10. R. Selwitz, "Manufacturing Goes Multinational," *Air Cargo World*, February 1988, 14–19.
11. M. Rusk, "The Allante Express," *Air Cargo World*, September 1987, 20–21.
12. E.A. Finn, Jr., "Twenty-first-Century Truckers," 80–86.
13. R. Doganis, *Flying Off Course: The Economics of International Airlines* (London: George Allen and Unwin, 1985), 248.
14. Taneja, *The U.S. Airfreight Industry*, 142–43.
15. J.E. Tyworth, J.L. Cavinato, and C.J. Langely, Jr., *Traffic Management: Planning, Operations, and Control* (Reading, Mass.: Addison-Wesley, 1987), 44.
16. D. Woolley, "Anybody Notice the Rules Change?" *Air Cargo World*, November 1987, 42–46.
17. J.H. Mahoney, *Intermodal Freight Transportation* (Westport, Conn.: ENO Foundation for Transportation, 1985), 16.
18. P. Hogan, "Ansett/TNT: Connecting the Empire," *Aviation Economist* (London: AVMARK, October 1987), 15–19.
19. T. Hazen, "The Postman Does Ring Twice," *Air Cargo World*, October 1987, 28–38.

8
General Aviation

General aviation (GA) is defined as all civil aviation other than scheduled and nonscheduled commercial air transport. Measured by any one of a number of variables, such as number of active aircraft, number of hours flown, number of airports used, or number of pilots, general aviation is by far the largest component of civil aviation. During 1987, for example, whereas the airlines belonging to the 158 ICAO contracting states flew nineteen million hours in scheduled services, the world's general aviation fleet, excluding operations in China and the USSR, flew forty-five million hours. In 1986, 325,044 general aviation aircraft were on register in the ICAO contracting states, excluding China and the USSR.[1] That same year, the FAA listed 220,044 active general aviation aircraft registered in the United States. Thus, at least in terms of number of aircraft, about two-thirds of the general aviation activity worldwide, excluding China and the USSR, takes place in the United States.

In recent years, general aviation has been facing a number of critical business issues, brought about by structural changes in this industry. As a result, it is operating, at least in the United States, in a new environment that offers both challenges and opportunities. This chapter examines the historical developments, structural changes, pilot training, fixed-base operators, corporate aviation, and the current trends in the general aviation industry.

Development and General Characteristics

Immediately after the Wright brothers' flight in 1903, there was virtually no commercial or military interest in the flying machine. Only the desire of a few dedicated individuals to achieve "great flying feats" kept aviation alive and furthered its development. Famous aviators like Glenn Curtiss in the United States and Louis Bleriot, Henri Farman, and Charles Voisin in France were designing their own airplanes for aerial competitions in the United States and Europe. One of the first great aviation meets took place in 1909 at Reims, France. Sponsored by the local champagne industry, it attracted not only the best pilots and airplanes but also thousands of enthusiastic spectators. Such meets, involving substantial amounts of prize money, proved instrumental in generating public enthusiasm for aviation, stimulating interest in learning to fly, and improving the performance of the airplane. In turn, these developments led the U.S. government to place an order with the Wright brothers for airplanes and to establish the U.S. Army's first flying school at College Park, Maryland.[2] Although limited, this combined demand for airplanes marked the early beginnings of the airplane manufacturing industry. Some of the earliest start-up companies included those founded by Glenn Curtiss in the United States and the Short brothers in Great Britain.

The earliest versions of the single-engine airplane—which is still used for personal flying and represents the oldest component of the general aviation industry—were fabric covered and generally utilized hand-cranked engines of less than 50 horsepower. They also had only rudimentary instruments and controls; therefore, their operation was limited to good weather. Still, these airplanes demonstrated that flying machines could be made widely available to the general public. Moreover, the military value of the airplane was demonstrated, too, when an Italian pilot in 1912 made an hour-long flight to observe Turkish positions near Tripoli.[3]

The "sport" aspects of flying ended abruptly with the outbreak of World War I in 1914. Simultaneously, wartime activities produced a tremendous need for pilots, pilot training programs, large numbers of standardized aircraft, and improved aircraft performance. The pressure for improved performance was especially intense. Manufacturers developed more powerful engines that enabled aircraft to fly faster, farther, and at higher altitudes, as exemplified by the development of the British de Havilland Four (DH-4). This airplane, which entered service in 1917, was fitted with a 250-horsepower, Rolls-Royce, water-cooled engine. It could fly at a speed of more than 100 miles per hour at an altitude of about 15,000 feet. Some fifteen hundred of these airplanes were produced in Great Britain and about five thousand in the United States. The Americans developed the Liberty engine, a powerful twelve-cylinder engine that was mounted on the British DH-4s produced in the United States. The Americans also produced about six thousand Curtiss Jenny training aircraft. This airplane, the JN-4, not only helped train thousands of American pilots but also was used to initiate airmail service in the United States in 1918.

As World War I came to an end in 1918, there were thousands of surplus airplanes and thousands of pilots who did not want to stop flying. With few legitimate commercial alternatives available, many returning pilots purchased war-surplus airplanes and barnstormed the country. Their well-publicized activities revived the sport, the game, and the circus images of aviation. Other pilots sought fame and fortune in the achievement of "great flying feats," which focused on long-distance flights, such as ocean crossings.

Wealthy private citizens and newspapers put up large sums of prize money for nonstop flights across the Atlantic and Pacific oceans. One such famous flight took place in 1919 when two British aviators, Captain John Alcock and Lieutenant Arthur Brown, flew nonstop from Newfoundland to Ireland in a Vickers Vimy, a converted two-engine biplane bomber. Other great flying feats included the flight from England to Australia by the Australian Smith brothers (1919), the first nonstop flight between New York and San Diego by Kelly and MacReady (1923), and a round-the-world flight by a fleet of U.S. Army airplanes (1924). The most famous flight, however, was Charles Lindbergh's 1927 solo nonstop flight from New York to Paris in a single-engine Ryan monoplane.

After the war, other components of general aviation—including bush pilots, agricultural flying, fixed-base operators, and corporate aviation—began to develop around the world. The bush pilots were war-trained pilots who used war-surplus airplanes to fly between remote settlements in wilderness areas of the world, such as Alaska, northern Canada, Latin America, and the Australian outback. Inadequate facilities, such as the lack of suitable landing sites, and poor environmental conditions, such as the extremely cold climate in northern Canada, forced these pilots to develop unique flying techniques. Because of the courage and resourcefulness of these bush pilots, many small, isolated communities had much better access to medicine, mail, essential commodities, and emergency aid.[4] The Flying Doctor Service in Australia, which brought medical care to the people living in the outback, is particularly noteworthy of the contribution of general aviation in the late 1920s.

War-trained pilots and war-surplus airplanes were also instrumental in the development of agricultural flying, particularly crop dusting. Using airplanes fitted with special storage bins, pilots flew at low altitudes to spread seeds, insecticides, or herbicides over large agricultural areas. Figure 8–1 shows the application of an airplane in the agricultural sector of the economy.

Barnstormers, who made their living from air shows, airplane rides, and airplane maintenance services, were not regulated with respect to their flying skills, their maintenance skills, or the airworthiness of their airplanes. With the passage of the Air Commerce Act in the United States, which established aviation regulations, some of the barnstormers quit touring around and set up permanent operations at airports, which communities developed to attract airmail and air transport. These facilities became known as fixed-base operators—service stations for the general aviation industry and in some cases managers of airports themselves.

Corporate aviation, which involved the use of aircraft by nonaviation companies to further their business, also began to grow in the late 1920s. According to one source, the number of nonaviation companies that operated their own airplanes in the United States increased from thirty-four in

Figure 8–1. Application of an Airplane in the Agricultural Sector

Photos Courtesy of Cessna Aircraft Company

1927 to three hundred by 1930.[5] Fixed-base operators and corporate aviation are addressed in separate sections later in this chapter.

Following the war, the growing interest in private flying and business flying led to the establishment of aircraft manufacturing companies that focused on the needs of the general aviation market. In Great Britain, the de Havilland Company in 1925 produced a light airplane for private use called the Moth. In the United States, those companies producing airplanes for private use included the Laird Company in Chicago, the Travel Air Manufacturing Company in Wichita, and the Taylor Brothers Aircraft Corporation in Bradford, Pennsylvania. Two of the partners in the Travel Air Manufacturing Company, Walter Beech and Clyde Cessna, subsequently separated from Travel Air and formed their own companies. Taylor Brothers Aircraft was acquired by William Piper, who changed the name to the Taylor Aircraft Company and eventually to the Piper Aircraft Corporation. Subsequently, these three American companies—Beech, Cessna, and Piper—became the dominant manufacturers of general aviation aircraft in the world. It is worthwhile to note that the U.S. general aviation manufacturers had two huge advantages over their European counterparts following the war. First, inasmuch as the general aviation market is closely tied to economic conditions, the U.S. economy emerged from the war in much stronger condition than most European countries. Second, the war-ravaged countries of Europe committed nearly all their resources to rebuilding their industrial infrastructure, leaving precious little for general aviation facilities. Nevertheless, the Europeans concentrated on the development of gliders—a popular and cheaper alternative—and today Europe maintains a tremendous edge in glider design.

Despite the difficulties in Europe, general aviation continued to make substantial contributions to aviation throughout the 1930s. For example, the sport aspects, such as endurance flights and racing, led to vast improvements in the design of the airplane in both Europe and the United States. Airplane designs began to incorporate enclosed cockpits, cantilevered wings, streamlined fuselages with insulated compartments for the pilot and passengers, air-cooled engines, controllable-pitch propellers, and retractable landing gears. In addition, the growing network of established airways and improved navigation equipment contributed to the increase in flying. The proliferation of flying clubs, which spread the costs of airplane ownership, facilitated a rapid increase in the number of pilots. In addition, the Civilian Pilot Training Program enabled more than a thousand educational institutions to provide flight training to more than 400,000 students.[6]

Immediately after World War II, manufacturers of light aircraft saw an enormous market potential based on the general public's increasing desire to travel by air. The optimistic forecasts of the civil market for light airplanes prompted a sudden increase in the number of aircraft manufacturers—in the United States alone, there were twenty companies producing light airplanes.

But the optimistic sales forecasts did not materialize. A.T. Wells and B.D. Chadbourne cite a number of reasons for this situation, among them that (a) the newly designed airplanes were expensive relative to the price of war-surplus airplanes and (b) the airplane could not compete with the all-around utility of the automobile.[7] Consequently, competing manufacturers struggled for survival and many ceased operations. The companies that survived did so by finding new and better uses for airplanes—producing, for example, improved agricultural airplanes for sowing, dusting crops, and spreading fertilizer and aerial tankers to fight fires by spraying water from the sky. The helicopter, developed after the war as a result of advanced engine technology, also began to play an important role in general aviation, particularly during the 1950s. It was used in traffic control, search-and-rescue efforts, surveying, flying-crane work, ambulance service, and transportation to and from oil rigs at sea. Converted war-surplus bombers, too, gained some acceptance among the business community. But it was ultimately the growth of the country's navigation network, particularly VOR stations and the widespread availability of turbine-powered aircraft, that truly spurred the growth of corporate aviation. In the late 1950s, the general aviation industry introduced turbine-powered aircraft for business travel, examples of which included the Lockheed JetStar (1957), the Rockwell Sabreliner (1958), the Grumman G-1 (1959), the British Aerospace BAe 125 (1962), the Dassault Falcon 20 (1963), and the Learjet (1963). These airplanes were operated to airline standards with respect to flight crew, navigational equipment, and flight performance. Additionally, some airplanes were equipped with special fuel tanks to enable them to operate in intercontinental and transoceanic markets.

The single-engine, fixed-wing piston airplane has continued to be the largest component of the general aviation fleet. In 1986, the general aviation fleet in the United States consisted of 220,044 aircraft, of which 171,777, or 78 percent, represented single-engine piston airplanes (see table 8–1). These airplanes range in sophistication from one-person, "experimental" ("homebuilt") vehicles to powerful planes that can outperform some twin-engine models. The upscale Cessna Pressurized Centurion (see figure 8–2), for example, can carry six persons a distance of about 1,000 miles. This high-wing airplane has a pressurized cabin and retractable landing gear. Its engine can deliver 325 horsepower, enabling the airplane to cruise at more than 200 knots.

Some pilots enjoy the challenge and sense of accomplishment of building an airplane. Other pilots elect to build their own planes because it is usually cheaper to build a do-it-yourself plane than to purchase a factory-built one. For these intrepid builder-pilots, there are a variety of options, ranging from rudimentary drawings that require the builder to cut and assemble the entire airplane to elaborate kits that require the builder to assemble larger pieces. The finished product is subject to special FAA certification requirements.

Table 8–1
Active U.S. Civil Aircraft

	1983	1984	1985	1986
General aviation				
Fixed-wing				
Piston, one-engine	166,427	171,922	164,385	171,777
Turboprop, two-engine	5,311	5,633	5,240	5,779
Turbojet, two-engine	3,447	3,780	3,914	4,037
Other	25,646	26,236	24,435	24,497
Rotorcraft	6,540	7,096	6,418	6,943
All other general aviation	5,923	6,276	6,262	7,011
Total general aviation	213,293	220,943	210,654	220,044
Total air carriers	4,203	4,370	4,678	4,909
Total U.S. civilian fleet	217,486	225,313	215,332	224,953

Source: Federal Aviation Administration (FAA), *FAA Statistical Handbook of Aviation* (Washington, D.C.: FAA), 1984–1987.

According to one source, a person does not need to acquire special skills to build an airplane at home (although some welding skills are useful) and the cost varies from $6,000 to $12,000 (based on 1987 data).[8] The capability of an experimental aircraft was well demonstrated by pilots Jeana Yeager and Richard Rutan in December 1986, when they flew their *Voyager* non-stop around the world in nine days. *Ultralights*—very light vehicles used for aerial recreational purposes—are a particular subset of experimentals; they and their pilots are not regulated by the FAA so long as both pilots and ultralights comply with certain rules pertaining to the weight of the machine and its operation in the airspace.

U.S. General Aviation Industry: Structure and Structural Changes

As shown in table 8–2, in 1986 there were 220,044 active general aviation aircraft in the industry. More than half the total general aviation fleet is used for personal flying, and almost all these airplanes have single-piston engines. About 20 percent of the fleet is used for business purposes, whereas instructional and executive uses account for 7.2 percent and 5.5 percent, respectively. The distinction between business and executive flying, according to the FAA classification of primary use, relates to whether the airplane is used by individuals or by organizations, such as corporations. The business-use category can be misleading, since an airplane can be flown for personal and business use simultaneously. The executive-use category is clearer, in that these airplanes are owned and operated by organizations, primarily for the use of their employees or members and their customers. The executive-use category also has the highest percentage of turboprops and turbojets; in

Figure 8–2. Cessna Pressurized Centurion

Source: Cessna Aircraft Company

Table 8–2
Active General Aviation Fleet Disaggregated by Primary Use, 1986

Primary Use	Number of Aircraft	Percentage of Total Aircraft
Personal	120,308	54.7
Business	43,780	19.9
Instructional	15,812	7.2
Executive	12,075	5.5
Air taxi	7,568	3.4
Aerial application	7,286	3.2
Aerial observation	4,716	2.1
Commuter	1,721	0.8
Other	6,996	3.2
Total	220,044	100.0

Source: Federal Aviation Administration (FAA), *FAA Statistical Handbook of Aviation* (Washington, D.C.: FAA, 1987), 165.

1986, for example, 3,094 of the total 5,964 turboprops and 3,119 of the total 4,480 turbojets were in executive use.[9]

During the past ten years, the U.S. general aviation industry has undergone several significant structural changes. Indicative of these changes are a decline in the number of general aviation aircraft produced, a consolidation and reorganization in the general aviation aircraft manufacturing industry, an increase in the market share held by non-U.S. manufacturers in the U.S. domestic market, and a decline in the number of active pilot certificates held. The structural changes include maturation of the U.S. general aviation market; skyrocketing costs of airplane ownership, insurance, and operation; and changes in the life-styles and preferences of the U.S. population.[10] Many people are unable or unwilling to make the substantial commitments of time and resources needed to become and remain proficient general aviation pilots. Unlike drivers of other modes of personal transportation—notably, of recreational vehicles and boats—pilots must undergo rigorous training and recurrent certification, including medical certification, to exercise the privileges granted by their pilot's license. In addition, government regulations concerning general aviation operations, such as airspace restrictions and airspace equipment requirements, are becoming more complex. Consequently, many potential pilots pursue other interests and many licensed pilots are no longer active. Table 8–3 shows an estimate of the active pilot certificates held as of December 1987. The total number of pilots holding certificates increased until 1980 (827,071) and then declined each year until 1983 (718,004); a slight increase occurred in 1984, followed by decreases in 1985, 1986, and 1987.

Table 8–4 shows historical data on the annual shipments of new U.S. general aviation aircraft, including units shipped, the number of companies reporting, and factory net billings in current dollars. The number of units

Table 8–3
Estimate of Active Pilot Certificates Held, December 1987

Category	1980	1987
Student	199,833	146,016
Private	357,479	300,949
Commercial	183,442	143,645
Airline transport	69,569	91,287
Helicopter		
(only)	6,030	8,702
Glider (only)[a]	7,039	7,901
Lighter-than-air[a]	3,679	1,153
Total	827,071	699,653

Source: Federal Aviation Administration data as reported in General Aviation Manufacturers Association (GAMA), *General Aviation Statistical Databook: 1988 Edition* (Washington, D.C.: GAMA, 1988), 14.

Note: [a]Pilots in the glider and lighter-than-air categories are not required to have a medical examination; however, the total figures above represent pilots who received a medical examination within the preceding twenty-five months.

shipped peaked in 1946, declined each year thereafter until 1951, and then steadily increased until 1966. Annual shipments decreased from 1966 to 1971 and then steadily increased to a high of 17,811 units in 1978. Since then, the number of units shipped has been declining each year, reaching a low of 1,085 in 1987, the lowest level since the end of World War II. The dollar value of all airplanes shipped has not declined so rapidly, however, since an increasing percentage of airplanes shipped are the larger and higher-priced multiengine and turbine-powered airplanes. Total factory billings in 1987 were $1.4 billion for about 1,100 airplanes, compared with $1.8 billion for about 18,000 aircraft in 1978.

Until the late 1970s, the fluctuations in annual shipments shown in table 8–4 were related to the cyclical nature of the U.S. economy. During periods of economic growth, the growth in annual shipments exceeded that in the economy (measured by the increase in GNP adjusted for price changes) by a factor of 4.2. Since 1979, however, changes in the number of general aviation aircraft shipments have not followed changes in the economy according to the patterns established prior to 1979. For example, since 1979, annual aircraft shipments actually declined each year despite real GNP growth in six of the eight years for which data are given. This phenomenon indicates the existence of other unfavorable factors that are overriding the positive impact of economic growth. These unfavorable factors include (a) the availability of low-cost alternatives for recreational flying, such as gliders and ultralights; (b) changes in life-styles and preferences, such as a proliferation of nonaviation activities; (c) declining student and private pilot enrollments; (d) rapidly rising prices and operating costs of conventional aircraft; and (e)

Table 8–4
Annual Shipments of New U.S. General Aviation Aircraft

Year	Units Shipped	Companies Reporting	Factory Net Billings (Millions)
1946	35,000	—	$ 110.0
1947	15,594	15	57.9
1948	7,037	12	32.4
1949	3,405	11	17.7
1950	3,386	13	19.1
1951	2,302	12	16.8
1952	3,058	8	26.8
1953	3,788	7	34.4
1954	3,071	7	43.4
1955	4,434	7	68.2
1956	6,738	8	103.7
1957	6,118	9	99.6
1958	6,414	10	101.9
1959	7,689	9	129.8
1960	7,588	8	151.2
1961	6,778	8	124.3
1962	6,697	7	136.8
1963	7,569	7	153.4
1964	9,336	8	198.8
1965	11,852	8	318.2
1966	15,768	10	444.9
1967	13,577	14	359.6
1968	13,698	14	425.7
1969	12,457	14	584.5
1970	7,292	13	337.0
1971	7,466	11	321.5
1972	9,774	12	557.6
1973	13,646	12	828.1
1974	14,166	12	909.4
1975	14,056	12	1,032.9
1976	15,451	12	1,225.5
1977	16,904	12	1,488.1
1978	17,811	12	1,781.2
1979	17,048	12	2,165.0
1980	11,877	12	2,486.2
1981	9,457	12	2,919.9
1982	4,266	11	1,999.5
1983	2,691	10	1,469.5
1984	2,431	9	1,680.7
1985	2,029	9	1,430.6
1986	1,495	9	1,261.9
1987	1,085	9	1,363.5

Source: General Aviation Manufacturers Association (GAMA), *General Aviation Statistical Databook: 1988 Edition* (Washington, D.C.: GAMA, 1988), 4.

growing pressure on GA activities as a result of "crowded skies" and the consequent additional regulations, such as mode C transponders.

According to studies conducted by the FAA, the demand for single-engine piston airplanes is highly sensitive to airplane prices, airplane operating and maintenance costs, and the state of the U.S. economy. Since the economy has undergone relatively consistent growth through most of the past decade and since the number of airplanes shipped has declined during the same years, it stands to reason that the increases in airplane prices and operating costs have more than offset the impact of the growth in the economy. Figure 8–3 shows the trends in aircraft prices and aircraft operating and maintenance costs since 1970. Since 1978, these prices and costs have been increasing at a rate much higher than the general rate of inflation. From 1978 through 1985, the price of single-engine piston airplanes increased at an annual rate of about 11 percent in current dollars and about 5 percent in constant dollars (after adjusting for price increases due to inflation). Similarly, the increase in operating and maintenance costs, particularly in operating costs, has exceeded the increase in inflation. Part of the explanation suggested in the FAA studies is that the recent decline in the price of fuel experienced by commercial air carriers may not have been passed on to the general aviation industry.

A major business issue facing the general aviation industry is the increase in premiums for insurance against product liability suits. According to one estimate, in 1985 the cost to manufacturers of product liability insurance premiums averaged $70,000 for each new aircraft sold; this cost is inevitably passed on to the purchaser of a new aircraft in the form of higher prices. Product liability insurance premiums have increased despite the fact that the safety record of the general aviation industry has been improving. Higher liability insurance premiums are the result of several factors associated with product liability litigation. For example, unlike most other products that wear out and are replaced, general aviation airplanes are extremely durable and the courts have held manufacturers liable even for airplanes that were manufactured decades earlier. Therefore, manufacturers and their insurers must make financial provisions for potential lawsuits arising both from airplanes manufactured years ago and from airplanes manufactured currently that will remain in the general aviation fleet for decades to come. In addition, general aviation accidents, although relatively infrequent, receive a great deal of publicity, which tends to sensationalize the situation. Further, frequently adopted in general aviation liability cases is the legal doctrine of joint and several liability, which in essence assesses penalties against all companies that participated in the manufacture of an airplane—and many small subcontractors supply parts to the major manufacturers—in proportion to their ability to pay, regardless of their role in any product default associated with the liability suit. This situation has not only had a negative impact on the number of new airplanes sold but also contributed to the lack of interest on the part of manufacturers to introduce new product innovations for the nonbusiness market.[11] Moreover, because the increase in the price of airplanes reduces demand, the corresponding reduction in production volume

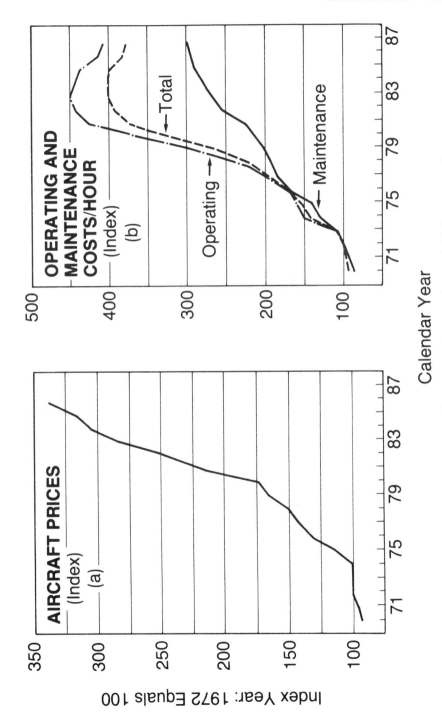

Figure 8–3. Trends in Single-Engine Piston Aircraft Prices and Operating and Maintenance Costs

Source: Federal Aviation Administration (FAA). *FAA Aviation Forecasts: Fiscal Years 1988–1999* (Washington, D.C.: FAA, February 1988), 73.

further raises the price of each airplane finally sold, since all of the manufacturer's fixed costs, such as research, development, and insurance, must be spread over smaller quantities.

Reductions in the sales of new airplanes and increases in the cost of developing new airplanes have forced many independent general aviation aircraft manufacturers in the United States to be taken over by conglomerates that have greater financial resources. Examples include the acquisition of Beech Aircraft by the Raytheon Company, Gulfstream Aerospace by the Chrysler Corporation, Cessna Aircraft by General Dynamics, and Learjet by a series of larger corporate owners. These manufacturers are hoping that their parent companies will provide financial resources to revitalize their product lines by introducing new airplanes with new technology to stimulate lackluster demand and to compete more effectively with foreign manufacturers, some of which are allegedly government-subsidized.

The FAA's aviation forecasts show no significant increase in the number of general aviation airplanes from 1987 to 1999; they indicate a decline of 0.2 percent between 1987 and 1992, followed by an increase of 0.2 percent between 1992 and 1999. These forecasts call for a decline in the number of single-engine piston airplanes, from 171,800 in 1987 to 162,500 in 1999, but an increase in the number of turbine-powered aircraft, from 13,500 in 1987 to 15,700 in 1999, or about 1.2 percent per year. In addition, the turbine rotorcraft fleet is expected to increase at a rate of about 1.9 percent per year.[12]

Although the U.S. domestic market is the single largest market for general aviation airplanes, it appears to be saturated. Not only has demand slumped, but foreign manufacturers have introduced a number of products that compete very effectively with U.S.-manufactured airplanes. Foreign markets for general aviation airplanes, particularly in Australia, Brazil, Canada, China, and Japan, appear to offer much greater potential. These foreign markets for general aviation airplanes will put pressure on (a) manufacturers, to develop standardized products; (b) regulatory agencies, to adopt uniform certification requirements; and (c) governments, to open their borders to foreign-made airplanes.

In an effort to bolster lagging sales, some U.S. manufacturers are incorporating advanced technology in new airplane designs, particularly in the business-aviation market. The development of Beech Aircraft's Starship 1 illustrates this trend (see figure 8–4). Raytheon's financial backing helped Beech experiment with such new technology as the use of composite materials that provide weight savings of approximately 20 percent; two pusher turboprop engines that enable the airplane to cruise at about 400 miles per hour; an integrated cockpit display system that reduces pilot work load while enhancing "heads up" time for increased safety in high-density airspace; and an avionics system that provides direct, point-to-point automatic navigation anywhere in the world, performs self-diagnostic checks of all internal com-

Figure 8–4. Beechcraft Starship 1

Source: Beech Aircraft Company

ponents, and points out faults. These revolutionary design ideas are a dramatic departure from the industry's conservative, evolutionary approach to new product design. Adoption of high technology in the design of new general aviation aircraft could, however, prove risky in light of the trends discussed earlier.

Pilot Training

Pilot training, one of the most important and useful general aviation activities, is provided by more than four hundred colleges and universities, by designated representatives of the airplane manufacturing companies, by private flying clubs, by qualified flight instructors, and by fixed-base operators—private businesses located at or close to airports. In light of the trends noted earlier, there could be a shift toward institutional training with such features as standardization, increased use of simulators, and economies of scale. Data shown in table 8–2 indicate that in 1986, 7.2 percent of all general aviation airplanes were used for training pilots, making this the third-largest category of such airplanes by type of use. Trainers tend to be low-powered, two-seater, single piston-engine airplanes.

In the United States, a person can obtain a license to fly by meeting the requirements of the FAA. The FAA issues five kinds of certificates: student, private, commercial, instructor, and airline transport. In addition, a pilot can qualify for special ratings on the certificate that indicate, for example, the ability to fly under instrument flight rules or in multiengine airplanes. Applicants need to pass a physical medical examination as well as written and practical examinations of flying knowledge and proficiency. Each certificate calls for the fulfillment of a different set of FAA requirements, as set forth in FAA's FAR part 61 ("Certification: Pilots and Flight Instructors"). The requirements become more stringent as the pilot upgrades the certificate from student to airline transport; in each case, the applicant is required to have acquired certain aeronautical knowledge, flight proficiency, and aeronautical experience.

Because a description of the detailed requirements for each type of certificate is beyond the scope of this book, interested readers are referred to FAA's FAR part 61.* Following, however, is a general outline of the requirements for a private pilot's license, extracted from the FAA's part 61 ("Subpart D: Private Pilots"). The training for a private pilot's license usually takes between forty and sixty hours of actual flight time, plus ground-school instruction, and the cost typically ranges between $2,000 and $3,000.

The actual steps to becoming a private pilot are as follows: First, the candidate must be at least seventeen years of age and hold a current medical

---

*Pilot schools comply with FAA part 141 regulations.

certificate issued under the FAA's part 67 requirements. Second, the applicant must demonstrate basic aeronautical knowledge in the areas of

- accident reporting requirements;
- VFR navigation;
- basic meteorology;
- safe and efficient operation of airplanes; and
- basic aerodynamics and principles of flight.

With respect to flight proficiency, the applicant must be able to demonstrate knowledge in

- preflight inspection;
- airport and traffic pattern operations;
- flight maneuvering by reference to ground objects;
- flight at critically slow speeds;
- takeoffs and landings under a variety of conditions;
- control of an airplane solely by reference to instruments;
- cross-country flying;
- night flying; and
- emergency operations.

With respect to aeronautical experience, the private pilot applicant must have acquired at least forty hours of flight time, which must include

- twenty hours of flight instruction, and
- twenty hours of solo flight time.

A private pilot license entitles the holder to operate the type of aircraft listed on the license and to carry passengers. The private pilot may not, however, charge money to operate an airplane; the FAA requires the fulfillment of additional requirements to become a "for hire" pilot. As a pilot progresses through the five FAA certifications—private through airline transport—the medical, flight training, and experience requirements become more stringent. Moreover, pilots of high-performance corporate airplanes and commercial airline transports undergo regular recurrent training.

To increase the efficacy and lower the cost of training, particularly recurrent training, aircraft simulators are playing an increasingly important role. With their high degree of fidelity, modern simulators can realistically duplicate an airplane's response to a wide variety of operating conditions.

Moreover, the use of simulators for training provides at least four advantages. First, the cost of training is reduced: Since airplanes are expensive, substituting flight training in simulators avoids out-of-pocket costs for fuel, maintenance, and so forth. Second, safety is enhanced with the use of simulators. Not only are the pilot and the airplane free of a potentially hazardous operating environment, but the pilot is able to gain experience in handling situations that cannot, without dire consequences, be repeatedly duplicated in the real world. Third, simulators allow environmental conditions to be easily controlled for the purposes of training. Thus, pilots can be exposed to specific weather conditions and effects—fog, icy surfaces, sudden changes in wind—to suit the convenience of the instructor. And fourth, simulators can be scheduled around the clock for flight training, their availability precluding the need to take an airplane out of commercial service for nonrevenue training purposes (and thereby also saving airplanes from unnecessary wear and tear).

Fixed-Base Operators

Fixed-base operators (FBOs) are an integral component of the U.S. general aviation industry. In addition to providing flight instruction, FBOs furnish a number of other services, such as airplane sales and rentals, airplane parts and service, aircraft charter service, air-taxi services (on-demand aircraft charters), fuel sales, and maintenance. Some FBOs also provide specialized services, such as aerial advertising, cropdusting, and sightseeing. Most general aviation airports have at least one FBO; larger airports usually have more than one. One source estimates that some thirty-five hundred FBOs are operating in the United States at different public-use airports.[13] Although the number of FBOs has remained fairly constant since the late 1970s, turnover in this industry is continuous.[14] The vast majority of FBOs have small operations geared to the needs of private pilots of single-engine airplanes. A few large FBOs, however, are capable of handling air carrier airplanes and providing full service to corporate fleets and are large enough to have established operations at more than one airport. Some large FBOs also provide comprehensive services on a contractual basis, to corporate users, handling such matters as corporate aircraft leases; flight operations, including crew; maintenance; and administrative functions, including keeping maintenance records and obtaining insurance. In effect, these large FBOs supply all the services a contracting corporation would otherwise need to provide through its own aviation department.

Earlier in this chapter, the history of FBOs was traced to the post–World War I nomadic barnstormers who eventually settled down at fixed sites. Many other FBOs got into the business as a type of maintenance facility and then expanded that narrowly defined business into other areas, such as selling fuel, providing airplane hangarage and tie-down facilities, selling spare parts and eventually airplanes, and operating general aviation terminal buildings. Other FBOs began as the appointed or leased operator for those airports, which, as noted earlier, were developed by local authorities to attract airmail and air transport and, once developed, tended to be used more by general aviation.

Like other components of the aviation industry, FBOs are regulated in the area of aviation safety. The FAA regulates, for example, FBO activities with respect to flight instruction, maintenance, charter and air-taxi flights, and special activities like agricultural operations. In their book *Aviation Industry Regulation*, H.P. Wolfe and D.A. NewMyer provide a good description of the levels, numbers, and kinds of regulations affecting FBOs.[15]

Briefly, in the area of flight instruction FBOs must conform to FAR parts 61 ("Certification of Pilots and Flight Instructors"), 141 ("Pilot Schools"), and 143 ("Ground Instructors"). As stated earlier, part 61 deals with pilot qualifications, privileges, and limitations. Part 141 describes the requirements for becoming a certified pilot training school, as well as the necessary approval process for courses offered by such schools. With respect to maintenance, FBOs must conform to FAR parts 23, 33, 35, 39, 43, 65, and 145, part 43 providing the rules for aircraft maintenance and specifying the persons authorized to perform such work. For charter and air-taxi operations, FBOs must conform to FAR parts 91 ("General Operating and Flight Rules") and 135 ("Air-Taxi Operators and Commercial Operators of Small Aircraft"). Air taxis, a component of the FBO industry, are common carriers for hire that hold an air-taxi operating certificate but do not provide service on fixed routes or according to a fixed schedule. Finally, the specialized activity of agricultural operations falls under FAR part 137 ("Agricultural Aircraft Operations").

Full-service FBOs normally operate such facilities as airplane tie-down areas, hangars, maintenance shops, airplane showrooms, and administrative offices and typically lease these facilities from airport owners/operators. Although many elements of the lease, such as lease term and rent, are standard clauses in real estate leases, a fairly large portion of the lease consists of the operating agreement between the airport and the FBO and covers such points as flight operations, line service, service charges, and exclusive rights. Generally, FBOs have to meet minimum standards established by the airport owners/operators, and the FAA publishes guidelines on those standards. When an airport has received federal funds for its development, it is required to make its facilities available to all potential FBOs. Consequently, a single FBO at an airport has little protection from potential competition. Although competition is desirable from the consumer's viewpoint, occasionally there may simply be insufficient business for more than one FBO, in which case the airport owner/operator might be able to set minimum standards at a level that would deter underfinanced FBOs from establishing competitive enterprises. Here, though, the prospective FBO could take its case to the FAA if there were legitimate reason to believe that "sponsor assurances" had been violated, such assurances existing to ensure that an airport docs not grant exclusive rights to a single FBO if the airport has received federal funds.

Just as FBOs vary in the size and scope of their business activities, they also vary in degree of business experience, expertise, and profitability. When in the late 1970s the aviation business was expanding, the FBO industry did not have to demonstrate particularly high levels of management skill to achieve reasonable returns on investment. Since 1980, however, the market environment has changed sufficiently to cause problems for those FBOs which are small or slow to adapt to the changing marketplace. For example, those FBOs which previously were heavily dependent on the sale of aviation fuel must now pursue other activities more aggressively, and those which cannot afford to provide flight training cost-effectively must now deemphasize that component of their business, even though it may have been profitable in the past. Just the same, some of the larger FBOs that have been able to specialize in certain areas, such as corporate services or maintenance, have done very well financially and should continue to do so.

The FBOs face many of the same issues as other components of the general aviation industry face. For example, the reduction each year in the number of new airplanes sold is having a negative impact on FBOs, since this sales activity has traditionally represented a significant proportion of their revenue base. Many FBOs have also been severely affected by the increase in the cost of product liability insurance. To be successful in the changing environment, it appears that an FBO must manage each component of its business—fuel sales, new and preowned aircraft sales, flight training, maintenance, hangarage, and so forth—as a unique profit center. Since some of the activities may be interrelated, it is necessary not only that each activity make a contribution to fixed costs but also that some activities earn more than their fully allocated costs to pay for those activities which earn less. These types of analyses require a reasonable knowledge of business techniques, information collection and processing, and the ability to interpret market trends.

An interesting trend to watch is the merging of small, individual FBO operations into groups or chains.[16] This strategy could introduce greater efficiencies into FBO operations by providing access to buying power, specialized services, and areas of management expertise without creating excessive costs for any one FBO. Fuel and parts contracts, for example, often carry substantial pricing advantage for higher-volume purchases, while in the case of management expertise, the group or chain could afford to hire the services of expert accountants, attorneys, and data analysts. Such strategies could enable small FBOs to survive and thrive in the new marketplace, albeit at a loss of some independence.

Corporate Aviation

The phrase *corporate aviation* refers to any use of an aircraft by a business for the purpose of transporting its employees and/or property not for compensation or hire, and employing professional pilots for the operation of the aircraft. Today, corporate airplanes have become cost-effective tools of business operations, transporting not only corporate staff but also potential customers. Consider the following examples: A businessperson can leave Rochester, New York, at 7:00 A.M. and arrive back home at a little after 9:00 P.M., having made four 2-hour stops for business meetings in Philadelphia, Pennsylvania; Richmond, Virginia; Atlanta, Georgia; and St. Petersburg, Florida.[17] In international operations, a businessperson can leave London at 7:15 A.M. and return at 8:00 P.M., having made three 3-hour stops for business in Paris, Zurich, and Amsterdam.

A corporate fleet can also be a unique business tool for demonstrating products and services. A real estate company seeking financial capital, for example, can use an airplane to transport potential investors to the proposed development site.[18] As a case in point, Steelcase, Inc., a Grand Rapids–based designer and manufacturer of office furnishings, made its corporate fleet an effective sales tool by flying potential customers to its head office for a tour of the company's manufacturing facilities.[19] Thus, the private airplane can be a valuable asset in expanding business, since it can open new markets and enable quick, face-to-face meetings to "seal the deal." Of course, many successful companies do not have corporate airplanes. The decision of whether or not to invest in an airplane—which requires a substantial financial commitment—is based not only on "hard" numbers but also on a company's willingness to adopt a new corporate philosophy that will enable the firm to fully appreciate the value and advantages of an airplane.

Changes in the airline industry as a whole have affected corporate aviation. For example, the number of airports served by the major airlines has been declining: Whereas in 1960 the major carriers served about 750 airports across the United States, by 1970 that number had declined to about 470 and by 1987 to 284. By contrast, the number of airports served by commuter/regional airlines in North America has increased, rising from 681 in 1978 to 834 in 1987.[20] Yet, in the eyes of many business travelers, the increase in commuter service is not equal compensation for the loss of service by the major airlines. Frequent business travelers complain—some quite vehemently—about major carrier jet service being replaced by a commuter carrier's turboprop service to a hub airport. Moreover, deregulation of the airline industry has led the larger carriers to radically change their operating patterns, reducing the scheduled services provided to and from smaller cities and increasing the development of hub-and-spoke systems. These trends have prompted some corporations with plants and offices spread over large geographic areas to operate their own airplanes so as to take maximum advantage of business opportunities while optimizing executives' time. Most corporate airplanes can land at more than 10,000 airports not served by commercial carriers, such airports frequently being closer to a traveler's ultimate destination and much less crowded than busier airports, thereby saving time for expensive corporate staff. Moreover, use of a corporate airplane provides greater flexibility in terms of arrival and departure times, particularly for travel to isolated spots within the United States and overseas. With a corporate jet, a businessperson in Jeddah, for example, can visit Amman, Kuwait, and Bahrain and be back in Jeddah the same day, having traveled more than 2,500 miles.[21]

Because of these benefits, more than two-thirds of the five hundred largest U.S. industrial companies operate their own airplanes. In 1988, almost three thousand companies belonged to the National Business Aircraft Association, an organization of businesses that own and operate aircraft. Collectively, these companies operated almost five thousand aircraft, ranging from single-engine piston airplanes to sophisticated jets weighing 30,000 pounds and over; jet aircraft weighing under 30,000 pounds made up about a third of the total fleet.[22] Some of the larger industrial companies—examples are Rockwell International and Chevron Corporation—operate fleets with as many as fifty aircraft and have corporate aviation departments that operate like small airlines.[23] These departments can provide cost-effective service to increase management productivity, especially considering the value of senior staff time.

In addition, the cost and availability of commercial service to small communities severely constrain management's ability to travel to outlying facilities. For some international businesses, plants to be visited are widely scattered and far from airports served by international airlines, and surface transportation may be poor or nonexistent. To gauge their value to the company and keep tabs on their continued effectiveness, some corporate aviation departments operate as profit centers, charging departments within the corporation rates that are competitive with commercial airline coach fares.

Corporate airplanes provide other advantages besides cost-effective air transportation between communities that are poorly served by commercial carriers, although quantifying those advantages may be difficult. First, corporate airplanes can provide both improved security against hijackers and terrorists and secluded conference areas for in-flight meetings that must be confidential. Second, such airplanes can be valuable assets when there is a need to dispatch technicians or spare parts to take care of mechanical problems or a need to deliver medical supplies. Third, corporate airplanes can provide a competitive advantage, in that they can get to some locations before a commercial flight and can transport clients back to the home office for in-house demonstrations. Fourth, corporate airplanes may enable staff members to get home more often, thus saving out-of-town expenses. And fifth, travel in corporate airplanes may be less tiring for company executives, inasmuch as modern corporate aircraft contain first-class, airliner-size seats in the main cabin (see figure 8–5 following page 144). When deciding on the acquisition of corporate airplanes, businesses attempt to quantify and include these kinds of intangible benefits along with the cost savings.

Corporate aviation departments are generally defined as staff operations; that is, they support line operations—the departments that generate revenue. In this sense, a corporate aviation department functions like an accounting or legal department. Small corporate aviation departments are usually managed by a chief pilot, whose time is divided among three functions: administrative duties; responsibilities related to operations, such as crew schedules and recurrent training; and flying the airplanes. Large departments usually have an aviation department manager, whose primary responsibility concerns administrative functions; depending on how the corporation views the role of this department, the aviation department manager may not only fulfill the transportation needs of the corporation but also suggest innovative ways of making the fleet an integral part of the company.

Within large corporate aviation departments, the administrative duties include identifying, developing, and implementing department objectives; developing and implementing departmental policies and procedures; preparing annual departmental budget proposals; coordinating with other departments; maintaining adequate staffing levels; developing an efficient maintenance record-keeping system; and overseeing the development of the operations manual. Operational duties are divided into flight operations and maintenance. *Flight operations* responsibilities include developing relevant operating manuals that comply with FAA regulations, hiring qualified personnel, establishing necessary training and refresher programs, ensuring that airworthiness standards are met, establishing flight dispatching policies and procedures, and developing crew assignments that are cost-effective and meet both FAA regulations and contractual agreements. *Maintenance* responsibilities include establishing and monitoring a maintenance program that is cost-effective and meets FAA requirements and the requirements of the company. For further information on corporate aviation departments, readers are referred to the National Business Aircraft Association's *Recommended Standards Manual*, which deals with business aircraft ownership and the management, administration, flight operations, and maintenance aspects of corporate aviation departments.[24]

In general, corporate aviation departments in the United States operate under FAR part 91, subpart D; these rules apply to departments that operate airplanes for noncommercial purposes. For organizations that operate large transport aircraft or conduct operations for hire or on a scheduled basis, the relevant FARs are contained in parts 121, 123, 125, and 135. In addition, corporate aviation departments must comply with the standard FARs that deal with the qualification and certification of flight crew and maintenance personnel. And, as noted earlier, most corporate aviation departments operate according to the policies, procedures, and standards established in the company's operations manual, the basic objective of which is to improve safety and efficiency by documenting all policies and procedures and making them known to all affected personnel.

As in the case of the FBOs, all repairs, overhauls, and alterations (materials and procedures) to corporate aircraft must conform to the standards set forth in FAR part 43. Further, each operator is required to establish an inspection program. For corporate aviation departments, the FAA generally accepts the manufacturer's maintenance instructions--either the hundred-hour, phased inspection program or the progressive inspection program. The majority of corporate aircraft are maintained on a phased basis, whereby major aircraft subassemblies are inspected according to a set schedule. Under the progressive program, an airplane is inspected in progressive, scheduled stages and is completely inspected at least once in each twelve-calendar-month period. Both types of inspections are conducted by certified mechanics, and any necessary work must be performed in certified repair stations. In addition, operators of large airplanes can be placed in the approved maintenance programs of commercial operators certified under part 121, air travel clubs certified under part 123, air-taxi/commercial operators certified under part 135, or the manufacturer's recommended inspection program. Alternatively, they can establish their own programs and obtain FAA approval for them.

For a corporate fleet to be cost-effective and an integral component of a business, a thorough cost-benefit analysis must be conducted prior to the acquisition of airplanes. A.T. Wells and B.D. Chadbourne in *General Aviation Marketing* provide a good description of the necessary steps for performing a complete cost-benefit analysis, as well as the relevant considerations for selecting the appropriate airplane.[25] The process starts with a thorough analysis of travel needs, based on past experience and on future projections—number of trips and passengers, length of haul, frequency, duration, and so forth. Next is an analysis of the quantity and quality of the available commercial airline service and its cost, the quality aspects examining such factors as *total* trip time, frequency, and the need to spend additional nights in a hotel and the cost aspects taking into consideration all cost components, including the cost of ground transportation, hotels, and food. Then comes computation of the total cost of owning and operating the corporate fleet, including not only acquisition and operating costs but also the cost of either establishing and maintaining a corporate flight department or having the services performed by a FBO.

The need to consider all benefits and costs cannot be overemphasized. Too often, such analyses fail to take into consideration the cost of money (capital tied up), spare parts inventory, the cost of record keeping for the purpose of maintenance, and indirect costs of flight department employee benefits, such as insurance and retirement programs. On the benefits side of the equation, it is also necessary to address, to the extent possible, the indirect benefits cited earlier in this discussion. Finally, the entire cost-benefit analysis should be performed using an acceptable financial technique, such as net present value analysis, which takes into consideration the time value of money as well as the relevant risk factors.

Corporate aviation is probably the most glamorous component of the widely diverse general aviation industry. Yet its existence is closely tied to the other components; corporate flight departments rely on FBOs for fuel and other ground services, and many corporate pilots begin as private pilots. Consequently, corporate aviation will be affected by the challenges and opportunities facing the entire general aviation industry—for example, the cost of insurance and the impact of noise legislation. Further, the structural changes experienced by the general aviation industry and the challenges and opportunities confronting it are reflective of the dynamics of the broader civil aviation industry. In the concluding chapter are summarized the global challenges and opportunities for civil aviation.

Notes

1. International Civil Aviation Organization (ICAO), *Bulletin* (Montreal: ICAO, July 1988), 44–45.

2. "Air Transportation," *The New Encyclopaedia Britannica*, 15th ed., vol. 28 (Chicago: Encyclopaedia, 1987), 829.

3. D. Mondey, *The International Encyclopedia of Aviation* (New York: Crown Publishers, 1977), 425.

4. Time-Life Books, *The Bush Pilots* (Alexandria, Va.: Time-Life Books, 1983), 19.

5. A.T. Wells and B.D. Chadbourne, *General Aviation Marketing* (Malabar, Fla.: Krieger, 1987), 5.

6. J. Christy, *American Aviation: An Illustrated History* (Blue Ridge Summit, Pa.: Tab Books, 1987), 313–14.

7. Wells and Chadbourne, *General Aviation Marketing*, 8–10.

8. Christy, *American Aviation*, 307.

9. Federal Aviation Administration (FAA), *FAA Statistical Handbook of Aviation: Calendar Year 1986* (Washington, D.C.: FAA, 1987), 165.

10. U.S. Department of Transportation, *FAA Aviation Forecasts: Fiscal Years 1988–1999* (Washington, D.C.: Federal Aviation Administration, February 1988), 69–70.

11. National Business Aircraft Association (NBAA), *NBAA Issues '88* (Washington, D.C.: NBAA, 1988).

12. U.S. Department of Transportation, *FAA Aviation Forecasts: Fiscal Years 1988–1999*, 80.

13. Wells and Chadbourne, *General Aviation Marketing*, 53.

14. J.D. Richardson and J.F. Rodwell, *Essentials of Aviation Management*, 3d ed. (Dubuque, Iowa: Kendall/Hunt, 1985), 8.

15. H.P. Wolfe and D.A. NewMyer, *Aviation Industry Regulation* (Carbondale: Southern Illinois University Press, 1985), 146–52.

16. E. Sturm, "FBO Future," in *Ninth Annual FAA Forecast Conference Proceedings* (Washington, D.C.: Federal Aviation Administration, 1984), 38–42.

17. Cessna Aircraft Company, *Cessna Citation S/II* (brochure) (Wichita, Kans.: Cessna, April 1986), 7.

18. Saudia, "Executive Aircraft: Wings for the Boardroom," *Ahlan Wasahlan* (in-flight magazine) 10, no. 2 (February 1986): 14.

19. "Case in Point: Steelcase, Inc.," *Dun's Business Month*, August 1985, 80.

20. Regional Airline Association (RAA), *1988 Annual Report* (Washington, D.C.: RAA, 1988), 8.

21. Saudia, "Executive Aircraft," 13.

22. Data provided by the National Business Aircraft Association, Washington, D.C.

23. J. Braham, "Offices in the Sky," *Industry Week*, April 1, 1985, 28.

24. National Business Aircraft Association (NBAA), *NBAA Recommended Standard Manual* (Washington, D.C.: NBAA, 1982).

25. Wells and Chadbourne, *General Aviation Marketing*, chap. 7–9.

9
Concluding Comments

C ivil aviation is an extraordinarily complex, dynamic, challenging, and important industry. The complexity of the industry stems from the very demanding task of integrating the disparate needs of its many components—airlines, general aviation, air cargo, airports, the air traffic control system, and regulatory agencies—into a safe and efficient transportation network. The dynamism of this industry is the result of (a) significant technological developments, such as new airframe designs, quieter and more efficient engines, highly automated flight controls, and improved air traffic control procedures and equipment; (b) significant technological advances outside the industry, such as computers and telecommunications systems, which have greatly improved the capability of airlines to forecast demand, market their services, and manage revenues; (c) unsettling economic events, such as vacillations in the price of fuel and the emerging strength of the global economy; and (d) more liberalized regulatory policies. In addition to integrating the diverse components of civil aviation in a rapidly changing environment, the industry is also being challenged to satisfy the growing demand for air travel worldwide without further stressing the capacity limits of airport and air traffic control facilities or violating increasingly stringent environmental restrictions, especially those pertaining to aircraft noise. Of course, the greatest ongoing task confronting the industry is to convert these internal and external challenges into lucrative business opportunities. The economic, political, and social importance of this industry is evidenced by its contributions to national economies in the way of creating jobs, generating foreign currency, and promoting tourism; its dominance as the preeminent mode of common-carrier intercity passenger travel in developed countries; and its influence on our quality of life in terms of where we live, work, and vacation.

The preceding chapters have described the major components of the civil aviation industry. The common thread among all these components is, of course, the airplane. When viewing the phenomenal growth of the industry and the technological leaps that have been made, it is easy to overlook the fact that only fifty years passed between the time the Wright brothers struggled to achieve powered flight and the time the British introduced 500-mile-per-hour commercial jet service and that it was only another twenty-five years before the British and the French introduced the supersonic Concorde. Nowadays, safe, comfortable, fast, and affordable air service is provided between virtually all pairs of cities of significant size. Passengers travel in comfort on long-haul, nonstop flights between New York and Tokyo, Los Angeles and Sydney, and London and Tokyo. Among the many other profitable uses for modern aircraft are overnight delivery of letters and small packages—a service now available between most pairs of cities in the United States; air-cargo services, which have enabled many shippers to profitably expand into new markets and which some companies have successfully incorporated into both their distribution and manufacturing processes; corporate fleets, which provide virtual door-to-door convenience for executives and thus conserve precious management time; helicopters, which rush accident victims to hospitals and enhance police surveillance activities; agricultural uses; and deliveries by bush pilots of passengers and cargo to isolated sites.

As the airplane's dependability, speed, comfort, and capacity have improved, the public's reliance on and demand for aviation services have changed and so, too, has the role of the federal government. During its formative years, the civil aviation industry relied heavily on direct government support to build dependable airplanes and develop an efficient infrastructure of airports, airways, rules, procedures, and traffic control. The government was also involved in promoting economic self-sufficiency and the interests of national carriers in foreign markets. And from the beginning, all governments have taken an active role in regulating aviation safety. As the industry prospered, the need for economic regulation lessened in many developed countries and ultimately the U.S. domestic airline industry was deregulated. Deregulation gave each carrier the opportunity to succeed—or fail—according to the forces of the marketplace rather than the subjective assessments of CAB members. (The FAA, of course, continues to uphold safety standards in the United States by regulating pilot and aircraft certification, airport operations, airspace utilization, maintenance procedures, and aircraft operating rules and procedures. Moreover, the government's heightened awareness of environmental issues is increasingly affecting the aviation industry, particularly in the area of noise regulation.) In other parts of the world, the movement to liberalize the regulatory framework has been gaining momentum, creating additional price/service options for consumers and increasing opportunities for aviation and nonaviation businesses.

Whereas much of the industry's growth can be attributed to technological advances, so, too, can some of the industry's problems. Although jet airplanes, for example, led to enormous growth in passenger traffic, their introduction also brought into focus the inadequacy of the airport and airway systems. In addition, the earliest jet engines were so noisy that they disrupted living conditions for many people residing near airports. Fortunately, in a relatively short period of time aircraft manufacturers came forward with newer, quieter technologies that solved many of the problems. The development of high-bypass-ratio engines, for example, not only reduced airplane noise but made wide-body airplanes economically and operationally feasible. Although advances in airplane technology were costly, related increases in capacity and efficiency more than offset the required initial investments, thereby reducing the carriers' unit operating costs. Lower unit costs, coupled with a less regulated and more competitive marketplace, led to lower fares and dramatic increases in traffic volume. Growth in traffic, however, has strained the capacity of airports, airways, and the air traffic control system. As a result, numerous proposals have been put forth to efficiently harmonize infrastructure capacity with the current and projected demand for aviation services. In the United States, for example, implementation of the National Airspace System Plan is transforming the air traffic control system. Other changes to the airport and airway system that are being considered include defederalization of airports and establishment of a private corporation to manage the air traffic control system.

If the introduction of the jet airplane is widely regarded as the single most important event in passenger service, the Airline Deregulation Act of 1978 is a very close second. In the United States, airline deregulation affected not only commercial carriers but every other component of the industry, on an international scale. In the commercial sector, U.S. airlines abandoned their linear route networks and set up hub-and-spoke systems; reduced their labor costs by various measures, including layoffs, two-tier wage structures, and even voluntary bankruptcies; altered their marketing techniques and introduced new price/service options; and consolidated their businesses. Hub-and-spoke systems, in turn, not only affected the structure of the airline industry itself—creating, for example, the need to develop code-sharing agreements with regional/commuter carriers—but also placed tremendous pressure on airport and airway capacity at major airports, causing congestion, delay, and a concomitant increase in operating costs. It is noteworthy that the combination of airport congestion and changes in airline route structures has also affected the general aviation industry. Many corporations have experienced severe disruptions in air service to outlying facilities; accordingly, some of these businesses have invested in corporate fleets and adopted new corporate travel practices.

Deregulation has affected aircraft manufacturers as well. In the regulated environment, each airline had a stable route structure and a fairly well defined fare structure; consequently, fleet planning decisions were relatively straightforward. With deregulation, the airline industry has been forced to become extremely cost-conscious and more flexible in capital budgeting decisions. The airlines' increased attention to costs and the need for financial planning flexibility, combined with significant inroads made by foreign aircraft manufacturers, have increased competition in this segment of the aviation industry. In addition, the enormous R&D costs required to produce an entirely new aircraft and the need to increase the size of the customer base for aircraft have led to the formation of several international alliances of manufacturers.

The impact of increased foreign competition has extended beyond large-aircraft manufacturers to general aviation. Rapidly rising airplane prices have significantly reduced the demand for all types of general aviation airplanes, and high operating costs have reduced the level of overall flight activity, including flight training. Confronted with dismal sales, general aviation manufacturers have had to seek affiliations with larger companies. In the current environment, only corporations can afford the convenience and efficiency of a privately owned aircraft, as evidenced by the high proportion of corporate airplanes sold relative to the number of single-engine piston airplanes sold. As a result of the declining trend in general aviation activity during the past ten years, positive efforts have been made to stimulate interest, examples being consideration of a less stringent recreational pilot's license and ongoing development of ultralight airplanes.

In summary, civil aviation is expected to remain a visible and vibrant industry for the foreseeable future, because of continuing advances in technology, creative applications of that technology, and changes in regulatory practices. If the jet revolution of the 1960s, for example, is any indication of the potential for advanced technology to spur traffic growth, then the introduction of a commercially viable and environmentally acceptable supersonic transport should once again lead the industry through double-digit growth. At the other end of the spectrum, the tilt-rotor aircraft may alleviate airport congestion problems by enabling operators to offer high-speed commercial service between city centers. As proof of the potential for new aviation services, one need only look to the expansion of expedited small-package carriers, the integration of air cargo into the distribution and manufacturing processes of various Fortune 1000 firms, and the value of helicopters for short-haul travel. And changes in regulatory practices are encouraging airlines to become more market oriented and innovative in developing, pricing, distributing, and promoting their product.

Throughout its history, the civil aviation industry has shown resilience and resourcefulness in coping with challenges and taking advantage of emerging opportunities. Aviation professionals are well accustomed to facing challenges and have repeatedly demonstrated an ability to confront, solve, and ultimately prosper from them. Moreover, in light of trends toward liberalization and privatization, it appears that the aviation industry will have an ever-increasing say in determining its own destiny.

Glossary

Advisory Circular (AC)   An FAA document that provides guidance on aviation issues.

aeronautics   Part of the science that deals with the design and operation of aircraft.

Aerospace Industries Association of America (AIA)   A trade association of major manufacturers of aerospace systems and components.

ailerons   Control surfaces on the wings (located on the outboard trailing edge), used to move an airplane around the longitudinal axis (roll).

airbill (air waybill)   A shipping document used by airlines as evidence of an airfreight shipment.

air cargo   Total volume of freight, express, and mail traffic transported by air.

Air Cargo, Inc. (ACI)   An organization owned jointly by the U.S. scheduled airlines to provide airfreight pickup and delivery.

air carrier operations   Aircraft arrivals and departures performed by air carriers certified in accordance with FAR parts 121 and 127.

air carriers   The commercial system of air transportation, consisting of the certified route air carriers, air taxis (including commuters), supplemental air carriers, commercial operators of large aircraft, and air travel clubs.

aircraft   Airborne vehicles supported by either buoyancy or dynamic action.

aircraft industry   A component of the aerospace industry that is primarily engaged in the manufacture of aircraft, aircraft engines and parts, aircraft propellers and parts, and auxiliary equipment.

Aircraft Owners and Pilots Association (AOPA)   An organization of owners and operators of general aviation aircraft.

airfoil   A surface or body (for example, a wing or a propeller blade) designed to achieve a dynamic interaction with the airflow to accomplish a specific purpose (for example, to generate lift or thrust).

airframe   The structure of an airplane (excluding the engine), such as fuselage or wings.

airfreight forwarders   Companies that assemble and consolidate shipments and utilize the services of airlines to move goods; they can also own and operate their own aircraft.

airman or airwoman   A pilot, mechanic, or other licensed aviation technician.

Airman's Information Manual (AIM)   A manual containing information needed by pilots for planning and conducting flights in the National Airspace System.

Airport Development Aid Program (ADAP)   A program originally established by the Airport and Airway Development Act of 1970 to provide federal funds for certain airport improvements and new airport development; the original legislation has been renewed a number of times, ending in the Airport and Airway Improvement Act of 1982.

Airport/Facility Directory (AFD)   An FAA publication containing information on all landing facilities open to the public, including communications data and navigation facilities.

airport radar service area (ARSA)   An area around designated airports in which all entering aircraft must be in radio contact with air traffic control.

airport surveillance radar (ASR)   Radar used by terminal area traffic control to provide positions of aircraft by azimuth and range data; it does not provide elevation data.

Air Route Traffic Control Center (ARTCC)   An FAA facility that provides air traffic control service to aircraft operating on an IFR flight plan within controlled airspace (principally during the en route phase of flight).

airside   The part of the airport facility where aircraft movements take place (runways, taxiways, aprons, and so forth).

air taxi   An air carrier certificated in accordance with FAR part 135 and authorized to provide, on demand, public transportation of persons and property by aircraft.

air traffic control (ATC)   A service operated by the FAA to promote the safe, orderly, and expeditious flow of air traffic.

air traffic control radar beacon system (ATCRBS)   A system consisting of an interrogator, an airborne transponder, and a radar scope.

air traffic control tower (ATCT)   An airport facility that provides air traffic control services to aircraft operating in the movement area and to airborne aircraft operating in the vicinity of an airport.

air traffic hub   A city or Standard Metropolitan Statistical Area that may include more than one airport.

Air Transport Association of America (ATA)   A trade association of U.S. scheduled airlines.

airway A control area in the form of a corridor, in which the centerline is defined by radio navigational aids.

airworthy Aircraft status indicating that an aircraft has been determined suitable for safe flight.

all-cargo aircraft An aircraft configured to carry only cargo.

all-cargo carrier An air carrier certified in accordance with FAR part 121 to provide scheduled and nonscheduled airfreight, express, and mail transportation.

angle of attack The angle between the chord line of the airfoil and the relative wind.

approach control facility A terminal area traffic control facility providing approach control service.

apron An area on the airside of the terminal where aircraft are maneuvered and parked and where activities associated with the handling of a flight take place.

area navigation (RNAV) A method of using navigation instruments that allows pilots flexibility to fly direct routes between waypoints or to offset from published or established routes/airways at specified distance and direction.

asset (tangible) A physical asset, such as plant, machinery, and offices.

automatic directional finder (ADF) An aircraft radio navigation system that senses and indicates the direction to a nondirectional beacon ground transmitter.

available seat miles (ASM) Aircraft miles flown in each flight stage multiplied by the number of seats available on that stage for revenue passenger use.

average stage length The weighted average of stage or sector lengths flown by an airline.

avionics Communications, navigation, flight control, and displays.

azimuth The angle from the north (moving eastward), graduated into 360 degrees.

based aircraft An aircraft permanently stationed at an airport by agreement between the owner and the airport management.

Bermuda Agreement A bilateral agreement between the United States and Great Britain in 1946, granting each other the five freedoms.

Bermuda II An agreement between the United States and Great Britain in July 1977, replacing the agreement signed in 1946.

bilateral agreement An agreement or treaty between two nations to establish international air services to be operated by the designated carriers of each country.

biplane An airplane with two wings, one above the other.

block speed The average speed for each stage computed from the block time.

block time The time for each stage between engines being switched on at departure and off at arrival.

bond Long-term debt.

bond rating A system used by major investor services to grade bonds according to investment quality.

bypass ratio The ratio of the weight of air that bypasses the compressor and the burners to the weight of air that flows through them.

by-product pricing The theory that airfreight is a by-product of passenger service and should be offered on an as-available basis.

cabotage rights The right of an airline from country A to carry revenue traffic between two points in country B.

capital budgeting Long-term planning for the acquisition of capital assets.

ceiling The height above the earth's surface of the lowest layer of clouds or obscuring phenomena that is reported as "broken," "overcast," or "obscured" and is not classified as "thin" or "partial."

combi aircraft Aircraft on which passengers and cargo are both carried on the main deck.

combination carriers Airlines that transport both passengers and cargo.

commercial service airport A public airport that enplanes twenty-five hundred or more passengers annually and receives scheduled passenger service.

common carrier A transportation company that offers its services for public hire.

commuter air carrier An air taxi that performs at least five round trips per week between two or more points and publishes flight schedules specifying the times, days of the week, and points between which such flights are provided; commuters are certified in accordance with FAR part 135 and operate aircraft with a maximum of sixty seats.

compensatory-cost approach An airport pricing approach in which an airport operator assumes the major financial risk of running the airport and the airline charges are set at a level to recover the actual costs of the facilities and services used.

concessionaire A company allowed by an airport owner/operator to locate and conduct business at the airport for the convenience of airport users.

constant-dollar deflator An index used to convert a price level to one comparable to the price level at a different time.

container rates Special cargo rates for shippers utilizing containers.

controlled airspace An airspace control area designated as a continental control area, or transition area, within which some or all aircraft may be subject to air traffic control.

corporate flying   The use of aircraft, owned or leased, that are operated by a corporate or business firm for the transportation of personnel or cargo and are flown by professional pilots who receive direct salary or compensation for piloting.

cost allocation   Assigning costs to one or more segments of an organization according to benefits received, responsibilities, or some other rationale.

cost-related pricing   A concept in which the object is to set fares that relate to the costs incurred in providing the service used by passengers paying the fares.

country-of-origin rules   The right of each country to establish whatever conditions it requires for air services originating from it.

crosswind   Wind blowing across the line of flight of an aircraft; the wind component is measured in knots at 90 degrees to the longitudinal axis of the runway or the aircraft's flight path.

curfew   A time-of-day restriction placed on all or certain classes of aircraft for the purpose of reducing or controlling airport noise.

current asset   An asset that will normally be turned into cash within a year.

current liability   A liability that will normally be repaid within a year.

debt-equity ratio   The ratio of that part of a business which is financed by creditors relative to that part which is financed by its owners.

debt service safety margin   Gross revenues less operating and maintenance expenses and annual debt service, divided by gross revenues; it measures both the percentage of revenues available to service an airport's new debt and the financial cushion in the event that an airport achieves unexpectedly low revenues.

debt-to-asset ratio   Gross debt minus bond principal reserves, divided by net fixed assets plus working capital; it measures the fraction of total assets provided by creditors.

decibel   A standard unit of noise measurement relating to a logarithmic scale in which ten units represent a doubling of acoustic energy.

demand-related pricing   A concept in which the object is to set fares based on what passengers are willing and able to pay (that is, what the traffic will bear), rather than on costs of service.

depreciation   The reduction in the book or market value of an asset and the part of an investment that can be deducted from taxable income.

dihedral   The angle between the plane of the wing and the horizontal plane at the root of the wing.

distance-measuring equipment (DME)   Airborne and ground equipment used to measure, in nautical miles, the slant range distance of an aircraft from the DME navigational aid.

dividend   Payment by a company to its stockholders.

double disapproval A situation in which a tariff can be refused only if both governments that are party to the agreement reject it.

drag The force opposing an airplane's movement through the air; total drag is made up of induced drag (due to lift) and parasite drag (due to all other sources).

economies of scale Reductions in a company's long-run average costs as the size of its operations increases.

elasticity of demand The ratio of the percentage change in the quantity demanded to the percentage change in price.

elevator A control surface (attached to the trailing edge of the horizontal stabilizer) used to move an airplane around the lateral axis (pitch).

en route The route of a flight from the departure point to the destination, including intermediate stops but excluding local operations.

Essential Air Service (EAS) Section 419 of the Airline Deregulation Act of 1978, relating to points that had certified service at the time of the act.

equity Net worth or common stock and preferred stock.

expediated service Service that emphasizes expedited handling, such as next-day delivery.

Federal Aviation Administration (FAA) An agency of the U.S. Department of Transportation.

Federal Aviation Regulations (FARs) Regulations established and administered by the FAA that govern civil aviation and aviation-related activities.

fifth freedom The right of an airline from country A to carry revenue traffic between country B and other countries, such as C or D.

first freedom The right to fly over another country without landing.

fixed-base operator (FBO) An airport facility that serves the general aviation community by selling and repairing aircraft and parts, selling fuel, and providing flight and ground-school instruction.

flight plan Specified oral or written information about the intended flight of an aircraft that is filed with air traffic control.

flight service station (FSS) An air traffic service facility within the National Airspace System that provides preflight pilot briefings and en route communications with VFR flights, assists lost IFR/VFR aircraft, assists aircraft in emergencies, relays ATC clearances, disseminates Notices to Airmen, broadcasts aviation weather and NAS information, receives and closes flight plans, monitors radio navigational aids, notifies search-and-rescue units of missing VFR aircraft, and operates the national weather teletypewriter system.

fourth freedom The right to carry traffic from another country back to your own country.

fuselage The main body of an airplane, which houses passengers, crew, and cargo.

General Agreement on Tariffs and Trade (GATT) A multilateral treaty subscribed to by more than eighty governments that together account for more than four-fifths of world trade; it is the only multilateral instrument that lays down agreed rules for international trade, the object being to liberalize world trade.

general aviation The portion of civil aviation that encompasses all facets of aviation except air carriers.

general aviation airport (public airport) An airport that is used for public purposes, that is under the control of a public agency, and whose landing area is publicly owned; these airports serve aircraft owned by private individuals or firms that are used primarily for business and recreational flying.

General Aviation Manufacturers Association (GAMA) A trade association of manufacturers of general aviation aircraft and components.

general commodity rates The basic rates applicable to all commodities in all markets.

general obligation bonds Long-term debt that pledges the unlimited taxing power and the full faith and credit of the state, municipality, or other general purpose government.

glide slope Vertical guidance provided during approach using an instrument landing system.

global positioning system (GPS) A navigation system based on the use of satellites.

gross national product (GNP) The market value of the total output of goods and services produced by a nation's economy before deduction of depreciation charges and other allowances for business and institutional consumption of durable goods.

helicopter A rotary-wing aircraft that depends primarily for its support and motion in the air on the lift generated by one or more power-driven rotors, rotating on substantially vertical axes.

heliport An area of land or water or any structure used for the landing and takeoff of helicopters.

Herfindahl-Hirschman Index (HHI) A measure of the degree of horizontal concentration in an industry; it is computed by squaring the market share of each participant and then summing the results for all participants.

hub-and-spoke network A traffic system that feeds air traffic from small communities through larger communities to the passenger's destination via connections at the larger community.

inertial navigation system (INS) A self-contained navigation system based on the principles of inertia.

instrument approach A series of predetermined maneuvers for the orderly transfer of an aircraft under instrument flight conditions from the beginning of the initial approach to a landing or to a point from which a landing may be made visually.

instrument flight rules (IFRs) Rules governing the procedures for conducting instrument flight; also, a term used by pilots and controllers to indicate type of flight plan.

instrument landing system (ILS) A precision instrument approach system that normally consists of the following electronic and visual aids: localizer, glide slope, and marker beacons.

instrument operation An aircraft operation in accordance with an IFR flight plan or an operation in which IFR separation between aircraft is provided by a terminal control facility or an Air Route Traffic Control Center.

intermodal transportation Transportation involving two or more modes.

International Air Transport Association (IATA) A trade association of international scheduled airlines that also provides a mechanism for the airlines to coordinate international passenger and cargo tariffs.

International Civil Aviation Organization (ICAO) An agency of the United Nations, consisting of contracting states, that develops the principles and techniques of international air navigation and fosters the planning and development of international air transportation.

itinerant operations All aircraft operations other than local operations.

jet route A route designated to serve aircraft operations from 18,000 to 45,000 feet.

joint-product pricing A concept in which passengers and freight services are both treated as profit centers and each is priced according to the cost of providing the service.

landside That part of an airport used for activities other than the movement of aircraft, such as vehicular access roads and parking.

large air traffic hub A community enplaning 1 percent or more of the total annual enplaned passengers.

large regional air carrier An air carrier with annual operating revenues between $10 million and $100 million.

lift The aerodynamic force on an airfoil produced by the action of the air moving over it.

localizer An instrument that provides course guidance to the runway in an instrument approach landing.

local operations Operations performed by aircraft that (a) operate in the local traffic pattern or within sight of an airport; (b) are known to be departing for, or arriving from, flight in local practice areas within a 20-mile radius of the airport; and (c) execute simulated instrument approaches or low passes at the airport.

loran A navigational aid used for long-range routes (usually over water).

Mach number The ratio of air velocity to the speed of sound.

major air carrier An air carrier with annual operating revenues greater than $1 billion.

marker beacon An instrument that provides aural and/or visual identification of a specific position along an instrument approach landing.

master plan A comprehensive long-range plan to guide airport development.

medium air traffic hub A community enplaning from 0.25 to 0.999 percent of the total annual enplaned passengers.

medium regional air carrier An air carrier with annual operating revenues of less than $10 million.

microwave landing system (MLS) An instrument landing system operating in the microwave spectrum that provides lateral and vertical guidance to aircraft that have compatible avionics equipment.

mode The number or letter referring to the specific pulse spacing of the signal transmitted by an interrogator.

mode C An altitude-reporting mode of secondary radar.

mode S A discrete, addressable secondary radar system with data link.

multiple designation The right of each party to a bilateral agreement to designate more than one airline to operate the agreed routes.

national air carrier An air carrier with annual operating revenues of between $100 million and $1 billion.

national airspace system (NAS) A common system consisting of public-use airports connected by a network of air routes defined by navigational aids that, in turn, control traffic flow.

National Business Aircraft Association (NBAA) A trade association of corporate aircraft owners and operators.

National Plan of Integrated Airport Systems (NPIAS) A national plan for the development of public-use airports in the United States.

National Transportation Safety Board (NTSB) An independent U.S. agency that investigates accidents and makes recommendations on safety measures and practices.

nautical mile (nmi) A unit of distance measurement used in air navigation; it is equal to 1.15 statute miles.

net profit margin   Net profit after interest and after taxes as a percentage of operating revenues.

new entrant   An airline that began service after October 24, 1978, the effective date of the Airline Deregulation Act of 1978.

noise abatement   A procedure for operating an aircraft at an airport so as to minimize the impact of noise on the local environment.

noise contour   A continuous line on a map of the airport vicinity that connects points of the same noise-exposure level.

non-directional beacon (NDB)   A radio beacon transmitting nondirectional signals whereby the pilot of an aircraft equipped with direction-finding equipment can determine headings to or from the radio beacon and "home" on a track to or from the station.

nonhub   A community enplaning less than 0.05 percent of the total annual enplaned passengers.

Notices to Airmen (NOTAM)   Notices containing information concerning the establishment, condition, or change in any component or hazard in the National Airspace System, the timely knowledge of which is essential to personnel concerned with flight operations.

Official Airline Guide (OAG)   A bimonthly publication of scheduled operations and services of air carriers in the United States.

Omega   A network of eight very-low-frequency stations located around the world that provides navigational signals for long-range flights over remote areas.

open-skies policy   A concept in international markets that promotes unrestricted entry and capacity as well as freedom in pricing.

operating profit margin   Operating profit (operating revenues minus operating expenses) as a percentage of operating revenues.

operating ratio   Operating and maintenance expenses divided by operating revenue; it measures the share of revenues absorbed by operating and maintenance costs.

payload   The useful weight on an aircraft, including passengers, cargo, and baggage.

payload-range diagram   A diagram that shows the relationship between payload and the distance an aircraft can fly with that payload.

pooling   An agreement between two or more airlines to share revenues in particular markets in some predetermined manner.

positive control   Control of all air traffic, within designated airspace, by air traffic control.

positive control area (PCA)   Designated airspace in which aircraft are required to be operated under instrument flight rules.

precision approach radar (PAR) Radar that provides the controller with positive distance, direction, and altitude to guide an aircraft to touchdown on a runway.

primary airport A commercial service airport that enplanes 0.01 percent or more of the total number of passengers enplaned annually at all commercial service airports.

publicly owned airport An airport that is owned by a city, state, county, or regional agency or the federal government.

public-use airport An airport that is open for the use of general public.

quick-change aircraft Aircraft used as passenger aircraft during the day and then reconfigured quickly for freight work during the night.

Regional Airline Association (RAA) A trade association of regional and commuter airlines.

reliever airport An airport designated as having the function of relieving congestion at a commercial airport and providing more general aviation access to the overall community.

residual-cost approach An airport pricing approach in which the airlines assume significant financial risk by agreeing to pay any costs of running the airport that are not allocated to other users or covered by non-airline sources of revenue.

return on investment (ROI) A measure of a firm's operating efficiency, computed by the ratio of net income to invested capital.

revenue bonds Long-term debt that pledges the user fees or lease revenues generated by the actual facility to be developed.

revenue passenger enplanements The total number of passengers boarding aircraft; it includes both originating and connecting passengers.

revenue passenger load factor Revenue passenger miles as a percentage of available seat miles in revenue passenger services—that is, the proportion of aircraft seating capacity that is actually sold and utilized.

revenue passenger mile (RPM) One revenue passenger transported 1 mile in revenue service; revenue passenger miles are computed by summing the products of the revenue aircraft miles flown on each interairport stage multiplied by the number of revenue passengers carried on that stage.

revenue ton mile (RTM) One ton of revenue traffic transported 1 mile.

seat pitch A standard way of measuring seating density on aircraft; it is the distance between the back of one seat and the same point on the back of the seat in front.

second freedom The right to land for technical reasons in another country without picking up or setting down revenue traffic.

section 406 The section of the ADA that contains provisions for the payment of subsidy to regional airlines.

section 419 The section of the ADA that provides for the guarantee of a minimum level of air service to eligible small communities.

separation In air traffic control, the spacing of aircraft to achieve safe and orderly movement in flight and during landing and takeoff.

sixth freedom The process by which the airline of country A uses third- and fourth-freedom rights to carry traffic between two other countries, using the home base at A as a transit point.

small air traffic hub A community enplaning from 0.05 to 0.249 percent of the total annual enplaned passengers.

specific commodity rates Airfreight rates developed for specific commodities between certain cities.

standard instrument departure (SID) A preplanned, ATC-coded IFR departure route for pilot use that simplifies clearance procedures.

standard terminal arrival route (STAR) A preplanned, ATC-coded IFR arrival route for pilot use that simplifies clearance procedures.

stolport An airport specifically designed for short takeoff and landing (STOL) aircraft; it is separate from conventional airport facilities.

supplemental air carrier An air carrier certified in accordance with FAR part 121 that provides nonscheduled or supplemental carriage of passengers or cargo, or both, in air transportation; also referred to as nonscheduled or charter air carrier.

tariff A schedule of fares and rates applicable to the transportation of persons and property and the rules and conditions relating to such fares and rates.

terminal area A general term used to describe airspace in which approach control or airport traffic control service is provided.

terminal control area (TCA) Controlled airspace around a terminal within which all aircraft are subject to operating rules and pilot and equipment requirements specified in FAR part 91.

terminal radar approach control (TRACON) An FAA traffic control facility using radar and air-to-ground communications to provide approach control services to aircraft arriving, departing, or transiting the airspace controlled by the facility.

terminal radar service area (TRSA) Airspace around designated airports in which air traffic control provides radar vectoring, sequencing, and separation on a full-time basis for all IFR flights and participating VFR flights.

third freedom The right to carry revenue traffic from one's own country to the country of one's treaty partner.

thrust The driving force exerted by an engine in propelling the vehicle to which it is attached.

total distribution costs (TDC)   A concept that takes into account all costs relating to the distribution system, including inventory- and transportation-related costs.

transponder   The airborne radar beacon receiver/transmitter portion of the air traffic control beacon system that automatically receives radio signals from interrogators on the ground and selectively replies only to those interrogations being received on the mode to which it is set to respond; each aircraft transponder is capable of replying to 4,096 codes as selected by the pilot. Provides the air traffic controller with positive location and, in some cases, altitude information.

turbine   A mechanical device or engine that spins in reaction to a fluid flow through or over it. Frequently used in turbojet, turbofan, and turboprop aircraft.

turbofan   A turbojet engine whose thrust is increased by the addition of a low-pressure compressor (oversize fan) at the front of the engine and in which part of the airflow bypasses the engine core.

turbojet   An engine that produces power from the reaction force to rapidly expanding hot gases that move at high speed from the back of the engine.

turboprop   A turbine engine in which the propeller is rotated by the turbine.

two-tier wage structure   A wage structure in which newly hired workers are paid substantially less than current workers for similar jobs.

variable costs   Costs that vary directly with the level of production.

Victor Airways   A low-altitude airway system based on the use of VOR facilities.

visual flight rules (VFRs)   Rules that govern the procedures for conducting flight under visual conditions; the abbreviation *VFR* is also used in the United States to indicate weather conditions that are equal to or greater than minimum VFR requirements; in addition, it is used by pilots and controllers to indicate type of flight plan.

VOR   Very high frequency omnidirectional range, used as the basis for navigation in the National Airspace System.

VORTAC   Integrated VOR and tactical air navigation; a navigation aid that provides azimuth and distance-measuring equipment at one site.

vortices   Circular movements of air generated by the movement of airfoils through the air; air patterns around and about the wingtips tend to roll up into rotating vortices and become hazardous to smaller aircraft.

wide-body aircraft   High-capacity aircraft with double aisles in the passenger cabin.

wing flaps   Sections of the wing (located at the trailing edge to change the wing's lift characteristics) used during takeoff and landing to increase effective lift and to achieve slower takeoff and landing speeds.

working capital   Current assets minus current liabilities.

yield   Air transport revenue per unit of revenue traffic transported.

Selected Bibliography

Aerospace Industries Association of America. *Aerospace Facts and Figures 86/87.* New York: McGraw-Hill, October 1986.

Air Transport Association of America. *Air Transport 1988.* Washington, D.C.: Air Transport Association, June 1988.

Anderson, J.D., Jr. *Introduction to Flight.* New York: McGraw-Hill, 1978.

Ashford, N., and P.H. Wright. *Airport Engineering*, 2d ed. New York: Wiley, 1984.

Bailey, E.E., D.R. Graham, and D.P. Kaplan. *Deregulating the Airlines.* Cambridge, Mass.: MIT Press, 1985.

Boeing Commercial Airplane Company. *Current Market Outlook.* Seattle, Wash.: Boeing Commercial Airplane Company, February 1986.

Bowers, P.M. *The DC-3: Fifty Years of Legendary Flight.* Blue Ridge, Pa.: Tab Books, 1986.

Brenner, M.A., J.O. Leet, and E. Schott. *Airline Deregulation.* Westport, Conn.: ENO Foundation for Transportation, 1985.

Bureau of Transport Economics. *Competition and Regulation in Domestic Aviation: Submission to Independent Review.* Canberra, Australia: Canberra Publishing and Printing Company, July 1985.

Burton, C.P. "Highlights of ATC History, 1945–1956." *Journal of Air Traffic Control* 27, no. 4 (October-December 1985): 25–29.

Christy, J. *American Aviation: An Illustrated History.* Ridge Summit, Pa.: Tab Books, 1987.

Clausing, D.J. *The Aviator's Guide to Modern Navigation.* Blue Ridge Summit, Pa.: Tab Books, 1987.

Collier, D.A. *Service Management: Operating Decisions.* Englewood Cliffs, N.J.: Prentice Hall, 1987.

Congressional Budget Office. *Financing U.S. Airports in the 1980s.* Washington, D.C.: Government Printing Office, April 1984.

Coyle, J.J., E.J. Bardi, and C.J. Langley, Jr. *The Management of Business Logistics,* 4th ed. St. Paul, Minn.: West Publishing, 1988.

Davies, D.P. *Handling the Big Jets,* 3d. ed. London: U.K. Civil Aviation Authority, December 1971.

Davies, G.M. *The Department of Transportation.* Lexington, Mass.: Lexington Books, 1970.

Davies, R.E.G. *A History of the World's Airlines.* London: Oxford University Press, 1964.

Ethell, J. *Fuel Economy in Aviation.* Washington, D.C.: NASA, 1983.

Doganis, R. *Flying Off Course: The Economics of International Airlines.* London: George Allen and Unwin, 1985.

Doganis, R., and A. Graham. *Airport Management: The Role of Performance Indicators.* London: Polytechnic of Central London, January 1987.

Federal Aviation Administration. *Airside Capacity Criteria Used in Preparing the National Airport Plan.* Advisory Circular 150/5060-1A. Washington, D.C.: Federal Aviation Administration, July 1968.

———. *Instrument Flying Handbook.* Washington, D.C.: Federal Aviation Administration, 1980.

———. *Airport Design Standards: Transport Airports.* Advisory Circular 150/5300-12. Washington, D.C.: Federal Aviation Administration, February 28, 1983.

———. *Noise Control and Compatibility Planning for Airports.* Advisory Circular 150/5020-1. Washington, D.C.: Federal Aviation Administration, August 5, 1983.

———. *Airport Capacity and Delay.* Advisory Circular 150/5060-5. Washington, D.C.: Federal Aviation Administration, September 23, 1983.

———. *Airport Master Planning.* Advisory Circular 150/5070-6A. Washington, D.C.: Federal Aviation Administration, June 1985.

———. *Eleventh Annual FAA Aviation Forecast Conference Proceedings.* Washington, D.C.: Federal Aviation Administration, February 1986.

———. *Airport Capacity Enhancement Plan.* Washington, D.C.: Federal Aviation Administration, 1987.

———. *National Airspace System Plan.* Washington, D.C.: Federal Aviation Administration, April 1987.

———. *National Plan of Integrated Airport Systems.* Washington, D.C.: Federal Aviation Administration, November 1987.

General Aviation Manufacturers Association. *General Aviation Statistical Databook: 1987 Edition.* Washington, D.C.: General Aviation Manufacturers Association, 1988.

Gidwitz, B. *The Politics of International Air Transport.* Lexington, Mass.: Lexington Books, 1980.

Glaeser, D., S. Gum, and B. Walters. *An Invitation to Fly: Basics for the Private Pilot.* Belmont, Calif.: Wadsworth, 1985.

Green, W., G. Swanborough, and J. Mowinski. *Modern Aircraft.* New York: Crown, 1987.

Greenslet, E.S. *Airline Industry: Passenger Profitability Index.* New York: Merrill Lynch, November 1983.

Greif, M. *The Airport Book.* New York: Mayflower Books, 1979.

Hart, W. *The Airport Passenger Terminal.* New York: Wiley, 1985.

Hawkins, F.H. *Human Factors in Flight.* Brookfield, Vt.: Gower, 1987.

Horonjeff, R., and F.X. McKelvey. *Planning and Design of Airports,* 3d ed. New York: McGraw-Hill, 1983.

International Air Transport Association. "Workable Competition: The Emerging Market Environment." Aviation Seminar held in Puerto Azul, Philippines, September 20–22, 1985.

———. *Membership Services Directory.* Geneva, Switzerland: International Air Transport Association, May 1986.

———. *Annual Report, 1987.* Geneva, Switzerland: International Air Transport Association, 1987.

———. *World Air Transport Statistics.* Geneva, Switzerland: International Air Transport Association, June 1988.

International Civil Aviation Organization. *Environmental Protection, Volume 1: Aircraft Noise.* Montreal, Canada: International Civil Aviation Organization, 1981.

———. *Third Air Transport Conference.* Montreal, Canada: International Civil Aviation Organization, January 1986.

———. *Airport Planning Manual, Part 1: Master Planning.* Montreal, Canada: International Civil Aviation Organization, November, 1987.

———. *Civil Aviation Statistics of the World 1986.* Montreal, Canada: International Civil Aviation Organization, September, 1987.

Jensen, R.S., ed. *Proceedings of the First Symposium on Aviation Psychology.* Columbus: Ohio State University, April 21–22, 1981.

Jeppesen Sanderson, Inc. *Aviation Fundamentals.* Englewood, Colo.: Jeppesen Sanderson, 1983.

Kane, R.M., and Vose, A.D. *Air Transportation,* 8th ed. Dubuque, Iowa: Kendall/Hunt, 1982.

King, F.H. *Aviation Maintenance Management.* Carbondale: Southern Illinois University Press, 1985.

Knight, G. *Concorde: The Inside Story.* London: Weidenfeld and Nicolson, 1976.

Koonce, J.M. "A Brief History of Aviation Psychology." *Human Factors* 26, no. 5 (October 1984): 499–508.

Lewis, H.T., and J.W. Culliton. *The Role of Air Freight in Physical Distribution.* Boston: Harvard Business School, 1956.

Loomis, J.P., ed. *High Speed Commercial Flight: The Coming Era.* Columbus, Ohio: Battelle Press, 1987.

Loos, J. "In the Beginning." *Journal of Air Traffic Control* 27, no. 3 (July-September 1985): 9–14.

———. "ATC History: The Modern Era, 1972–1985." *Journal of Air Traffic Control* 28, no. 2 (April-June 1986): 9–12.

Mahoney, J.H. *Intermodal Freight Transportation.* Westport, Conn.: ENO Foundation for Transportation, 1985.

Molloy, J.F., Jr. *The U.S. Commuter Airline Industry: Policy Alternatives.* Lexington, Mass.: Lexington Books, 1985.

Mondey, D., ed. *The International Encyclopedia of Aviation.* New York: Crown, 1977.

National Business Aircraft Association. *NBAA Recommended Standard Manual.* Washington, D.C.: National Business Aircraft Association, 1982.

O'Connor, W.E. *An Introduction to Airline Economics,* 3d ed. New York: Praeger, 1985.

Office of Technology Assessment. *Airport and Air Traffic Control System.* Washington, D.C.: Government Printing Office, January 1982.

———. *Airport System Development.* Washington, D.C.: Government Printing Office, August 1984.

Rae, J.B. *Climb to Greatness: The American Aircraft Industry, 1920–1960.* Cambridge, Mass.: MIT Press, 1968.

Regional Airline Association. *1988 Annual Report*. Washington, D.C.: Regional Airline Association, 1988.

Richardson, J.D., and J.F. Rodwell. *Essentials of Aviation Management*. 3d ed. Dubuque, Iowa: Kendall/Hunt, 1985.

Sampson, A. *Empires of the Sky: The Politics, Contests, and Cartels of World Airlines*. New York: Random House, 1984.

Shaw, S. *Airline Marketing and Management*, 2d ed. London: Pitman, 1985.

Shevell, R.S. *Fundamentals of Flight*. Englewood Cliffs, N.J.: Prentice Hall, 1983.

Smith, D.I., J.D. Odegard, and W. Shea. *Airport Planning and Management*. Belmont, Calif.: Wadsworth, 1984.

Smith, H. *Aerodynamics: The Illustrated Guide*. Blue Ridge Summit, Pa.: Tab Books, 1985.

Solberg, C. *Conquest of the Skies: A History of Commercial Aviation in America*. Boston: Little, Brown, 1979.

Stroud, J. *Famous Airports of the World*. London: Frederick Muller, 1959.

Sturm, E. "FBO Future." In *Ninth Annual FAA Forecast Conference Proceedings*. Washington, D.C.: Federal Aviation Administration, 1984.

Taneja, N.K. *The Commercial Airline Industry: Managerial Practices and Regulatory Policies*. Lexington, Mass.: Lexington Books, 1976.

———. *Airline Traffic Forecasting: A Regression Analysis Approach*. Lexington, Mass.: Lexington Books, 1978.

———. *The U.S. Airfreight Industry*. Lexington, Mass.: Lexington Books, 1979.

———. *U.S. International Aviation Policy*. Lexington, Mass.: Lexington Books, 1980.

———. *Airlines in Transition*. Lexington, Mass.: Lexington Books, 1981.

———. *Airline Planning: Corporate, Financial, and Marketing*. Lexington, Mass.: Lexington Books, 1982.

———. *The International Airline Industry: Trends, Issues, and Challenges*. Lexington, Mass.: Lexington Books, 1988.

Taylor, R.L. *Understanding Flying: A Commonsense Practical Approach to the Basics of Flying*. New York: Delacorte Press/Eleanor Friede, 1977.

Time-Life Books. *The Bush Pilots*. Alexandria, Virginia: Time-Life Books, 1983.

Thomas, D.D. "ATC in Transition, 1956–1963." *Journal of Air Traffic Control* 27, no. 4 (October-December 1985): 30–38.

Thurston, D.B. *Design for Flying*. New York: McGraw-Hill, 1978.

Tyworth, J.E., J.L. Cavinto, and C.J. Langley, Jr. *Traffic Management: Planning, Operations, and Control*. Reading, Mass.: Addison-Wesley, 1987.

U.K. Civil Aviation Authority. *Competition on the Main Domestic Trunk Routes*. London: Civil Aviation Authority, March 1987.

U.S. Department of Transportation. *FAA Statistical Handbook of Aviation, 1986*. Washington, D.C.: Federal Aviation Administration, 1987.

———. *FAA Aviation Forecasts: Fiscal Years 1988–1999*. Washington, D.C.: Federal Aviation Administration, February 1988.

Wells, A.T. *Air Transportation: A Management Perspective* 2d ed. Belmont, Calif.: Wadsworth, 1989.

———. *Airport Planning and Management*. Blue Ridge Summit, Pa.: Tab Books, 1986.

Wells, A.T., and B.D. Chadbourne. *General Aviation Marketing*. Blue Ridge Summit, Pa.: Tab Books, 1987.

Wheatcroft, S., and G. Lipman. *The Air Transport in a Competitive European Market.* London: The Economist, 1986.

Wolfe, H.P., and D.A. NewMyer. *Aviation Industry Regulation.* Carbondale: Southern Illinois University Press, 1985.

Index

About the Author

Nawal K. Taneja is a professor in the Department of Aviation, College of Engineering, and in the Department of Marketing, College of Business, at The Ohio State University. Prior to these appointments, he was president and chief executive officer of an airline that operated jet equipment, president of a research organization that provided consulting services to the aviation community worldwide, associate professor of aeronautics and astronautics at the Massachusetts Institute of Technology, and senior economic analyst with Trans World Airlines. At OSU, Dr. Taneja teaches and conducts research in airline analysis and planning. He is the author of seven other books published by Lexington Books: *The Commercial Airline Industry: Managerial Practices and Regulatory Policies; Airline Traffic Forecasting: A Regression Analysis Approach; The U.S. Airfreight Industry; U.S. International Aviation Policy; Airlines in Transition; Airline Planning: Corporate, Financial, and Marketing;* and *The International Airline Industry: Trends, Issues, and Challenges.* Dr. Taneja is a consultant to airlines, airport authorities, aircraft manufacturers, and governmental organizations throughout the world.